C000005742

exam success

in

ECONOMICS

for Cambridge International AS & A Level

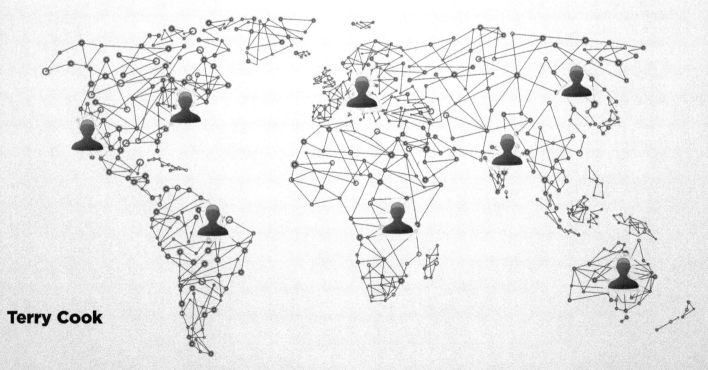

Terry Cook

OXFORD
UNIVERSITY PRESS

Great Clarendon Street, Oxford, OX2 6DP, United Kingdom

Oxford University Press is a department of the University of Oxford. It furthers the University's objective of excellence in research, scholarship, and education by publishing worldwide. Oxford is a registered trade mark of Oxford University Press in the UK and in certain other countries

British Library Cataloguing in Publication Data
Data available

978-0-19-841271-7

3 5 7 9 10 8 6 4

Paper used in the production of this book is a natural, recyclable product made from wood grown in sustainable forests. The manufacturing process conforms to the environmental regulations of the country of origin.

Printed by CPI Group (UK) Ltd, Croydon CR0 4YY

Acknowledgements
The publishers would like to thank the following for permissions to use copyright material:

Cover illustrations: vectoriart/iStockphoto

Although we have made every effort to trace and contact all copyright holders before publication this has not been possible in all cases. If notified, the publisher will rectify any errors or omissions at the earliest opportunity.

Contents

A Level

AS Level and A Level

Introduction

The *Exam Success* series has been designed to help you reach your highest potential and achieve the best possible grade. Each book fully covers the syllabus and is written in syllabus order to help you prepare effectively for the exam. In contrast to traditional revision guides, these new books contain advice and guidance on how to improve answers, giving you a clear insight into what examiners are expecting of candidates, and include a unique section on how students can repair an answer that is incorrect or inadequate. Each of the *Exam Success* titles consists of two parts: the first part covers the content of the subject, with clear syllabus references, while the second part contains exam-style questions and advice on how to improve your performance in the exam. All of the titles are written by authors who have a great deal of experience in knowing what is required of candidates in exams.

Exam Success in Cambridge International AS and A Level Economics has been written specifically to meet the requirements of the AS Level and A Level Cambridge 9708 Economics syllabus. The first part of the guide consists of 10 units. The first five of these cover the content that is required for the AS exam, while the last five cover the additional content that is required for the A Level exam. Each unit closely follows the syllabus and includes diagrams to help you fully understand the content, with exam tips and worked examples throughout. There is a revision checklist at the end of each unit, which you can use to ensure you have covered all of the topics. There are also examples of exam-style questions at the end of each unit, covering both multiple choice questions (featured in Papers 1 and 3) and structured questions (featured in Papers 2 and 4). In the second part of the guide, in Units 11 and 12, there are further examples of exam-style questions and useful advice on how you can best prepare for the Economics exam. There is also an appendix on maths skills for Economics, which includes worked examples to show how mathematics can be used by economists, and a list of the more important formulae that you may need to use in the exam.

Each of the titles in the *Exam Success* series contains common features to help you do your best in the exam. These include the following:

Key terms

These give you easy-to-understand definitions of important terms and concepts of the subject.

X Common errors

These give you a clear indication of some of the errors that students have made in exams in the past, helping you to avoid making the same kinds of mistakes.

★ Exam tips

These give you guidance and advice to help you understand exactly what the examiners are looking for from you in the exam.

✓ What you need to know

These provide you with useful summaries of the main features of topics you would need to demonstrate an understanding of in the exam.

Raise your grade

In these sections, you will be able to read answers by candidates who do not achieve maximum marks. This feature provides advice on how to improve the grade for these answers.

Revision checklist

Each unit has a revision checklist, which gives you the opportunity to check whether you have fully understood all of the material that is covered in the unit.

 Exam-style questions

Each unit contains examples of exam-style questions so you understand the sort of questions you can expect to see on each topic when you take your exam. There is also a complete unit of exam-style questions towards the end of the book in Unit 12, which are arranged by paper. These questions provide ample opportunities to practise the skills and techniques required of you in the exam.

The answers to all of the exam-style questions included in the book can be found on the OUP support website.

Repairing an answer

Unit 11, 'Raising your achievement', contains advice and guidance on how an incorrect or inadequate answer can be improved or 'repaired', through making appropriate revisions or additions to the answer.

Tables

Unit 11 also includes tables to show how to analyse knowledge and ideas on particular topics.

The *Exam Success* series is clearly focused on giving you practical advice that will help you to do your best in the exam. The 'sample' candidate answers, in particular, are extremely useful as they include examiner commentary and feedback. The expectations of examiners are made very clear throughout the books, so you can fully understand what is expected of you in the exam. This will also help to boost your confidence as you approach the exam.

 Access your support website for additional content here:
www.oxfordsecondary.com/9780198412717

Basic economic ideas and resource allocation AS 1(a)–(g)

Key topics

➤ scarcity, choice and opportunity cost

➤ positive and normative statements

➤ factors of production

➤ resource allocation in different economic systems and issues of transition

➤ production possibility curves

➤ money

➤ classification of goods and services.

1.1 Scarcity, choice and opportunity cost AS 1(a)

This topic is concerned with:

➤ the fundamental economic problem

➤ the meaning of scarcity and the inevitability of choice at all levels (individuals, firms, governments)

➤ the basic questions of what will be produced, how and for whom

➤ the meaning of the term, '*ceteris paribus*'

➤ the margin and decision making at the margin

➤ short run, long run and very long run.

The fundamental economic problem

The fundamental economic problem refers to a situation where there is a relative scarcity of resources in relation to the unlimited wants and needs of people.

> **✓ What you need to know**
>
> You need to understand that the fundamental economic problem occurs in all economies, including both developed and developing economies.

> **✗ Common error**
>
> It may appear that certain resources are not scarce in some countries. For example, there may be a high level of unemployment, suggesting an abundant supply of labour, and yet there may be an insufficient supply of labour with the right skills and/or in the right places.
>
> It is important that the fundamental economic problem, which applies to all economies, is not confused with particular economic problems that can occur in specific countries, such as a relatively high rate of inflation or level of unemployment.

> **Key term**
>
> Economic problem: the situation of the relative scarcity of resources in relation to the unlimited wants and needs of people.

> **★ Exam tip**
>
> Do not confuse the existence of the fundamental economic problem, which is a universal problem, with particular economic problems in specific countries, such as a high level of unemployment.

> **💡 Remember**
>
> Resources are limited, whereas the needs and wants of people are unlimited.

The meaning of scarcity and the inevitability of choice at all levels

Scarcity refers to a condition where there are insufficient resources to satisfy all the needs and wants of people. This makes choice inevitable, because there will be a requirement to make decisions about the possible alternative uses of scarce economic resources. These decisions will be taken in terms of opportunity cost; this is the next best alternative that is foregone, as a result of taking a decision. Choice will involve all levels of economic decision making, i.e. at the level of individuals, firms and governments.

> **Key terms**
>
> **Scarcity**: a condition where there are insufficient resources to satisfy all the wants and needs of people.
>
> **Needs**: the demand for something that is essential, such as food or shelter.
>
> **Wants**: the demand for something that is less important than the demand for a need (such as a new television) and which is not necessarily achieved by a consumer.
>
> **Choice**: the need to make decisions about the possible alternative uses of scarce resources, given the existence of limited resources and unlimited wants and needs.
>
> **Opportunity cost**: the cost of something in relation to a foregone opportunity, i.e. it indicates the benefits that could have been obtained by choosing the next best alternative.

> ★ **Exam tip**
>
> The concept of opportunity cost does not only apply to production decisions; it can be applied to consumption decisions as well.

> 💡 **Remember**
>
> Economic resources have alternative possible uses and so a choice will need to be made about the use of each particular resource.

> ✗ **Common error**
>
> Make sure you don't refer to opportunity cost in terms of any choice that is made. The foregone opportunity needs to be seen in terms of the next best alternative that is foregone, not just any possible alternative.
>
> The inevitability of choice applies at all levels in an economy, i.e. at the level of individuals, firms and governments.

> ✓ **What you need to know**
>
> You need to understand that the existence of scarcity makes choice inevitable.

The basic questions of what will be produced, how and for whom

There are three basic questions that need to be asked in every economy:

➤ **What will be produced?**: decisions will need to be taken about what is going to be produced with the economic resources and how much will be produced. For example, a decision will need to be made in terms of how many agricultural products will be produced in an economy and how many industrial products.

➤ **How will it be produced?**: production involves the combination of the four factors of production – land, labour, capital and enterprise – and decisions will need to be taken in terms of exactly how these factors will be combined to produce the required output.

➤ **For whom will it be produced?**: if it is not possible to satisfy the needs and wants of people in an economy, decisions will need to be taken as to which needs and wants will be satisfied, i.e. how is the output to be distributed?

> ★ **Exam tip**
>
> These three basic questions will be asked in every economy, however developed it is.

✓ What you need to know

You need to understand that answers to the three questions on the previous page will provide a very good indication of the nature of different economies.

X Common error

You need to recognise that a decision to produce more of one product, such as agricultural products, may lead to a lower production of another product, such as industrial products. This will be considered later in terms of the production possibility curve.

Candidates often focus on production, but it is also necessary to consider how the output that has been produced is to be distributed to different people in an economy.

Remember

There are different ways of producing a given output. For example, to what extent production is capital-intensive, i.e. where there is a relatively high proportion of capital used relative to labour, or labour-intensive, i.e. where there is a relatively high proportion of labour used relative to capital.

The meaning of the term '*Ceteris paribus*'

The term '*ceteris paribus*' literally means 'all other things being equal'. This is important in Economics because it emphasises that the other factors which could influence a relationship between two variables are assumed to remain constant.

Economics is regarded as one of the social sciences and yet it would be very difficult to regard it as a science, in the same way that chemistry, biology or physics can be regarded as sciences, given that it is concerned with human behaviour. The very nature of the subject matter of Economics can therefore cause difficulties.

Remember

The use of '*ceteris paribus*' means that for the purposes of establishing a theory or a model in Economics, it can be assumed that other possible influences on behaviour, apart from what is the focus of the theory or model, are held constant.

Key term

Ceteris paribus: literally 'all other things being equal', i.e. the other factors which could influence a relationship between two variables are assumed to be constant.

★ Exam tip

Make sure that you fully understand what is meant by the term '*ceteris paribus*' and can explain its importance in relation to the claim of Economics to be a social science.

Decision making at the margin

Economists, when analysing decision making, will often concentrate on decisions that are taken at the margin. This is the point at which the last unit of a product is consumed or produced.

★ **Exam tip**

In answering a question on the satisfaction of people when consuming a good, it is important to distinguish between marginal utility and total utility.

✗ **Common error**

Make sure you can clearly distinguish between average, total and marginal data. For example, there can be confusion between average cost, total cost and marginal cost. You need to understand that **average cost** is the total cost divided by the output produced, **total cost** is all the costs of production added together and **marginal cost** is the cost involved in producing just one more product.

✓ **What you need to know**

You need to be able to distinguish between marginal and average data.

Short run, long run and very long run

Economists distinguish between three different time periods:

➤ The short run refers to a time period in which only some variables may change, i.e. some factors of production will be fixed and some will be variable. Technical progress is held to be constant.

➤ The long run refers to a time period in which all of the factors of production will be variable. Technical progress is held to be constant.

➤ The very long run refers to a time period in which it is possible for supply to change as a result of technical progress. This distinguishes the very long run from both the short run and the long run.

Key terms

Short run: a period of time in which at least one factor of production is fixed in supply and output can only be increased by using more of the variable factors.

Long run: a period of time when all factors of production are variable and output can be increased by using more of all factors.

Very long run: a time period when technical progress is taking place, affecting the ability of firms to supply products.

✗ **Common error**

Don't be confused into thinking that the short run and the long run refer to a specific period of time, this is not the case. The period of time involved before the short run becomes the long run will vary from one industry to another. It could be a matter of weeks or months in one industry and a matter of years in another.

Raise your grade

Explain why the fundamental economic problem makes choice inevitable at all levels of
an economy. [8]

The fundamental economic problem refers to the fact that the needs of people are unlimited[1]
and that there are not enough economic resources to satisfy those needs. There is therefore a
situation of scarcity[2] and, as a result, choices will have to be made and decisions taken in relation
to the alternative possible uses of those resources.[3] Choice is therefore inevitable for individual
consumers and individual firms.[4]

How to improve this answer

1. The candidate has referred to the fact that the needs of people were unlimited, but not to the
   fact that this also applies to wants as well as needs.

2. The candidate could have explained the term 'scarcity' more clearly, making it clear that this
   situation arises where there are insufficient economic resources to satisfy all the people.

3. The candidate could have referred to the concept of 'opportunity cost', as this concept
   focuses on the different possible uses that can be made of the scarce resources in terms of
   the next best alternative that is foregone as a result of taking one decision rather than another.

4. The candidate recognises that choice is inevitable for individual consumers and for individual
   firms, but makes no reference to the third level, i.e. government. Governments also have
   to take decisions in relation to the different possible outcomes of resource allocation. For
   example, whether to build a new road or a new school.

Knowledge and understanding:	2/4
Application:	2/4
Total:	4/8

1.2 Positive and normative statements

AS 1(b)

This topic is concerned with:

➤ the distinction between facts and value judgements.

The distinction between facts and value judgements

Candidates need to be able to clearly distinguish between a positive statement and a normative statement. A positive statement is one that is based on factual evidence, i.e. it will be objective rather than subjective. A normative statement is one that involves making a value judgement or expressing an opinion, i.e. it will be subjective rather than objective.

> ★ **Exam tip**
>
> Don't confuse positive and normative statements and objective and subjective statements. Understand how they are different.

> 💡 **Remember**
>
> A positive statement usually uses the word 'is', e.g. 'value added tax is an example of an indirect tax'. Whereas a normative statement usually uses the words 'ought' or 'should', e.g. 'the government should spend more money on defence than on transport'.

Key terms

Positive statement: a statement that is based on facts and factual evidence.

Normative statement: a statement that is based on beliefs rather than on factual evidence.

Value judgement: a judgement that is a reflection of particular values or beliefs.

1.3 Factors of production

AS 1(c)

This topic is concerned with:

➤ the rewards to the factors of production: land, labour, capital and enterprise

➤ the role of the factor enterprise in a modern economy

➤ specialisation and division of labour.

The rewards to the factors of production

It has already been pointed out that there are four factors of production, and each one is paid its own reward:

➤ rent is paid to land

➤ wages or salaries are paid to labour

➤ interest is paid to capital

➤ profit is paid to enterprise.

Key terms

Land: the factor of production that is concerned with the natural resources of an economy, such as farmland or mineral deposits.

Labour: the factor of production that is concerned with the workforce of an economy in terms of both the physical and mental effort involved in production.

Capital: the factor of production that relates to the human-made aids to production, such as tools and equipment.

Enterprise: the factor of production that takes a risk in organising the other three factors of production. The individual who takes this risk is known as an entrepreneur.

> ★ **Exam tip**
>
> Make sure that you can distinguish between labour, in the form of human capital, and capital, in the form of machinery or equipment.

Make sure you don't get confused by the term 'land'. It doesn't just mean land in the sense of a space that can be used for agricultural production, e.g. a farm, or industrial production, e.g. a factory. It has a wider meaning in the sense of referring to the natural resources of an economy, including forests, lakes and rivers.

The term 'labour' can also be confusing. It refers to all aspects of labour, including both physical and mental work. The term can also be used to apply to the skills, knowledge, experience and abilities of the labour force, which is why labour is also frequently referred to by economists as human or intellectual capital.

Capital, in the sense of being an economic resource or factor of production, can also be a misleading term. In this sense, it refers to the human-made aids to production, such as tools, machinery and equipment. It can also refer to factories. It should not be confused with the word 'capital' when it is used to mean money.

The term 'enterprise' can also cause difficulties. It refers to the role of the entrepreneur in combining, organising and coordinating the other three factors of production to enable production to take place and this involves taking a risk.

The role of the factor enterprise in a modern economy

The factor enterprise has already been referred to above and it is important to understand its role in a modern economy, both in terms of organising the other factors of production and, in doing so, taking a risk.

In many countries, there has developed what can be called an 'enterprise culture' which encourages the emergence of entrepreneurs, although in some of these countries the encouragement has come from a variety of government initiatives.

Specialisation and division of labour

Specialisation refers to concentration on the provision of particular goods and services rather than other products. Specialisation allows for, and encourages, a concentration on what producers are best at doing and so enables production to increase. When there is specialisation of economic activity by product or process, this is known as the division of labour.

Key terms

Specialisation: the process by which individuals, firms, regions and whole economies concentrate on producing those products in which they have an advantage.

Division of labour: the process whereby workers specialise in, or concentrate on, particular tasks.

✓ **What you need to know**

You need to understand that specialisation does not only refer to the situation where individual workers concentrate on performing particular tasks. Specialisation can also refer to the process by which firms, regions and whole economies concentrate on producing those products in which they have an advantage.

💡 **Remember**

The element of risk-taking is fundamental to the factor enterprise and it is that characteristic that distinguishes the entrepreneur from other workers. The risk involved in what they do arises from the situation of uncertainty that is associated with any initiative that they take.

★ **Exam tip**

Make sure you can write about both the advantages and disadvantages of specialisation and division of labour. These advantages and disadvantages can be seen from the viewpoint of the worker, the firm and the whole economy.

1.4 Resource allocation in different economic systems and issues of transition `AS 1(d)`

This topic is concerned with:

➤ decision making in market, planned and mixed economies

➤ issues of transition.

Decision making in market, planned and mixed economies

There are three types of economic system:

➤ market economies

➤ planned economies

➤ mixed economies.

A market economy, or market system, is one that is characterised by a relatively low level of state or government intervention in the economy where decisions about the allocation of resources are taken in the private sector by producers and consumers. The price mechanism is the means through which these decisions are taken, bringing about changes in the allocation of resources in such an economy.

A planned economy, or command economy, is one that is characterised by a relatively high level of state or government intervention in the economy where decisions about the allocation of resources are taken by a central planning agency on behalf of the government. These decisions are usually taken within the context of a five year plan.

The disadvantages of a planned economy, operating through government commands or instructions, are often stressed, but it also has to be understood that such a system can have some advantages, such as the fact that unemployment could be lower than in a market economy and the distribution of income and wealth more equal.

Mixed economy: a type of economic system in which decisions about the allocation of resources are taken in both the private sector and the public sector.

It should be clear that both market and planned economies have a variety of advantages and disadvantages and so most economic systems in the world today can be regarded as mixed economies, combining elements of both a market economy and a planned economy.

The balance of the mixed economy can change over a period of time. For example, in 2008-2009, a number of financial institutions in different countries experienced difficulties and many of these had to be supported by government. In the UK, two of the major banks, Royal Bank of Scotland and Lloyds Banking Group, had to be supported by the government to prevent them from going out of existence.

A planned economy can also be known as a command economy, because the government 'commands' or 'controls' the allocation of resources to a large extent.

Don't be confused into thinking that there is one 'type' of mixed economy that will be the same all over the world, but in actual fact this type of economic system can vary enormously between countries. For example, in one economy, the mixture might be 25% public sector and 75% private sector, while in another economy the mixture might be 75% public sector and 25% private sector.

Transitional economy: an economy that is in the process of changing from a planned or command economy to more of a mixed economy where market forces have greater importance.

Issues of transition

Economies are not 'static'. They can be regarded as 'dynamic' entities and many economies are going through a process of transition from one type of economic system to another. In most cases, this process of transition will be from a planned economy to a market or mixed economy.

This development has given rise to what has been called a transitional economy, i.e. an economy that is in the process of changing from a planned economy to more of a mixed economy.

Nationalisation and privatisation will change the nature of a mixed economy. Nationalisation increases the size of the public sector relative to that of the private sector and with privatisation having the opposite effect.

You need to understand that this process of transition is one that will take a number of years and will not happen 'overnight'.

During this process, the economy is likely to experience difficulties, such as when government commands are increasingly replaced by price signals as the main determinant of a change in the allocation of resources.

You should also be aware that encouragement of economic reforms that involve a change from government control to competitive markets has come from the World Bank.

Show that you understand that a mixed economy is not 'static', and give an example of how the balance of the economy can change.

Raise your grade

Discuss to what extent a transition from a planned economy to a market economy will always be a smooth process. [12]

Many economies have in the past been planned economies. These are economies where major economic decisions are taken by the state. Most of the economic resources are owned, or at least controlled, by the state and in most cases there is no price mechanism operating as there would be in a market economy, with prices generally determined by the government.[1]

These economies, known as transitional economies,[2] are now going through the process of change towards more of a market economy.[3] China is an example of such a transitional economy. There are also a number of examples in eastern Europe, including Russia, Poland, Hungary, Bulgaria and Ukraine.[4] The state is reducing the extent of its influence on economic decision making, with a greater role being given to market forces and the price mechanism and as the public sector has reduced in importance, the private sector has increased in importance.[5]

In some of these countries, the process has been relatively smooth, if slow. However, in others, the process has been accompanied by increases in unemployment and/or inflation.[6]

How to improve this answer

1 The candidate's analysis could have been developed more fully, such as in relation to exactly how prices are determined by the government, although there is a useful contrast with what happens in a market economy.

2 There is a reference to the fact that these economies are in the process of changing from one type of system to another are known as transitional economies, but there is no definition of exactly what is meant by a transitional economy.

3 The candidate has again referred to a market economy, but has not really gone very far in their analysis of this type of economic system.

4 The candidate has included some appropriate examples of countries that are going through this process of change.

5 There are some passing references to 'market forces', the 'price mechanism' and the 'private and public sectors', but this needed to be developed more fully.

6 There is some attempt at evaluation in the final paragraph, but this is rather limited and really needed to be developed more fully.

Analysis:	4/8
Evaluation:	1/4
Total:	5/12

1.5 Production possibility curves AS 1(e)

This topic is concerned with:

➤ the shape and shifts of the curve

➤ constant and increasing opportunity costs.

The shape and shifts of the curve

Key term

Production possibility curve (PPC): a curve that joins together the different combinations of products that can be produced in an economy over a particular period of time given the existing resources and level of technology available.

A production possibility curve (PPC) can be used to show the maximum possible output that can be achieved in an economy given the use of a particular combination of resources and technology in a given time period. If an economy is operating on its PPC, in order to increase the output of one type of product, it will be necessary to reduce the output of the other. This can be seen in Figure 1.1, where a movement from X to Y along the PPC leads to an increase of BD industrial output and a decrease of AC agricultural output. It can be seen that the shape of the PPC is a curve.

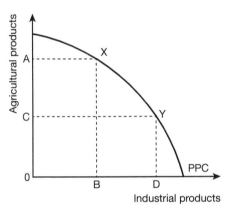

▲ **Figure 1.1** A production possibility curve

Figure 1.1 shows a movement from one point on a PPC to another, but it is also possible for there to be a shift of the whole PPC. This is shown in Figure 1.2, where there is a movement of the PPC to the right from PPC_1 to PPC_2. When this happens, an economy can produce more of both types of good, i.e. there can be an increased output of both agricultural products and industrial products.

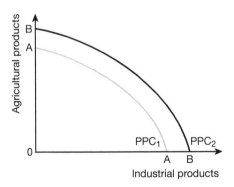

▲ **Figure 1.2** A shift to the right of a PPC

You need to understand that a production possibility curve can also be called a 'production possibility frontier' or a 'production possibility boundary'.

You need to understand that a PPC illustrates the total output of two products given the availability of resources in an economy in a given time period. This output of two products is within the constraint of a given level of technology in a given time period.

There will be an element of opportunity cost involved with a movement from one position to another on a PPC, i.e. it is not possible to have an increase of output of both products. However, if it is possible to shift a PPC to the right, then it becomes possible to produce a greater output of both products.

Constant and increasing opportunity costs

It has already been pointed out that a PPC is drawn as a curve rather than as a straight line. If there was a situation of constant opportunity costs, then it would be possible to draw a PPC as a straight line. However, it is usually the case that there will be a situation of increasing opportunity costs, i.e. there will not be an equal sacrifice of resources as there is a movement along a PPC.

Increasing opportunity costs: this occurs when the extra production of one product involves ever-increasing sacrifices of another.

You need to understand that a PPC can only be drawn as a straight line, rather than as a curve, when there are constant opportunity costs, i.e. when there is a movement along a PPC, the amount of production sacrificed by agricultural products and gained by industrial products are the same.

However, this is unlikely to happen because of the existence of the law of diminishing returns. This stresses that as extra units of a resource are used in production, they will lead to successively smaller increases in output. This is because not all factor inputs are equally suited to the production of different products.

As a position is reached that is closer to either end of a PPC, ever increasing amounts of one type of product will need to be sacrificed to produce more of the other, because of the fact that different factors of production have different qualities, and that is why a PPC is usually drawn as a curve rather than as a straight line.

Raise your grade

Describe a production possibility curve and explain why it is usually drawn as a curve rather than as a straight line. [8]

A production possibility curve shows the maximum output that it is possible to produce given the availability of resources in an economy at any one time.[1] It shows the output of just two products, one on the vertical axis, such as agricultural output, and one on the horizontal axis, such as industrial output.[2]

It could be drawn as a straight line, but this would only apply if there were constant opportunity costs.[3] This is not likely to be the case in most situations, and it is more likely that there would be increasing opportunity costs as a movement up or down a PPC is made.[4] This is why a PPC is usually drawn as a curve rather than as a straight line.

How to improve this answer

1   The candidate has demonstrated some knowledge and understanding of a production possibility curve, but this could have been developed more fully, e.g. by pointing out that the output is also constrained by the technology of a given time period.

2   The candidate could have emphasised how a PPC is a simplified version of what can be produced in an economy with its resources, contrasting this with the reality of production of many different types of products.

3   The candidate refers to the idea of 'constant opportunity costs', but there is no attempt to explain what this actually means.

4   The candidate refers to the idea of 'increasing opportunity costs', but again there is no attempt to explain what this actually means. For example, it would have been helpful if the candidate had brought in the law of diminishing returns to help explain why a PPC is drawn as a curve rather than as a straight line.

Knowledge and understanding:	2/4
Application:	2/4
Total:	4/8

1.6 Money

This topic is concerned with:

➤ the functions and characteristics of money in a modern economy

➤ barter, cash and bank deposits, cheques, near money and liquidity.

The functions and characteristics of money in a modern economy

Money performs four functions in a modern economy:

➤ a medium of exchange

➤ a measure of value or a unit of account

➤ a standard for deferred payment

➤ a store of value or a store of wealth.

Money has a number of distinctive characteristics and these include the following:

➤ acceptability	➤ durability	➤ recognisability
➤ divisibility	➤ scarcity	➤ uniformity
➤ portability	➤ stability of supply	➤ stability of value.

✓ What you need to know

Money as a medium of exchange essentially depends on its general acceptability in an economy as a way of financing transactions.

Money as a measure of value or as a unit of account makes it relatively easy to compare the value of different goods and services, something that was very difficult to do with barter.

Money as a standard for deferred payment enables people to borrow money and pay it back at a later date; this encourages the provision of credit and so is vital to the development of trade.

Money as a store of value or wealth could be adversely affected if a country experiences a relatively high rate of inflation because inflation will erode the purchasing power of a given sum of money over a period of time, so even though money enables saving to take place, the real value of those savings will fall if an economy experiences inflation.

💡 Remember

In a 'modern economy' money in the form of cash is becoming less important and should be seen not just as cash, but in terms of balances held in different financial institutions.

✗ Common error

A common error of candidates is to confuse the functions of money with the characteristics or attributes of money.

Barter, cash and bank deposits, cheques, near money and liquidity

Barter refers to the situation that occurs where, instead of using money, transactions involve the direct exchange of goods and services without the use of any monetary mechanism. The main reason that barter was replaced

Key terms

Barter: the direct exchange of one good or service for another.

Money: anything which is universally acceptable as a means of payment for goods and services and a settlement of debt.

by money is that it relies on a double coincidence of wants, i.e. one person offering a good or service needs to be able to find someone who wants the particular good or service and that person also needs to be offering something in exchange that the seller wants.

Money is often regarded as cash, but in many economies there is a move towards a cashless society. It is therefore important, in a modern economy, that money is seen as bank deposits in a variety of financial institutions, including banks, building societies, friendly societies and credit unions. A cheque is simply a means of transferring money; it is not money. Near money refers to financial assets that could settle some, but not all, debts. Liquidity refers to how easy or quick it is to turn a financial asset into money.

Key terms

Double coincidence of wants: the situation where, in a barter system of exchange, a seller needs to find a buyer who not only wants what the seller is selling, but also has something that the buyer wants.

Cash: the notes and coins in existence in an economy; this is the most liquid form of asset.

Bank deposits: money that is held in accounts with a financial institution, such as a bank, a building society, a credit union or a friendly society.

Cheque: a written instruction to a financial institution to pay an amount of money from an account; although a method of payment, a cheque is not a form of money.

Near money: an asset that can be transferred into money relatively easily and quickly, but is not actually money; it is therefore sometimes known as 'quasi money'.

Liquidity: a term used to indicate when a financial asset is turned into cash.

Remember

Money should not be viewed in terms of just cash. As economies move towards a cashless society, most money is held in the form of bank deposits, frequently accessed through a variety of cards and electronic transactions.

X Common error

Make sure you recognise that barter refers to the direct exchange of goods and services without the use of money, as well as understanding that the main limitation of barter is that it relies on the existence of a double coincidence of wants, with two people each wanting what the other has to sell.

A number of candidates regard a cheque as a form of money, but this is incorrect; a cheque is simply a means of transferring money from one account to another.

You should also understand that near money refers to financial assets that can settle some, but not all, debts and so it is unable to perform all of the functions of money. In particular, it cannot be used as a medium of exchange because it will not be generally acceptable.

Make sure you can explain the concept of liquidity. The term simply refers to the ease with which it is possible to turn a financial asset into money. For example, cash is the most liquid type of financial asset.

Raise your grade

Explain how money, in performing its various functions, can facilitate a country's economic progress. [8]

Money is said to have four functions or roles that it performs in a modern economy. Firstly, it acts as a medium of exchange, enabling individuals, firms and governments to finance transactions. In this role, it is much better than barter which relied on a direct exchange of goods and services without the use of money.[1]

Secondly, it acts as a measure of value or unit of account. This allows the value of a product to be directly compared, something that was not easily provided for in a barter system.[2]

Thirdly, it has the function of operating as a standard for deferred payment. This is very important in a modern economy as it enables people to borrow money and to pay it back at a later date. Payments can be spread over a period of time and this encourages the provision of credit.[3]

Finally, the fourth function of money is as a store of value or wealth. This is where wealth can be stored in the form of money and savings are therefore encouraged.[4]

How to improve this answer

1   The candidate has referred to money as a medium of exchange, but it would have been helpful if the candidate had pointed out that this role could only be performed effectively if money was generally accepted as a means of payment for goods and services in an economy. For example, there could have been a reference to the idea of 'legal tender'.

2   The candidate correctly refers to this second function of money, but it would have been helpful if the candidate had also pointed out that this function helps consumers to make economic decisions in terms of buying one product rather than another.

3   The candidate has stressed the importance of money operating as a standard for deferred payment, especially in terms of encouraging the provision of credit, but this point could have been developed more fully, especially in relation to the purchase of products through the use of credit cards, a major factor in the increase in consumption.

4   The candidate has referred to the function of money as a store of value or wealth and has linked this to the encouragement of savings. However, this point could have been developed more fully, such as through pointing out that the savings that are deposited in financial institutions enable these firms to lend to others. The candidate could also have pointed out a limitation of this function in countries with relatively high rates of inflation where saving may be discouraged due to the erosion of the real value of those savings.

Knowledge and understanding:	2/4
Application:	2/4
Total:	4/8

1.7 The classification of goods and services AS 1(g)

This topic is concerned with:

➤ free goods, private goods (economic goods) and public goods

➤ merit goods and demerit goods as the outcome of imperfect information by consumers.

Free goods, private goods (economic goods) and public goods

A free good is one which does not involve the basic condition of scarcity, i.e. there is a sufficient quantity of it to satisfy demand and so there is no necessity for there to be an allocative mechanism. Examples of free goods include sunshine, air and sea water.

A private or economic good, on the other hand, is one which does involve the basic condition of scarcity. As a result of such scarcity, there needs to be an allocative mechanism to decide which people are able to consume it and which are not. This will be through the existence of the price mechanism. A private good, such as a bicycle, a car or an item of clothing, will have three essential characteristics: it is rival, excludable and rejectable.

Another type of good is that of a public good, such as street lighting or a flood control system. Public goods have three essential characteristics and these are the opposite of those of a private good: they are non-rival, non-excludable and non-rejectable. A particular feature of non-excludability is that it would be impossible to exclude anybody who had not paid for a product, e.g. street lighting; this gives rise to the existence of the free rider problem, i.e. a person who has no incentive to pay for the use of a public good because there can be consumption without any payment being made.

Key terms

Free good: a good which is not scarce and so therefore does not need a mechanism to allocate it; the demand for a free good is equal to the supply of it at zero price.

Allocative mechanism: a method whereby scarce resources are distributed in an economy.

Private or economic good: a private good that is relatively scarce and so will need to be allocated to a particular use in some way through an allocative mechanism.

Public good: a good which has the three characteristics of being 'non-rival', 'non-excludable' and 'non-rejectable'.

Non-rival: if one person consumes a product, it does not reduce the extent of its availability to other people.

Non-excludable: a situation where it is not possible to exclude any person from its use.

Non-rejectable: the idea that certain public goods cannot be rejected by people.

Free rider: a person who has no incentive to pay for the use of a public good because there can be consumption without any payment being made.

★ Exam tip

Do not confuse a free good, such as air, with a product that is provided for free by a government. A product such as healthcare may be free, in that a fee may not be paid directly to a doctor, but it is still an economic good because the resources involved in the provision of the healthcare have alternative uses.

You need to know that as free goods are not scarce, there is no cost involved in the consumption of them, unlike the consumption of a private good, so no price is charged. There is no need for there to be a mechanism to allocate a free good because the demand for, and the supply of, the free good are equal at zero price.

Although air may be regarded as an example of a free good, fresh air may be a less helpful example.

When one person consumes a private good, it reduces the quantity that is available to others. It is excludable in that potential consumers can be excluded from consuming a product because of the producer charging a price for it. It is rejectable in that if a person wishes to reject the opportunity to purchase a private good, they can do this simply by not buying it.

The characteristics of a public good are the opposite of those of a private good. It is non-rival in that if one person consumes a product, it does not reduce its availability to others. It is non-excludable in that it is not possible to exclude people from benefiting from the consumption of the good, giving rise to the free rider problem where it is impossible to charge consumers for the use of a public good. It is also non-rejectable in that people cannot reject the security they are afforded by the existence of a police force or a country's armed forces.

It is therefore possible to distinguish between private goods and public goods, but candidates should understand that in some cases it may not be easy to clearly differentiate between private and public goods and so in this situation, these products are referred to as quasi-public goods ('quasi' meaning 'near' or 'almost').

Merit goods and demerit goods as the outcome of imperfect information by consumers

A merit good is a private good and so has the characteristics of being rival, excludable and rejectable. However, it is likely to be under-produced and under-consumed in a market because of imperfect information on the part of consumers. They may not be fully aware of the potential benefit of the product, not only to themselves but to the whole society, i.e. they fail to take into account the possible external benefits, or positive externalities, of the consumption of such goods. Examples of merit goods include education, health care, public libraries and museums.

Figure 1.3 shows how a merit good can be under-produced and under-consumed in a market. The demand curve D_1 represents the marginal private benefit of consuming a good such as education. However, the demand curve D_2 represents the marginal social benefit of the consumption of education, i.e. it comprises not only marginal private benefit, but also marginal external benefit. The equilibrium position of MSB and MSC (marginal social cost) would therefore be at quantity Q_2 and price P_2.

Key term

Merit good: a product which has positive externalities, but which would be under-produced and under-consumed in a market economy as a result of the imperfect information held by consumers.

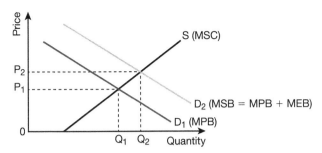

▲ **Figure 1.3** The under-production and under-consumption of a merit good in a market

A demerit good, like a merit good, is an example of a private good, but it is likely to be over-produced and over-consumed in a market because of imperfect information on the part of consumers. They may not be fully aware of the potential damage to themselves of consuming the product, nor of the potential damage to the whole society, i.e. they fail to take into account the possible external costs, or negative externalities, of the consumption of such goods. Examples of demerit goods include cigarettes and alcohol.

> **Key terms**
>
> Demerit good: a product which has negative externalities and which would be over-produced and over-consumed in a market economy as a result of the imperfect information held by consumers.
>
> Imperfect information: a situation in which people, including both consumers and producers, do not have the full information needed to make rational decisions, reducing the extent of efficiency.

Figure 1.4 shows how a demerit good can be over-produced and over-consumed in a market. The demand curve D_1 represents the marginal private benefit of consuming a good such as tobacco. However, the demand curve D_2 represents the marginal social benefit of the consumption of tobacco, i.e. it comprises not only marginal private benefit, but also marginal external benefit. The equilibrium position of MSB and MSC (marginal social cost) would therefore be at quantity Q_2 and price P_2.

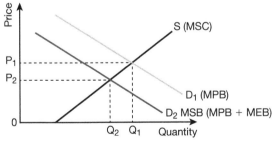

▲ **Figure 1.4** The over-production and over-consumption of a demerit good in a market

You need to know that both merit goods and demerit goods are private goods.

The under-consumption of merit goods and the over-consumption of demerit goods by consumers is the outcome of the imperfect information held by consumers, i.e. consumers underestimate the potential benefits of merit goods, both for themselves and for society as a whole, and underestimate the potential dangers of demerit goods, both for themselves and/or society as a whole.

You need to be able to understand these wider implications of the consumption of merit and demerit goods. For example, in the case of a merit good such as education, a more educated workforce in a country is not only likely to gain higher wages or salaries for themselves, but is also likely to benefit the whole society in the form of higher productivity. In the case of a demerit good such as tobacco, smokers are not only likely to damage their own health, but also the health of those in close contact with them ('passive smokers') and they are also likely to take up a significant proportion of a country's health expenditure.

Make sure you don't confuse a merit good with a free good because some merit goods, such as education, are free at the point of consumption. However, a free good does not require an allocative mechanism whereas a merit good does.

Raise your grade

Outline what is meant by imperfect information and explain how this can apply to the consumption of merit goods and demerit goods. [8]

Imperfect information refers to the fact that consumers do not always have sufficient information to make an informed decision about the consumption of particular products available in an economy.[1] For example, consumers may underestimate the potential benefits of some products, both to themselves and to the wider society, and underestimate the potential dangers of other products, both to themselves and to the wider society.[2]

In the case of merit goods, consumers may under-consume certain products because they do not fully realise the potential benefits. For instance, education can be regarded as an example of a merit good because there is a close link between a person's educational qualifications and the wages or salaries they receive for their work. Not only do they benefit, but the society also benefits in the form of a better educated workforce being more productive and more innovative, contributing positively to a country's economic progress.[3]

In the case of demerit goods, consumers may over-consume certain products because they do not fully realise the potential dangers of such consumption. For example, cigarettes can be regarded as an example of a demerit good because not only can they damage the health of a person, they can also damage the health of other people, known as 'passive smokers', and can cost a great deal in hospital treatment.[4]

How to improve this answer

1 The candidate has outlined what is meant by imperfect information, but could have developed this more fully, such as in relation to the idea of 'information failure'.

2 Although some examples are provided later in the answer, it would have been useful if the candidate had supplied some examples at this point.

3 The candidate could have referred to other appropriate examples, such as health care, museums or libraries.

4 This section could have been developed more fully, both in terms of bringing in other examples, such as the consumption of alcohol, and in relation to the fact that other people may not be able to receive hospital treatment of their problems.

Knowledge and understanding:	2/4
Application:	2/4
Total:	4/8

I can:

➤ understand what is meant by the fundamental economic problem ☐

➤ understand the meaning of scarcity and why this makes choices inevitable, leading to decision making by individuals, firms and governments; and I understand how decision making is linked to the concept of opportunity cost ☐

➤ fully appreciate the three basic questions of what will be produced, how will it be produced and for whom will it be produced ☐

➤ understand the meaning of the term, '*ceteris paribus*', and how this relates to the idea of Economics as a social science ☐

➤ understand what is meant by the margin and why much decision-making in Economics is at the margin ☐

➤ distinguish between the short run, the long run and the very long run ☐

➤ understand what is meant by positive statements and normative statements ☐

➤ understand the distinction between facts and value judgements ☐

➤ understand the four factors of production and the rewards that are paid to these factors ☐

➤ appreciate the role of the factor enterprise in a modern economy ☐

➤ understand the concepts of specialisation and division of labour ☐

➤ understand how resources are allocated in different economic systems, including decision making in market, planned and mixed economies ☐

➤ understand that there are likely to be issues of transition as a country moves from one economic system to another ☐

➤ understand the shape and shifts of production possibility curves ☐

➤ distinguish between constant and increasing opportunity costs ☐

➤ understand how opportunity costs can affect the shape of production possibility curves ☐

➤ understand the functions and characteristics of money in a modern economy ☐

➤ understand what is meant by barter, cash, bank deposits, cheques, near money and liquidity ☐

➤ understand how goods and services provided in an economy can be classified ☐

➤ distinguish between free goods, private or economic goods and public goods ☐

➤ understand that the consumption of merit goods and demerit goods is the outcome of imperfect information held by consumers. ☐

? Exam-style questions

1 Which is the best definition of opportunity cost?

   A An alternative that is foregone.

   B The best alternative foregone by firms.

   C The next best alternative foregone.

   D The next best alternative foregone by consumers. [1]

2 The term, '*ceteris paribus*', means:

   A all other things being equal

   B at the margin

   C choice is inevitable

   D opportunity cost. [1]

3 Which of the following statements about the short run is correct?

   A All variables are fixed.

   B All variables can change.

   C Some variables can change and some are fixed.

   D The short run is never more than three months. [1]

4 Which of the following is a positive statement?

   A Economic growth is measured through changes in Gross Domestic Product.

   B Governments should spend more on education.

   C The pay of nurses should be doubled.

   D Trade unions ought to avoid taking industrial action. [1]

5 The reward to capital is:

   A interest

   B profit

   C rent

   D salary. [1]

6 A transitional economy is one which is:

   A in the process of reducing its rate of inflation

   B increasing the length of the plan from five to ten years

   C introducing more nationalisation

   D moving from one type of economic system to another. [1]

7 Which of the following will shift a production possibility curve to the left?

   A An increase in unemployment.

   B Improved technology.

   C Improved training of workers.

   D New mineral deposits. [1]

8 A production possibility curve is likely to be curved rather than straight because of:

   A *ceteris paribus*

   B constant opportunity costs

   C inflation

   D the law of diminishing returns. [1]

9 Which of the functions of money has encouraged people to buy on credit?

   A Medium of exchange.

   B Standard for deferred payment.

   C Store of value.

   D Unit of account. [1]

10 The free rider problem refers to the fact that:

   A a demerit good is likely to be over-produced and over-consumed

   B a free good requires some form of allocative mechanism

   C a merit good is likely to be under-produced and under-consumed

   D it would be impossible to exclude those who had not paid for a public good. [1]

11 (a) Explain why opportunity cost is crucial to the decisions of individuals. [8]

   (b) Discuss why some goods and services are provided through the private sector and some through the public sector in a mixed economy. [12]

12 (a) Explain why enterprise is so important in the development of a modern economy. [8]

   (b) Discuss whether lighthouses should be provided as a private good or a public good. [12]

Key topics

- ➤ demand and supply curves
- ➤ price elasticity, income elasticity and cross-elasticities of demand
- ➤ price elasticity of supply
- ➤ interaction of demand and supply
- ➤ market equilibrium and disequilibrium
- ➤ consumer and producer surplus.

2.1 Demand and supply curves

AS 2(a)

This topic is concerned with:

- ➤ effective demand
- ➤ individual and market demand and supply
- ➤ factors influencing demand and supply.

Effective demand

It is important to stress the distinction between demand and *effective demand*. Demand refers to the quantity of a good or service that an individual would like to buy, but effective demand refers to the quantity of a good or service that an individual is willing and able to purchase over a range of prices over a given period of time.

> **Key term**
>
> **Effective demand:** the quantity of a good or service that an individual is able and willing to purchase over a range of prices over a given period of time.

> ✓ **What you need to know**
>
> You need to be precise in referring to effective demand and not simply to demand, i.e. there is a clear difference between the desire for a good or service and the demand for a product that is backed by the ability and willingness of consumers to pay for it.
>
> It is important to be able to distinguish between the notional demand for a product, i.e. where consumers want a product, and effective demand, i.e. where that want is backed by actual purchasing power.
>
> The definition of effective demand is often supported by a reference to *ceteris paribus*, i.e. all other things being equal.

> ★ **Exam tip**
>
> Make sure you clearly understand the difference between the desire for a product and the effective demand for it.

> 💡 **Remember**
>
> In a market, effective demand means that consumers are able to afford to pay for particular products.
>
> Effective demand focuses on a situation where consumers enter into a market with the clear intention of being able to buy a product in that market.

Individual and market demand and supply

Individual demand

An individual demand curve shows the quantity of a product that a particular consumer is willing and able to buy at each and every price in a given period of time, other things being equal. The individual demand curve, indicating individual demand, will slope downwards from left to right, demonstrating that a consumer is more likely to buy a particular product at a lower price than at a higher price. This is known as the law of demand.

> **Key terms**
>
> Demand curve: a curve showing the relationship between changes in the quantity demanded and changes in prices, other things being equal.
>
> Individual demand: the quantity demanded of a good or service that a particular consumer is willing and able to buy at each and every price over a given period of time, other things being equal.
>
> Law of demand: for most goods and services, the quantity demanded varies inversely with the price.

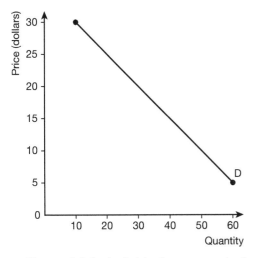

▲ **Figure 2.1** An individual consumer's demand curve for a product

> **✓ What you need to know**
>
> You need to appreciate that the law of demand indicates that there is an inverse relationship between the quantity demanded of a product and the price of the product and this is why the demand curve is downward sloping.
>
> The *ceteris paribus* situation needs to be stressed, i.e. the demand curve shows how demand is determined by changes in price, other things being equal.
>
> An individual's demand curve is derived from a demand schedule, which shows the quantity of a product demanded by an individual over a range of prices in a given period of time.

> **X Common error**
>
> Although there is an inverse relationship between demand and price for most products, this is not the case with all products. A Giffen good is one where the quantity demanded rises when the price of a product rises. Another type of product where there is not an inverse relationship is an ostentatious or Veblen good.

Market demand

It is possible to derive a market demand curve for a product from a number of individual demand curves. This involves bringing together, or aggregating, all the individual consumers of a product to produce market demand, i.e. the total quantity of a product that all consumers would be able and willing to buy at a given price in a given period of time.

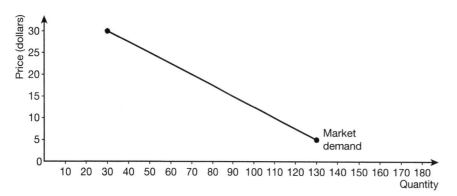

▲ **Figure 2.2** A market demand curve for a product

Individual supply

Whereas an individual demand curve shows the quantity of a product that a particular consumer is willing and able to buy at each and every price in a given period of time, other things being equal, an individual supply curve shows the quantity of a product that a particular producer is willing and able to supply at each and every price in a given period of time, other things being equal. The individual supply curve will slope upwards from left to right, demonstrating that a producer is more likely to sell a particular product at a higher price than at a lower price. This is known as the law of supply.

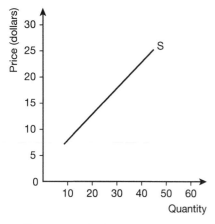

▲ **Figure 2.3** An individual producer's supply curve of a product

✓ **What you need to know**

Make sure you understand that in many cases, as the price of a product rises, a producer will be more likely to supply more than at a lower price because it is likely to be more profitable to do so.

It is also very likely that the costs of production will increase and so it will become necessary to increase the price of a product to maintain profit margins.

The *ceteris paribus* situation needs to be stressed, i.e. the supply curve shows how supply is determined by changes in price, other things being equal.

An individual producer's supply curve is derived from a supply schedule which shows the quantity of a product supplied by an individual producer over a range of prices in a given period of time.

Market supply

It has already been stated that it is possible to derive a market demand curve for a product from a number of individual demand curves and it is also possible to derive a market supply curve for a product from a number of supply curves of individual producers. This involves bringing together, or aggregating, all the individual producers of a product to produce market supply, i.e. the total quantity of a product that all producers would be able and willing to sell at a given price in a given period of time.

Key term

Market supply: the total quantity of a product that all producers in a market would be able and willing to sell at a given price in a given period of time.

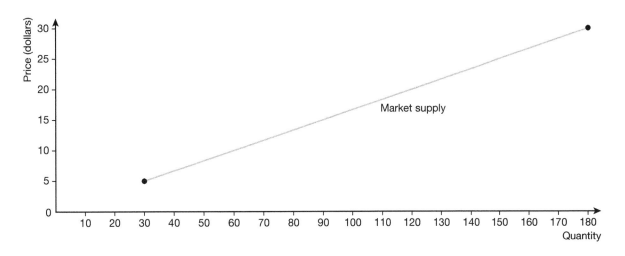

▲ **Figure 2.4** A market supply curve for a product

✓ **What you need to know**

You need to understand that the market supply curve is derived from a supply schedule, which shows the quantity of a product supplied by all producers over a range of prices in a given period of time.

Factors influencing demand and supply

Factors influencing demand

It has already been stated that price is a significant influence on the demand for a product and that there is an inverse relationship between a change in the price of a product and the quantity demanded of a product, all other things being equal.

However, price is not the only factor that can influence the demand for a product. If the assumption of *ceteris paribus* is removed, it is possible to consider a range of other factors that could influence demand. These include the following:

➤ a change in the incomes of consumers

➤ a change in the distribution of income in an economy

➤ a change in the price of a substitute product

➤ a change in the price of a complementary product

➤ a change in the tastes and preferences of consumers

➤ an advertising campaign

➤ a change in the size of the population

➤ a change in the age or gender distribution of the population

➤ a change of interest rates

➤ a change in the weather

➤ expectations of future prices.

Key terms

Substitute product: a product that is an alternative to another.

Complementary product: products that are consumed together.

Remember

Make sure you can distinguish between a change in quantity demanded, i.e. when demand for a product is influenced by a change in the price of a product, and a change in the conditions of demand, i.e. when something other than a change in the price of a product causes its demand to change.

✓ **What you need to know**

In many cases, an increase in the incomes of consumers will bring about an increase in the demand for products; these are called normal goods. However, it is also possible that an increase in the incomes of consumers will bring about a decrease in the demand for products; these are called inferior goods. It is important you understand that the demand for normal and inferior goods shows the relationship between a change in the quantity demanded of a product and a change in income, not price.

It is not only changes in income that are important, but also changes in the distribution of income in an economy; if the distribution of income becomes more even, the demand for normal goods is likely to increase and the demand for inferior goods is likely to decrease.

The demand for a product can be influenced by changes in the prices of other products, e.g. the demand for two substitutes, such as coffee and tea, will be affected by a change in the price of the other. If the price of tea increases and the price of coffee remains constant, there is likely to be an increase in the demand for coffee. The extent of the change in demand as a result of changes in the prices of substitutes will depend on the degree of substitutability of the two products.

The demand for a product can also be influenced by a change in the price of a complement, e.g. petrol is a complement to a car and if the price of cars rises considerably, not only may there be a decrease in the demand for cars but also a decrease in the demand for fuel.

A change in the tastes and preferences of consumers could affect demand, e.g. over a period of time, the demand for some products could rise while the demand for other products could fall.

The tastes and preferences of consumers could be influenced by an advertising campaign. This could influence the demand for a product, e.g. it would be expected that an increase in advertising would be likely to influence the demand for the product being advertised.

A change in the size of the population of an economy could influence the demand for products in that economy, although the increase in a population would need to be relatively large to have any significant effect on demand.

It is not only the size of a country's population that could be significant. There could be changes in the age and gender distribution of a population that influence demand, e.g. if a country has an ageing population, this is likely to increase the demand for those products needed by the elderly.

In many countries, a number of purchases are financed by credit, i.e. consumers buy products over a period of time. The demand for credit will be influenced by the cost of that credit, i.e. the rate of interest that needs to be paid. A fall in interest rates will make the cost of borrowing cheaper and this is likely to increase the level of demand for many products.

The demand for certain products could be influenced by changes in the weather, especially where demand is seasonal.

The demand for some products could be influenced by expectations of future prices, e.g. if consumers believe that the prices of certain products are likely to rise significantly in the future, this may encourage them to buy the products now rather than to leave it until some time in the future.

Key terms

Normal good: a good whose demand rises as income rises and falls as income falls.

Inferior good: a good whose demand falls as income rises and rises as income falls.

Factors influencing supply

It has already been stated that price is a significant influence on the supply of a product and that there is a direct relationship between a change in the price of a product and the quantity supplied of a product, all other things being equal.

However, price is not the only factor that can influence the supply of a product. If the assumption of *ceteris paribus* is removed, it is possible to consider a range of other factors that could influence supply. These include the following:

➤ costs of production

➤ the availability of resources

➤ climate and weather

➤ technology

➤ improved management of resources

➤ changes in the prices of other goods that the producer could supply

➤ the size of the industry

➤ taxes and subsidies (these will be looked at more closely in Unit 3).

Remember

If there is an increase in the costs of production of a product, supply will fall and firms will produce less at each and every price. However, if there is a fall in the costs of factors of production, e.g. if the cost of labour becomes cheaper, more can be supplied at each and every price.

✓ What you need to know

You need to understand that supply is likely to be influenced by the availability, as well as the cost, of resources. If resources become more readily available, this is likely to lead to an increase in the supply of a product.

Supply, especially of agricultural products, could be influenced by changes in the climate and the weather.

Supply is also likely to be influenced by the level of technological knowledge, e.g. an increase in technological knowledge is likely to lead to an increase in supply.

A change in the management of resources could influence supply, e.g. a better management structure could improve the productivity of a workforce leading to more being supplied at each and every price.

If it is possible for a producer to switch from the production of certain goods to other goods, then this decision will be influenced by changes in the prices of other goods that the producer could supply.

The supply of a product in a market is likely to be influenced by the size of the industry, e.g. if the barriers to entry into an industry are low or non-existent, new firms may be attracted into an industry, increasing supply.

Raise your grade

Describe what is meant by effective demand and explain why the demand for a product is influenced not only by its own price but by the prices of other products. [8]

Consumers will desire various products, but this will not be of economic significance in a market unless such desires are backed up by the willingness to pay[1,2].

The law of demand states that the demand for a product will be related to the price of the product[3,4], but changes in the prices of other products can also be an influence. For example, the demand for substitute goods is related. If the price of tea increases and the price of coffee remains constant, there is likely to be an increase in the demand for coffee[5,6].

How to improve this answer

1. The candidate has referred to the importance of the consumers' willingness to pay, but they could also have referred to their ability to pay.

2. There needed to be a clearer distinction between the idea of notional demand and effective demand, especially in relation to the actual purchasing power of consumers.

3. This could have been made clearer, especially in terms of pointing out that the relationship was usually an inverse one.

4. The candidate could also have referred to the idea of *ceteris paribus*, i.e. assuming that other things are equal and are held constant.

5. The candidate has given an example of two substitute goods, but there was no reference to the extent of the substitutability of the two products.

6. The answer is very limited in being restricted to a consideration of substitute goods. The answer would have been improved by a reference to complementary goods and by the inclusion of two appropriate examples.

Knowledge and understanding:	1/4
Application:	2/4
Total:	3/8

2.2 Price elasticity, income elasticity and cross-elasticities of demand

AS 2(b)

This topic is concerned with:

➤ the meaning and calculation of elasticity of demand

➤ the range of elasticities of demand

➤ the factors affecting elasticity of demand

➤ the implications for revenue and business decisions of price, income and cross-elasticities of demand.

The meaning and calculation of elasticity of demand

The concept of elasticity of demand refers to the responsiveness of demand to a change in one of its determinants, such as price, income or the price of another product.

It is calculated by dividing the percentage change in the quantity demanded of a product by the percentage change in the determinant, such as the percentage change in the price of a product (in the case of price elasticity of demand), the percentage change in income (in the case of income elasticity of demand) or the percentage change in the price of another product (in the case of cross-elasticity of demand).

The range of elasticities of demand

Elasticity of demand can range from perfectly inelastic to perfectly elastic, i.e. from zero to infinity. If demand is elastic, the figure for the elasticity will be greater than 1. If demand is unitary elastic, the figure for the elasticity will be equal to 1. If demand is inelastic, the figure for the elasticity will be less than 1.

> **Key terms**
>
> Elastic demand: the percentage (or proportionate) change in demand is greater than the percentage (or proportionate) change in the determinant bringing about the change in demand.
>
> Inelastic demand: the percentage (or proportionate) change in demand is less than the percentage (or proportionate) change in the determinant bringing about the change in demand.

> **X Common error**
>
> It is often thought that an inelastic figure, i.e. one less than 1, is negative; it is, in fact, positive.
>
> Make sure you refer to a particular good as being elastic; it is important to realise, however, that it is not a good or service that is being described as elastic, but the demand for that good or service.

The factors affecting elasticity of demand

The various factors affecting elasticity of demand can be understood in relation to the three different types of elasticity, i.e. price elasticity of demand, income elasticity of demand and cross-elasticity of demand.

Price elasticity of demand

Price elasticity of demand (PED) measures the responsiveness of the demand for a product to a change in its price. It is calculated by the following formula:

$$\frac{\text{Percentage change in the quantity demanded of a product}}{\text{Percentage change in the price of a product}}$$

Price elasticity of demand can range from perfectly inelastic to perfectly elastic. Figure 2.5 illustrates perfectly elastic demand, Figure 2.6 illustrates perfectly inelastic demand and Figure 2.7 illustrates unitary elasticity of demand.

> **Key term**
>
> Elasticity of demand: the responsiveness of demand to a change in one of its determinants.

> **Remember**
>
> Elasticity involves the examination of percentage changes, not absolute changes. Price changes are not usually presented as percentage changes and you will therefore need to be able to calculate these.

> **X Common error**
>
> Remember that the percentage change in the quantity demanded of a product goes on top of the formula and what is causing that change on the bottom.

> **Key terms**
>
> Price elasticity of demand (PED): the responsiveness of demand for a product to a change in its price.
>
> Perfectly elastic demand: demand is totally responsive to changes in price; PED is equal to infinity.
>
> Perfectly inelastic demand: demand is totally unresponsive to changes in price; PED is zero.

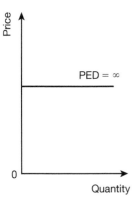

▲ **Figure 2.5** Perfectly elastic demand

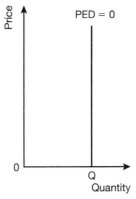

▲ **Figure 2.6** Perfectly inelastic demand

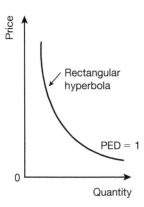

▲ **Figure 2.7** Unitary elasticity demand

Price elasticity of demand will vary along the length of a straight line demand curve, as can be seen in Figure 2.8. At the midway point, the PED will be equal to 1. When there is a movement up the curve, the PED will become increasingly elastic until it eventually reaches the vertical axis when it becomes perfectly elastic. When there is a movement down the curve, the PED will become increasingly inelastic until it eventually reaches the horizontal axis when it becomes perfectly inelastic.

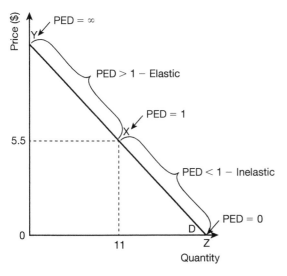

▲ **Figure 2.8** Changes in PED along the length of a straight line demand curve

> **✓ What you need to know**
>
> In the case of perfectly elastic PED, shown by a horizontal straight line, perfectly inelastic PED, shown by a vertical straight line, and unitary elastic PED, shown by a rectangular hyperbola, the PED value is constant along the entire length.
>
> In other situations, however, there will be different values of PED along the length of a straight line.

The factors affecting price elasticity of demand

There are a number of factors affecting price elasticity of demand, including the following:

➤ the number and availability of substitutes

➤ the width of the definition of a product

➤ the amount of money spent on a product

➤ the proportion of income that is spent on a product

➤ the period of time

➤ the degree of necessity

➤ the durability and perishability of products.

> **✓ What you need to know**
>
> You need to understand that the more substitutes that are available for a particular product, such as different brands of tea or coffee, the more price elastic will be the demand.
>
> It is important to understand that the wider the definition of a product, the more price inelastic will be the demand, e.g. the demand for tea or coffee will be more inelastic than the demand for particular brands or types of tea or coffee.
>
> You need to realise that if the amount of money spent on a product is relatively small, the demand is likely to be inelastic, e.g. the amount of money spent on newspapers is likely to be a relatively small proportion of total expenditure and so the demand for such a product is likely to be relatively inelastic.
>
> If the proportion of income taken by a product is relatively high, the price elasticity of demand will be more elastic compared to a situation where the proportion of income spent on a product is relatively low.
>
> The price elasticity of demand for a product is likely to be more inelastic in the short run than in the long run, when it might be possible to think about possible alternatives to a product.
>
> You should understand that the more necessary and essential a product is, the more inelastic the demand for it is likely to be, whereas the demand for luxuries is likely to be more elastic.
>
> The more durable a product is, the more price elastic the demand is likely to be, whereas the demand for more perishable goods is likely to be more price inelastic.

> **Key terms**
>
> **Elastic PED**: demand is relatively responsive to changes in price; PED is more than 1 and less than infinity.
>
> **Inelastic PED**: demand is relatively unresponsive to changes in price; PED is more than 0 and less than 1.
>
> **Unitary elastic PED**: the proportionate change in demand is exactly equal to the proportionate change in price; PED is equal to 1.

> **✗ Common error**
>
> It is important not to confuse arc price elasticity of demand, which is a measurement of price elasticity of demand over a range of prices, with point price elasticity of demand, which is a measurement of price elasticity of demand at a particular price.

Income elasticity of demand

Income elasticity of demand (YED) measures the responsiveness of the demand for a product to a change in income. It is calculated by the following formula:

$$\frac{\text{Percentage change in the quantity demanded of a product}}{\text{Percentage change in income}}$$

The income elasticity of demand for most products will be positive, i.e. as incomes rise, the demand for products will rise. These are known as normal goods. However, the income elasticity of demand for some products will be negative, i.e. as incomes rise, the demand for products will fall. These are known as inferior goods.

An Engels curve shows the relationship between changes in income and changes in the quantity demanded. This is shown in Figure 2.9.

Key term

Income elasticity of demand (YED): the responsiveness of demand for a product to a change in the incomes of consumers.

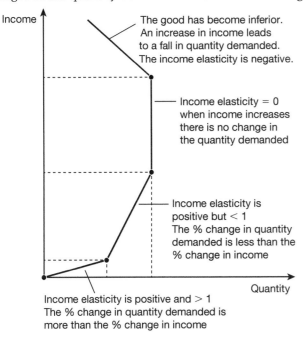

▲ **Figure 2.9** The relationship between changes in income and changes in the quantity demanded

✓ **What you need to know**

It is important that you are able to clearly distinguish between normal goods, the demand for which will rise as incomes increase, and inferior goods, the demand for which will fall as incomes increase.

With a normal good, the income elasticity of demand will be positive, i.e. as incomes rise, the quantity demanded rises. If the value is greater than 1, demand is income elastic, as in the case of luxuries. If the value is less than 1 (but therefore still positive), demand is income inelastic, as in the case of necessities.

With an inferior good, the income elasticity of demand will be negative, i.e. as incomes rise, the quantity demanded falls.

You should understand that normal and inferior goods will not always be the same in all economies, i.e. it will depend on the economic development of particular economies.

You also need to realise that the size of the YED coefficient, either positive or negative, indicates the strength of the relationship between changes in income and changes in demand; the higher the figure, the greater the relationship between demand and income.

The factors affecting income elasticity of demand

There are a number of factors affecting income elasticity of demand, including the following:

➤ the proportion of income that is spent on a product

➤ the width of the definition of a product

➤ the economic development of a particular economy.

Cross-elasticity of demand

Cross elasticity of demand (XED), or cross-price elasticity of demand, measures the responsiveness of the demand for a product to a change in the price of another product. It is calculated by the following formula:

$$\frac{\text{Percentage change in the quantity demanded of good A}}{\text{Percentage change in the price of good B}}$$

If the two products are substitutes, such as tea and coffee, the cross-elasticity of demand will be positive, i.e. if there is an increase in the price of good B, many people are likely to switch to the substitute, good A, and so the demand for good A rises.

If the two products are complements, such as DVDs and DVD players, the cross-elasticity of demand will be negative, i.e. if there is an increase in price of good B, fewer people are likely to buy it and so fewer people will buy good A as well.

The implications for revenue and business decisions of price, income and cross-elasticities of demand

Price elasticity of demand

Price elasticity of demand is extremely important to an understanding of business decisions, especially in relation to revenue. If the demand for a good or service is price elastic, a business should lower the price because more products will be bought and this will lead to a higher total revenue. If the demand for a good or service is price inelastic, a business should raise the price because although fewer items of the product will be sold, the increased revenue from each product will more than compensate for this.

✓ What you need to know

It is important to understand that if PED for a product is inelastic, total revenue will rise if there is a price increase and fall if there is a price decrease.

If PED for a product is elastic, total revenue will fall if there is a price increase and rise if there is a price decrease.

If the demand for a product is unitary elastic, total revenue will remain constant whether there is a price increase or a price decrease.

Businesses can use PED not only to help determine policies on price, but also policies on the number of goods to produce or stock and the number of people to employ.

Businesses can also use PED to anticipate the likely impact on their cashflow.

Income elasticity of demand

Income elasticity of demand is also important to an understanding of business decisions. Economic development, especially changes in incomes, can affect the decision making of businesses. For example, if the general level of incomes is rising in an economy, it would be expected that there would be an increase in the demand for normal goods and a decrease in the demand for inferior goods and businesses would need to take account of this in their planning.

✓ What you need to know

You need to understand that if an economy is experiencing an increase in the general level of incomes, the demand for normal goods is likely to rise and the demand for inferior goods is likely to fall.

If an economy is experiencing a recession, businesses should focus on the production of products with a relatively low income elasticity of demand, e.g. people will still buy food in a recession, but they are less likely to buy expensive cars.

Income elasticity of demand can therefore help to inform decisions on production or stocking and on the number of people to employ.

✓ What you need to know

A business would be able to use the concept of XED to estimate the effect on the demand for their products of a competitor changing the prices of its products.

✗ Common error

When considering the implications of XED for a business, you should ensure that they clearly distinguish between the effects in relation to substitutes and complements and not get these confused.

Cross-elasticity of demand

Cross-elasticity of demand is also important to an understanding of business decisions. In the case of substitutes, a firm needs to appreciate that if there is an increase in the price of tea, the demand for coffee is likely to rise and so a retailer would need to take this situation into account when deciding on the quantity of each product to order. In the case of complements, if there is an increase in the price of DVD players, this is likely to lead to a decrease in the demand not only of DVD players, but also DVDs.

Raise your grade

Discuss the usefulness of price elasticity of demand, income elasticity of demand and cross-elasticity of demand to a car manufacturer. [12]

There are three different types of elasticity of demand. Price elasticity of demand is defined as the relationship between the change in demand for a product and the price of that product[1]. Income elasticity of demand is defined as the relationship between the percentage change in the demand for a product and the change in incomes in an economy[2]. Cross-elasticity of demand is defined as the relationship between the percentage change in demand for a product and the percentage change in price[3].

In the case of a car manufacturer, if the demand for a car is price elastic, the business should increase the price of the cars to raise total revenue[4]. If incomes in an economy are rising, this is likely to lead to an increase in total revenue[5]. If the price of fuel is increasing, this is likely to lead to a reduction in sales of cars and therefore a decrease in total revenue[6].

How to improve this answer

1   The candidate needs to make it clear that PED is defined as the percentage change in the quantity demanded of a product divided by the percentage change in its price; there is no reference in this first sentence to percentage or proportionate changes. Also, the candidate has written very little on the concept of PED; the answer could have been developed more fully, such as in relation to analysing the difference between elastic and inelastic demand.

2   The candidate has referred to the percentage change in the quantity demanded of a product, but has not referred to the fact that it is the percentage change in incomes that needs to be considered, not simply the change in incomes. The treatment of YED is very limited, e.g. there is no reference to the contrast between normal goods and inferior goods.

3   The candidate has referred to both changes in terms of percentage changes, but has not made it clear that the change in price is not in terms of the same good, but that of another good. The analysis of XED is again limited, with no distinction between substitutes and complements.

4   The candidate has made a significant error here. If the demand for a car is price elastic, the manufacturer should reduce the price of the cars to increase total revenue, not increase it.

5   The candidate could have developed this evaluation more fully, e.g. by commenting on the significance of the extent of the increases in income, perhaps in terms of whether the business is producing cheaper car models or more expensive types.

6   It needs to be made clear that fuel and cars are complements.

Analysis:	3/8
Evaluation:	1/4
Total:	4/12

2.3 Price elasticity of supply

This topic is concerned with:

➤ the meaning and calculation of elasticity of supply

➤ the range of elasticities of supply

➤ the factors affecting elasticity of supply

➤ the implications for speed and ease with which businesses react to changed market conditions.

The meaning and calculation of elasticity of supply

Price elasticity of supply measures the responsiveness of the supply of a product to a change in its price. It is calculated by the following formula:

$$\frac{\text{Percentage change in the quantity supplied of a product}}{\text{Percentage change in the price of a product}}$$

If the percentage change in supply is greater than the percentage change in price, then supply is price elastic. If the percentage change in supply is less than the percentage change in price, then supply is inelastic.

> **Remember**
>
> You need to understand that elasticity involves the examination of percentage changes, not absolute changes. Price changes are not usually presented as percentage changes and you will therefore need to be able to calculate these.

> **Common error**
>
> It is important to remember that the percentage change in the quantity supplied of a product goes on top of the formula and what is causing that change on the bottom.

The range of elasticities of supply

The price elasticity of supply can range from perfectly elastic to perfectly inelastic, i.e. from infinity to zero. If supply is price elastic, the figure for PES will be greater than 1. If supply is price inelastic, the figure for PES will be less than 1.

A perfectly elastic supply curve is drawn as a horizontal straight line, as shown in Figure 2.10.

> **Key term**
>
> **Price elasticity of supply**: the responsiveness of the quantity supplied of a product to a change in its price.

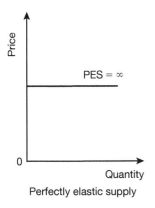

Perfectly elastic supply

▲ **Figure 2.10** Perfectly elastic supply

A perfectly inelastic supply curve is drawn as a vertical line, as shown in Figure 2.11.

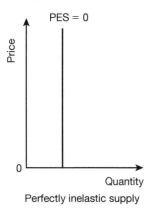

Perfectly inelastic supply

▲ **Figure 2.11** Perfectly inelastic supply

It is also important to see where a supply curve would intersect with the axes in a price/quantity diagram. Any straight line supply curve, drawn from the origin, has unitary price elasticity of supply, as shown in Figure 2.12. Any straight line supply curve which intersects with the price axis is price elastic, as shown in Figure 2.13. Any straight line supply curve which intersects with the quantity axis is price inelastic, as shown in Figure 2.14 on the next page.

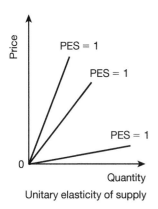

Unitary elasticity of supply

▲ **Figure 2.12** Unitary elasticity of supply

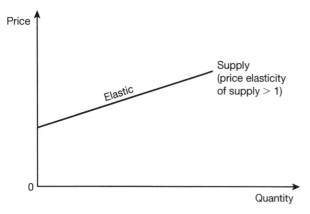

▲ **Figure 2.13** Price elastic supply

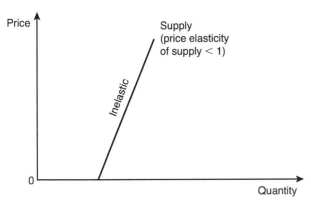

▲ **Figure 2.14** Price inelastic supply

✓ **What you need to know**

You need to understand that any straight line supply curve drawn from the origin has unitary elasticity of supply.

Any straight line supply curve that intersects with the price axis indicates elastic supply.

Any straight line supply curve that intersects with the quantity axis indicates inelastic supply.

The factors affecting elasticity of supply

There are a number of factors than can affect the elasticity of supply, including the following:

➤ the number of producers in an industry

➤ the amount of stock available

➤ the time period

➤ the existence of spare capacity

➤ the length of the production period

➤ the degree of factor mobility.

The implications for speed and ease with which businesses react to changed market conditions

It should be clear that that it is easier for businesses to react to changed market conditions over a relatively long period of time. Figure 2.15 shows how supply tends to be more inelastic in the short run and more elastic in the long run.

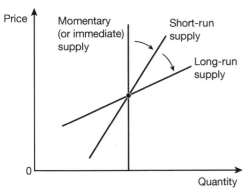

▲ **Figure 2.15** Differences in the speed of reaction of businesses to changed market conditions

You need to understand that the greater the number of suppliers in an industry, the easier it will be to increase output in response to a price increase, i.e. supply is likely to be relatively elastic. If there are no, or few, barriers of entry of firms into an industry, this will enable production to be increased relatively easily.

If there is an abundance of stocks, this will make supply relatively more elastic, whereas where products are perishable or difficult to stock, this will make supply relatively less elastic.

Supply is likely to be more elastic over a longer period of time as this will enable firms to invest in more factors of production and it will also allow more time for new firms to enter into an industry.

If there is a great deal of spare capacity in an industry, this is likely to make supply more elastic.

Supply will usually be more elastic when there is a shorter production period, e.g. the supply of manufactured products is likely to be more elastic than the supply of agricultural products.

If it is relatively easy to switch factors of production from one use to another, the more elastic supply is likely to be.

You need to understand that price elasticity of supply will vary over different periods of time.

Momentary supply refers to the situation of immediate supply when supply is perfectly inelastic.

Short-run supply refers to the situation when there are many constraints on the ability of businesses to substantially increase output, so supply is relatively inelastic.

Long-run supply refers to the situation when all factors of production are variable and so supply is relatively elastic.

You also need to understand that these time periods will vary from one industry to another. For example, the supply of agricultural products tends to be much more inelastic than the supply of manufactured goods because it can take a number of years to bring certain products to the market, depending on the length of the growing season.

In addition to the long run, it is also possible to refer to a period of time, known as the very long run, when there is a change of technological knowledge.

Raise your grade

Explain why price elasticity of supply is more elastic in the long run and why this makes the supply of manufactured products more elastic than the supply of agricultural products. [8]

Price elasticity of supply measures the responsiveness of the supply of a product to a change in its price. If the percentage change in supply is greater than the change in price, then supply is price elastic[1]. The elasticity of supply is more elastic in the long run because it gives more time for producers to increase output. For example, it will allow more time for new firms to enter an industry[2].

The supply of manufactured goods is more elastic than the supply of agricultural products because there is usually a shorter production period involved. It is relatively easy to increase the production of manufactured goods by employing more factors of production, e.g. more labour and capital, whereas agricultural production can take much longer to respond to changed market conditions because it can take many years for agricultural products to grow[3,4].

How to improve this answer

1   The formula for PES is not entirely accurate, as it makes no reference to the fact that it is the percentage or proportionate change in price that is significant, not just simply the change in price.

2   The candidate has given one example of why price elasticity of supply is likely to be more elastic in the long run than in the short run, but there are other examples that could have been given, such as giving more time to increase the capacity of the industry to respond to increased demand.

3   It would have been helpful if the candidate had included some appropriate examples to support the point being made. For example, it is easier to increase the production of cars than it is to increase the production of coffee.

4   The candidate could also have referred to the fact that the production of agricultural products can be affected more easily by adverse conditions than the production of manufactured goods. For example, it can be severely disrupted by adverse weather conditions and by disease.

Knowledge and understanding:	2/4
Application:	2/4
Total:	4/8

2.4 Interaction of demand and supply A 2(d)

This topic is concerned with:

➤ the effects of changes in supply and demand on equilibrium price and equilibrium quantity

➤ applications of demand and supply analysis

➤ movements along and shifts of the demand and supply curves

➤ joint demand (complements) and alternative demand (substitutes)

➤ joint supply

➤ the workings of the price mechanism; rationing, signalling and the transmission of preferences.

The effects of changes in supply and demand on equilibrium price and equilibrium quantity

An increase in demand

The effect of an increase in demand for a product can be seen in Figure 2.16. The original equilibrium was at price $0P_1$ and quantity $0Q_1$. If there is a change in the conditions of demand, e.g. there is a rise in incomes, the demand curve will shift to the right from D_1 to D_2. There has been an increase in demand and an extension of supply, leading to a new equilibrium position being established at a price of $0P_2$ and a quantity of $0Q_2$.

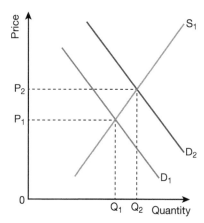

▲ **Figure 2.16** The effect of an increase in the demand for a product

A decrease in demand

The effect of a decrease in demand for a product can be seen in Figure 2.17. The original equilibrium was at price $0P_1$ and quantity $0Q_1$. If there is a change in the conditions of demand, e.g. there is a decrease in the advertising of the product, the demand curve will shift to the left from D_1 to D_2. There has been a decrease in demand and a contraction of supply, leading to a new equilibrium position being established at a price of $0P_2$ and a quantity of $0Q_2$.

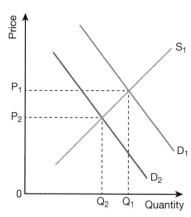

▲ **Figure 2.17** The effect of a decrease in the demand for a product

An increase in supply

The effect of an increase in supply of a product can be seen in Figure 2.18. The original equilibrium was at price $0P_1$ and quantity $0Q_1$. If there is a change in the conditions of supply, e.g. there is an improvement in the technology of production, the supply curve will shift to the right from S_1 to S_2. There has been an increase in supply and an extension of demand, leading to a new equilibrium position being established at a price of $0P_2$ and a quantity of $0Q_2$.

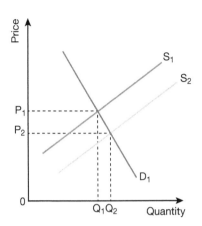

▲ **Figure 2.18** The effect of an increase in the supply of a product

A decrease in supply

The effect of a decrease in supply of a product can be seen in Figure 2.19. The original equilibrium was at price $0P_1$ and quantity $0Q_1$. If there is a change in the conditions of supply, e.g. there is an increase in the costs of production, the supply curve will shift to the left from S_1 to S_2. There has been a decrease in supply and a contraction of demand, leading to a new equilibrium position being established at a price of $0P_2$ and a quantity of $0Q_2$.

✓ **What you need to know**

It is important to be able to distinguish between an increase or decrease in demand or supply and an extension or contraction of demand or supply.

If there is a change in the conditions of demand or supply, there will be a shift of the demand or supply curve to the right or to the left.

If there is no change in the conditions of demand or supply, there will simply be a movement along a demand or supply curve, but not a shift; this is known as an extension or a contraction of demand or supply.

✗ **Common error**

Make sure you don't confuse a movement along a demand or a supply curve with a shift of a demand or a supply curve.

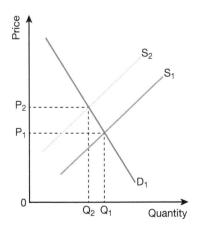

▲ **Figure 2.19** The effect of a decrease in the supply of a product

Applications of demand and supply analysis

There are many different possible applications of demand and supply analysis in a modern economy. For example, if an economy is experiencing an increase in the general level of incomes, there is likely to be an increase in the demand for televisions, shifting the demand curve for televisions to the right. This can be seen in Figure 2.20, where the demand curve has shifted to the right from D_0 to D_1. At the same time, an improvement in the technology of production may have reduced the cost of producing televisions, shifting the supply curve to the right from S_0 to S_1. The effect of these two shifts is that quantity has increased from $0Q_0$ to $0Q_2$. The effect of the shifts of the curves on price will depend on the extent of the two shifts. In Figure 2.20, price has returned to the original price of $0P_0$.

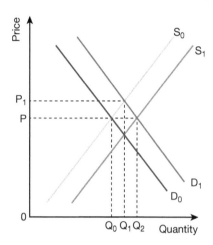

▲ **Figure 2.20** An application of demand and supply analysis to televisions

---

✓ **What you need to know**

You need to understand that in many situations, it is not simply a case of either the demand curve or the supply curve shifting, but both shifting at the same time.

It is also important to understand that the demand and supply curves may not shift in the same direction. For example, there could be a situation in a market where there is a shift to the right of the demand curve, but a shift to the left of the supply curve.

It is important to appreciate how a new equilibrium price and a new equilibrium quantity will be established in a market as a result of these shifts in demand and supply.

Movements along and shifts of the demand and supply curves

It has already been stressed that it is important to distinguish between a movement along a demand or supply curve and a shift of a demand or supply curve.

Movements along demand and supply curves

A movement along a demand or supply curve occurs when there is a change in the price of a product, but nothing else changes. This means that there is an assumption of *ceteris paribus*, i.e. all other influences on demand or supply are assumed to be constant and unchanged.

Shifts of demand and supply curves

If the situation of *ceteris paribus* does not apply, i.e. there has been a change in the conditions of demand or supply, then there will be a shift of the demand or supply curve. If the change in the conditions of demand or supply has been favourable, the curve will shift to the right. If the change in the conditions of demand or supply has been unfavourable, the curve will shift to the left.

> **✗ Common error**
>
> Make sure you don't confuse a change in demand or supply with a change in the conditions of demand or supply. It is important to be able to distinguish between a change in the price of a product and a change in other possible influences on demand or supply, other than a change in price.

Joint demand (complements) and alternative demand (substitutes)

It is important to distinguish between joint demand, in the case of complements, and alternative demand, in the case of substitutes.

Joint demand

Some products are jointly demanded, i.e. they are consumed together. Products that are jointly demanded are known as complements. Examples of complementary goods are CDs and CD players, or DVDs and DVD players.

Figure 2.21 shows what happens in the case of DVDs and DVD players. The demand for DVD players is shown on the left hand side. There is an increase in the demand for DVD players shown by a shift of the demand curve to the right from D to D_1. As DVDs and DVD players are complementary goods, there is also a shift of the demand curve to the right for DVDs, shown on the right hand side.

> **Key terms**
>
> **Joint demand**: a situation in which two complementary goods are normally demanded together.
>
> **Alternative demand**: a situation, also known as competitive demand, in which two goods are regarded as substitutes.

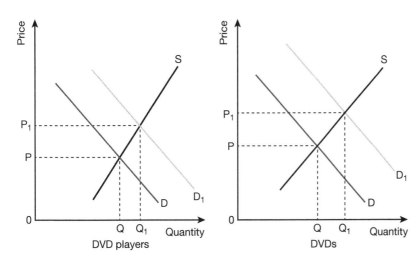

▲ **Figure 2.21** Joint demand for DVD players and DVDs

Alternative demand

Some products, however, are examples of alternative demand, i.e. they are in competition with each other. Products that are in competition with each other are known as substitutes. Examples of substitute goods are tea and coffee, or CDs and vinyl records.

Figure 2.22 shows what happens in the case of tea and coffee. The demand for tea is shown on the left hand side. There is an increase in the demand for tea shown by a shift of the demand curve to the right from D to D_1. As tea and coffee are substitute goods, there is a shift of the demand curve to the left for coffee, shown on the right hand side.

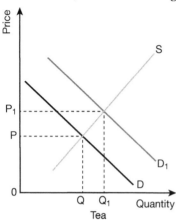 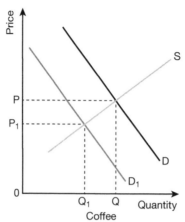

▲ **Figure 2.22** Alternative demand for tea and coffee

✓ **What you need to know**

It is important that you are able to clearly distinguish between a complement and a substitute.

You need to be able to provide appropriate examples of complements and substitutes.

You should understand that products will not necessarily be perfect substitutes for each other. For example, in the case of tea and coffee, some people may consume both products.

Joint supply

Joint supply occurs when the production of one product involves the production of another. This can sometimes happen in the chemical industry where one product may be produced as a by-product of another.

The workings of the price mechanism; rationing, signalling and the transmission of preferences
The workings of the price mechanism

The price mechanism plays a key role in the allocation of resources in a market. The Scottish economist Adam Smith (1723–1790) stressed the importance of the workings of the price mechanism to a successful economy, describing prices as an 'invisible hand' in allocating scarce resources.

Rationing

Prices also perform a key function as a rationing mechanism, e.g. if the supply of a product can't match the demand for it, the price of the product is likely to rise and this will ration the product because only those who are able to pay the higher price will be able to afford it.

Signalling and the transmission of preferences

Changes in the prices of different products, in response to changes in the demand and supply of them, can act as signals, indicating which resources will be needed to produce some products rather than others. In this way, the price mechanism provides a means by which consumers can transmit their preferences for certain products. This is termed signalling.

Key term

Joint supply: a situation where the production of one good automatically brings about an increase in the supply of another.

Remember

Products in joint supply are produced together, e.g. the production of beef will also lead to the supply of hides for making leather.

Key terms

Rationing: a limit on the amount of a product that can be consumed.

Signalling: the way in which the price mechanism operates by allowing consumers to transmit their preferences for certain products.

✓ **What you need to know**

You need to understand how the price mechanism operates as a rationing and signalling device through the operation of market forces in a free market, in contrast to a system where the government takes the major decisions in relation to the prices of products, as is the case in a planned or command economy.

Adam Smith perhaps expressed this role of prices in an economy best when he referred to them as an 'invisible hand'.

 Raise your grade

Distinguish between a movement along a demand curve and a shift of a demand curve in relation to the demand for a television.   [8]

A movement along a demand curve occurs when the price of a product changes and all other possible influences on demand are unchanged[1,2]. A shift of a demand curve occurs when there is a change in other possible influences on demand, other than price[3].

In the case of a television, more are likely to be demanded when there is a fall in price of them, i.e. there will be a movement along the demand curve[4]. If there is a change in other possible influences on the demand for televisions, other than the price of the product, leading to an increase in the demand for them, then there will be a shift of the demand curve[5,6].

How to improve this answer

1   The candidate could have referred to this situation of other possible influences on demand remaining unchanged as *ceteris paribus*.

2   The candidate simply refers to a movement along a demand curve, but the answer would have been improved if there had been a clear distinction between an extension of demand and a contraction of demand.

3   The candidate could have included some examples of other possible influences on demand, such as changes in incomes or the prices of substitutes and complements.

4   The candidate could have pointed out that if there was a fall in the price of televisions, this could be shown by an extension of demand.

5   The candidate could have made it clear that in this particular situation, there would be a shift of the demand curve to the right.

6   In terms of application to the context of the question, the candidate could have given some examples that would be appropriate for televisions, such as increase in incomes or an increase in the advertising of the product.

Knowledge and understanding:	2/4
Application:	2/4
Total:	4/8

2.5 **Market equilibrium and disequilibrium** `AS 2(e)`

This topic is concerned with:

➤ the meaning of equilibrium and disequilibrium.

The meaning of equilibrium and disequilibrium

Demand and supply have each been considered and it is now necessary to bring them together to establish market equilibrium. This position is where the quantity demanded and the quantity supplied in a market are equal and there is neither excess demand or excess supply. This position of equilibrium is where there is no tendency to change. If there was a change in the demand and/or supply of a product, the market would be said to be in a state of market disequilibrium, although a state of equilibrium will eventually be restored.

A situation of excess supply can be seen in Figure 2.23. If the price is above the equilibrium price of P_0, e.g. it is at P_1, there will be a situation of excess supply, i.e. the quantity that producers are willing to supply at that price is greater than the quantity that consumers are willing to demand at that price. This can be seen in the diagram by the horizontal distance between Q_1 and Q_2. As a result of the excess supply, the price will fall until equilibrium is reached at a price of P_0 and a quantity of Q_0.

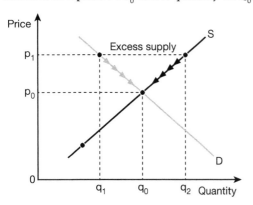

▲ **Figure 2.23** Excess supply bringing about a state of equilibrium in a market

A state of excess demand can be seen in Figure 2.24. If the price is below the equilibrium price of P_0, e.g. it is at P_3, there will be a situation of excess demand, i.e. the quantity that producers are willing to supply at that price is less than the quantity that consumers are willing to demand at that price. This can be seen in the diagram by the horizontal distance between Q_3 and Q_4. As a result of the excess demand, the price will rise until equilibrium is reached at a price of P_0 and a quantity of Q_0.

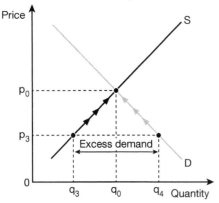

▲ **Figure 2.24** Excess demand bringing about a state of equilibrium in a market

> **Remember**
>
> You need to understand that a state of equilibrium in a market is where there is no tendency to change, i.e. the market is said to be in a state of rest or balance.

✓ **What you need to know**

A situation of excess supply, where producers are willing to supply more at a given price than consumers are willing to demand, will create disequilibrium in a market. However, a state of equilibrium will be restored in the market by price falling until a point where supply and demand are equal.

A situation of excess demand, where producers are willing to supply less at a given price than consumers are willing to demand, will create disequilibrium in a market. However, a state of equilibrium will be restored in the market by price rising until a point where supply and demand are equal.

 Raise your grade

Describe what is meant by a situation of market equilibrium and explain how market disequilibrium can arise. [8]

A situation of market equilibrium is said to exist when there is no tendency to change. This means that the quantity demanded in a market is exactly equal to the quantity supplied in a market and there is a state of rest or balance[1].

A situation of market disequilibrium can occur when there is a change in this situation. This could come about through either excess demand or excess supply[2,3]. A new equilibrium position will eventually be reached at a new equilibrium price and a new equilibrium quantity[4].

How to improve this answer

1   The candidate has described what is meant by a situation of market equilibrium, but could have made the answer clearer by stating that this equilibrium position will be a particular price and a particular quantity.

2   The candidate really needed to develop this much more fully. In the case of excess demand, price will eventually rise to restore a state of equilibrium in the market.

3   In the case of excess supply, price will eventually fall to restore a state of equilibrium in the market.

4   The candidate could have developed the answer more fully by referring to the fact that the new equilibrium will be at a market clearing position where demand is equal to supply and there is no excess demand or excess supply.

Knowledge and understanding:	2/4
Application:	2/4
Total:	4/8

2.6 Consumer surplus and producer surplus AS 2(f)

This topic is concerned with:

- the meaning and significance of consumer surplus and producer surplus
- how these are affected by changes in equilibrium price and equilibrium quantity.

The meaning and significance of consumer and producer surplus

Consumer surplus

This refers to a situation where consumers are able to obtain a value from consuming a good or service that is above the price that is actually paid for the product. In Figure 2.25, 0P is the equilibrium price and 0Q the equilibrium quantity. At any price above 0P, consumers would have been willing to pay a higher price than 0P and so the size of the consumer surplus is shown by the triangle PAB.

Producer surplus

This refers to a situation where producers would have been willing to accept a lower price for a product, but actually received a higher price than this. In Figure 2.25, 0P is the equilibrium price and 0Q the equilibrium quantity. Producers would have been willing to accept a price below 0P up to point B and so the size of the producer surplus is shown by the triangle PCB.

> **Key terms**
>
> **Consumer surplus**: the difference between the maximum price an individual is prepared to pay for a product and the price that is actually paid.
>
> **Producer surplus**: the difference between the minimum price a producer is prepared to accept for a product and the price that is actually received.

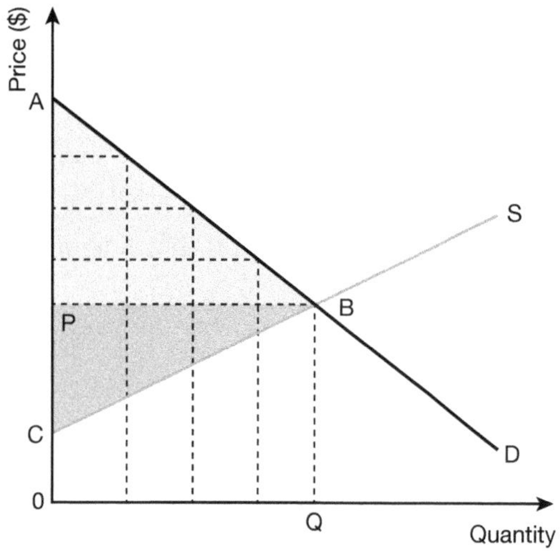

▲ **Figure 2.25** Consumer surplus and producer surplus

> **✓ What you need to know**
>
> You need to understand that consumer surplus refers to a situation where there is a difference between the maximum price that consumers are willing to pay for a product and the price prevailing in a market that they actually pay. This is shown by the triangle between the price line and the demand curve.
>
> Producer surplus, on the other hand, is the difference that producers are willing to accept for what is sold and the price that is actually received. This is shown by the triangle between the price line and the supply curve.

How consumer surplus and producer surplus are affected by changes in equilibrium price and equilibrium quantity

Consumer surplus and producer surplus are affected by changes in equilibrium price and equilibrium quantity. For example, if equilibrium price were to increase above 0P in Figure 2.25, the size of the consumer surplus would be reduced.

Revision checklist

I can:

➤ understand the difference between demand and effective demand ☐

➤ appreciate the difference between an individual demand curve and a market demand curve ☐

➤ understand the relationships between the changes in the prices of products and the changes in the demand for them ☐

➤ be clear about the meaning and significance of *ceteris paribus* ☐

➤ distinguish between an individual supply curve and a market supply curve ☐

➤ understand the relationship between the changes in the prices of products and the changes in the supply of them ☐

➤ be clear about the various factors that can influence the demand for a product ☐

➤ understand the various factors that can influence the supply of a product ☐

➤ fully understand the meaning and calculation of price elasticity of demand ☐

➤ clearly understand the meaning and calculation of income elasticity of demand ☐

➤ be clear about the meaning and calculation of cross-elasticity of demand ☐

➤ understand the factors that affect the different elasticities of demand ☐

➤ be clear about the implications for revenue and business decisions of the different elasticities of demand ☐

➤ fully understand the meaning and calculation of price elasticity of supply ☐

➤ be clear about the factors affecting the price elasticity of supply ☐

➤ fully understand the implications for speed and ease with which businesses react to changed market conditions ☐

➤ understand the meaning of equilibrium and disequilibrium in a market ☐

➤ understand the significance of the interaction of demand and supply ☐

➤ appreciate the effects of changes in supply and demand on equilibrium price and equilibrium quantity in a market ☐

➤ understand the variety of applications of demand and supply analysis in a modern economy ☐

➤ distinguish between movements along demand and supply curves and shifts of demand and supply curves ☐

➤ be clear about the distinction between joint demand and alternative demand ☐

➤ understand how there can be joint supply of some products ☐

➤ understand significance of the price mechanism as a rationing and signalling device in a market ☐

➤ distinguish between consumer surplus and producer surplus ☐

➤ understand how consumer surplus and producer surplus can be affected by changes in equilibrium price and equilibrium quantity. ☐

1 Effective demand is defined as demand that is:

   A adjusted to take account of the rate of inflation in an economy

   B backed by the ability and willingness of consumers to pay

   C the outcome of the dreams of all consumers in a market

   D what consumers would like to purchase. [1]

2 Which of the following will cause the shift of the demand curve for a product to the right?

   A A decrease in the price of a substitute.

   B A decrease in the price of the product.

   C An increase in the price of a complement.

   D An increase in the price of a substitute. [1]

3 Which of the following will cause the shift of the supply curve of a product to the left?

   A A decrease in the costs of production.

   B An improvement in the technology of production.

   C An increase in the costs of production.

   D An increase in the productivity of factors of production. [1]

4 Which of the following is drawn as a rectangular hyperbola?

   A Elastic price elasticity of demand.

   B Perfectly elastic price elasticity of demand.

   C Perfectly inelastic price elasticity of demand.

   D Unitary price elasticity of demand. [1]

5 The income elasticity of demand is negative for:

   A a luxury

   B a necessity

   C a normal good

   D an inferior good. [1]

6 Any straight line supply curve, drawn through the origin, will have:

   A elastic price elasticity of supply

   B inelastic price elasticity of supply

   C perfectly inelastic price elasticity of supply

   D unitary price elasticity of supply. [1]

7 Which of the following will cause a movement along a demand curve for a product?

   A A change in incomes.

   B A change in the price of a complement.

   C A change in the price of a substitute.

   D A change in the price of the product. [1]

8 Which of the following are examples of alternative demand?

   A Beef and hides.

   B CDs and CD players.

   C DVDs and DVD players.

   D Tea and coffee. [1]

9 Adam Smith described the price mechanism as:

   A an invisible hand

   B *ceteris paribus*

   C normal

   D ostentatious. [1]

10 Consumer surplus is shown in a diagram by:

   A half of the area between the demand curve and the supply curve

   B the triangle between the demand curve and the supply curve

   C the triangle between the price line and the demand curve

   D the triangle between the price line and the supply curve. [1]

11 (a) Explain why it is important to distinguish between changes in the prices of cars and changes in the conditions of demand for cars. [8]

   (b) Discuss why income elasticity of demand is elastic for some models of cars and inelastic for others. [12]

12 (a) Explain what is meant by market equilibrium and why a market may be in a state of disequilibrium for only a short period of time. [8]

   (b) Discuss how effective the price mechanism is likely to be in the transmission of consumer preferences. [12]

Government microeconomic intervention

Key topics

- ➤ maximum and minimum prices
- ➤ taxes (direct and indirect)
- ➤ subsidies
- ➤ transfer payments
- ➤ direct provision of goods and services
- ➤ nationalisation and privatisation.

3.1 Maximum and minimum prices

This topic is concerned with:

- ➤ the meaning of maximum and minimum prices and their effect on the market.

Maximum price control

The price and quantity in a market are usually determined by market forces, i.e. by demand and supply. However, a government could decide to intervene in a market by establishing a maximum price that acts as a ceiling, ensuring that price cannot go any higher than this maximum price. The effect of imposing a maximum price in a market can be seen in Figure 3.1.

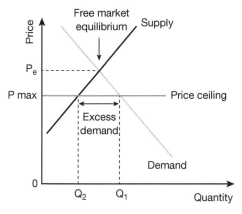

▲ **Figure 3.1** Maximum price control in a market

> **Key term**
>
> **Maximum price:** a situation where a maximum price, or price ceiling, is established in a market below what would have been the equilibrium price without government intervention.

> ★ **Exam tip**
>
> Make sure you can demonstrate you understand that a maximum price has to be established in a market below the equilibrium price if the imposition of the price ceiling is going to have any effect.

> 💡 **Remember**
>
> Remember that the maximum price has to be established at a price below equilibrium price if the price control is going to be effective.

> ✗ **Common error**
>
> Make sure you don't draw the maximum price above, rather than below, the equilibrium price in a market. Such a situation would have no effect.

Minimum price control

A government could also decide to intervene in a market by establishing a
minimum price that acts as a floor, ensuring that price cannot go any lower
than this minimum price. The effect of imposing a maximum price in a
market can be seen in Figure 3.2.

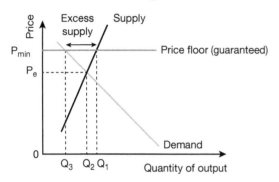

▲ **Figure 3.2** Minimum price control in a market

 Raise your grade

Discuss to what extent the establishment of a maximum price in a market is likely to be effective.   [12]

Instead of allowing an equilibrium price to be established in a market by the intersection of
demand and supply, a government could intervene in a market by establishing its own price[1].
This would be especially important as a way of keeping down the prices of certain products[2].

However, such an initiative by a government could lead to certain problems and difficulties.
For example, a maximum price could lead to excess demand[3] and this could create some form
of queue or waiting list[4]. Such a situation could possibly lead to an element of corruption and
bribery. It is also possible that the imposition of a price ceiling in the official market for the
product could lead to the creation of an informal market[5] and the price in this market is likely
to be different from that in the legal or official market[6].

How to improve this answer

1 The candidate has implied that the price would be different as a result of government intervention, but has not made it clear that the imposition of a maximum price control would establish a price below the equilibrium price. The candidate could have included a diagram to show this and to support the answer.

2 The candidate has referred to keeping down the prices of certain products, but it would have been helpful if some appropriate examples had been included, such as important food items, the amount of rent paid for housing or in the transport market e.g. the cost of rail transport.

3 The candidate has referred to the situation of excess demand, but has not really made it clear how this would come about as a result of the price being lower than it would have been without government intervention.

4 The candidate has referred to the possible existence of a queue or a waiting list, but this point could have been developed further by reference to the need for an alternative allocative mechanism, such as through the use of rationing.

5 The candidate has referred to the existence of an informal, in contrast to a formal, market, but there could also have been a reference to such markets also being known as black markets.

6 The candidate has stated that the price in the informal market would be different from that in the formal market, but has not made it clear that this price would be likely to be higher.

Analysis:	2/8
Evaluation:	2/4
Total:	4/12

3.2 Taxes (direct and indirect)

AS 3(b)

This topic is concerned with:

➤ the impact and incidence of taxes

➤ specific and *ad valorem* taxes

➤ average and marginal rates of taxation

➤ proportional, progressive and regressive taxes

➤ the canons of taxation.

The impact and incidence of taxes

It is important to distinguish between the impact of a tax and the incidence of a tax. The impact of a tax refers to the person, company or transaction on which a tax is levied, i.e. it is essentially the legal responsibility for the payment of tax. The incidence of a tax, however, refers to the burden of a tax, i.e. who actually pays a tax.

It is also important to distinguish between direct and indirect taxes. A direct tax is one that is imposed on money that is received, e.g. income tax on the earnings of individuals or corporation tax on the profits of companies. An indirect tax is one that is imposed on money that is spent, e.g. an excise duty on a particular product or a sales tax such as VAT (value added tax) or GST (goods and services tax).

> **Key terms**
>
> **Impact of a tax:** the person, company or transaction on which a tax is levied.
>
> **Incidence of a tax:** how the burden of taxation is shared between the producer and the consumer.
>
> **Direct tax:** a tax levied on income or wealth.
>
> **Indirect tax:** a tax levied on expenditure.

> ★ **Exam tip**
>
> You need to be able to clearly distinguish between a direct and an indirect tax and you may be required to provide appropriate examples of each type of tax.

The incidence of a tax will depend on the elasticity of the demand and supply curves. The more inelastic is the demand, and the more elastic is the supply, the greater the burden of a tax will be on the consumer rather than the producer.

Specific and *ad valorem* taxes

It is important to be able to distinguish between specific and *ad valorem* indirect taxes.

A specific tax, such as an excise duty, is where a fixed amount has to be paid. This is shown by a parallel shift to the left of the supply curve so that the vertical distance between the two supply curves remains constant, as in Figure 3.3.

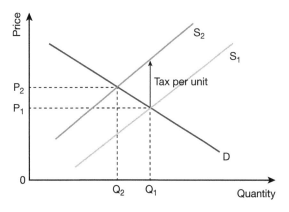

▲ **Figure 3.3** The imposition of a specific tax

An *ad valorem* tax, such as VAT (value added tax), is where a particular percentage has to be paid, e.g. 20% on the price of a product. This is shown by a shift to the left of the supply curve, but as the tax is in the form of a percentage, rather than a specific amount, the gap between the two supply curves will widen.

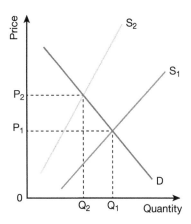

▲ **Figure 3.4** The imposition of an *ad valorem* tax

Key terms

Specific tax: this is where a specific amount of money has to be paid in taxation.

Ad valorem tax: this is where the tax on the consumption of a product is a percentage of the value of the product rather than a fixed amount.

💡 **Remember**

When a specific tax is imposed, the supply curve shifts to the left parallel to the original supply curve. When an *ad valorem* tax is imposed, the supply curve shifts to the left, but the vertical distance between the two supply curve widens.

Producers will try to pass the increased cost, in the form of the tax, on to the consumer. The ability of producers to do this depends on the relative elasticities of demand and supply. If demand is more inelastic than supply, the consumers will pay the greater proportion of the tax, i.e. the greater incidence of the tax will be placed on them. If supply is more inelastic than demand, the producers will pay the greater proportion of the tax, i.e. the greater incidence of the tax will be placed on them. If demand and supply are equally inelastic, the incidence of the tax will be equally shared by the producers and the consumers.

Average and marginal rates of taxation

It is important to be able to distinguish between average and marginal rates of taxation.

The average rate of taxation refers to the average percentage of total income which is paid in taxes. The marginal rate of taxation refers to the proportion of any increase in income that is paid in tax.

Proportional, progressive and regressive taxes

It is important to be able to distinguish between proportional, progressive and regressive taxes.

A proportional tax, also known as a flat tax, has a constant marginal rate of tax (MRT) irrespective of any changes in the income level. With a proportional tax, the marginal rate of tax and the average rate of tax are the same.

A progressive tax is one where not only the amount of tax paid rises when there is an increase in income, but the rate of tax increases. For example, rates of tax could start at 10% and then increase to 20%, 30%, 40%, 50% and even higher as income rises. In this situation, the MRT increases with a rise in income and the marginal rate of tax will be higher than the average rate of tax.

A regressive tax is the opposite of a progressive tax. This occurs where a fixed percentage of tax is imposed on expenditure, as with VAT (value added tax). In this case, the MRT falls as income increases.

Key terms

Proportional tax: a situation where the proportion of income paid in tax remains constant regardless of the level of income.

Progressive tax: a situation where the proportion of income paid in tax increases as income increases.

Regressive tax: a situation where the proportion of income paid in tax falls as income increases.

Key terms

Average rate of taxation: the average percentage of total income that is paid in taxes.

Marginal rate of taxation: the proportion of additional income that is taken in tax.

★ **Exam tip**

Make sure that you are able to clearly distinguish between a person's average rate of tax and their marginal rate of tax.

💡 **Remember**

In Unit 1, the importance of decisions taken at the margin was stressed. The distinction between average and marginal rates of taxation is an example of the importance of being able to distinguish between average and marginal data.

The distinction between these three types of tax can be seen in Figure 3.5.

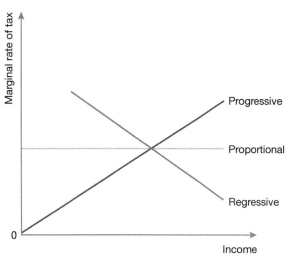

Figure 3.5 Proportional, progressive and regressive taxation

Remember

It is important to distinguish between average rates of taxation and marginal rates of taxation.

✓ **What you need to know**

With a proportional tax, the MRT is constant when there is a rise in income.
With a progressive tax, the MRT increases when there is a rise in income.
With a regressive tax, the MRT decreases when there is a rise in income.

The canons of taxation

The canons of taxation refer to a number of principles that should apply to taxation. They include the following:

➤ equity or fairness

➤ certainty or transparency

➤ convenience

➤ cost

➤ efficiency.

Key term

Canons of taxation: the principles of taxation by which a particular tax should be judged.

 Raise your grade

Explain, with the use of examples, the differences between progressive and regressive taxes.　　[8]

A progressive tax is one where not only the amount of income paid in tax rises as incomes rise, but also the rate of tax on income increases[1]. An example of such a tax is income tax[2].

A regressive tax is one where the rate of tax remains the same for all people irrespective of their income[3]. In this situation, a person's income is not taken into account[4].

How to improve this answer

1 The answer could have been developed more fully by referring to the fact that there will be an increase in both marginal and average rates of tax as incomes rise.

2 The candidate has given an appropriate example of a progressive tax, i.e. income tax, but could have written more about what happens in many countries in relation to income tax, i.e. that the marginal rate of tax will rise as incomes rise above a particular threshold, e.g. 10%, 30%, 50%.

3 The candidate correctly states what happens in relation to a regressive tax, but the answer could have been developed further by referring to the fact that there will be a decrease in both marginal and average rates of tax as incomes rise.

4 The candidate has not actually given an example of a regressive tax, despite the fact that the question explicitly requires the candidates to do so. Examples could include VAT or GST.

Knowledge and understanding:	2/4
Application:	1/4
Total:	3/8

3.3 Subsidies

AS 3 (C)

This topic is concerned with:

➤ the impact and incidence of subsidies.

Subsidies are where a government gives money to a producer, shifting the supply curve to the right. This can be seen in Figure 3.6. The vertical distance between S_1 and S_2 indicates the extent of the subsidy.

> **Key term**
>
> Subsidies: the amount of money paid by a government to a producer so that the price to the consumer will be lower than it otherwise would have been.

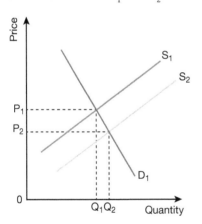

Figure 3.6 The effect of a subsidy

The impact and incidence of subsidies in a market will depend on differences in the elasticity of demand for, and the elasticity of supply of, a product.

> **Remember**
>
> The impact and incidence of a subsidy will depend on the elasticity of demand for, and the elasticity of supply of, a product.

> ✓ **What you need to know**
>
> If the demand for a product is relatively elastic, the provision of a subsidy would lead to a relatively small reduction in price, but a relatively large increase in consumption.
>
> If the demand for a product is relatively inelastic, the provision of a subsidy would lead to a relatively large reduction in price, but a relatively small increase in consumption.

3.4 Transfer payments
AS 3 (d)

This topic is concerned with:

➤ the meaning of transfer payments and their effect on the market.

A government could intervene in a market through the provision of transfer payments. This is where revenue received by a government, such as through the proceeds from taxation, is used to provide financial support for people, particularly those who are less well off. Examples of transfer payments include pensions and social security payments.

The provision of transfer payments could have an effect on the market. For example, unemployment benefit is paid in many countries to those people who are unemployed. This can be seen as advantageous to those who have been unable to find employment, but it could also be argued that it has a distorting effect on the labour market. For example, if the unemployment benefit is relatively high, it may make some people unwilling to seek employment.

> **✗ Common error**
>
> Make sure you don't confuse transfer payments with transfer earnings in relation to wage determination.

> **Key term**
>
> **Transfer payments**: a situation where revenue is received from one part of society, such as taxpayers, and paid to another part of society, such as pensioners.

> **💡 Remember**
>
> Although transfer payments can be seen as worthwhile, transferring money from one group of people to another, they can also be seen as potentially having a distorting effect on a market.

Direct provision of goods and services
AS 3 (e)

This topic is concerned with:

➤ the meaning of direct provision of goods and services and the effect of this provision on the market.

Another way in which a government could intervene in a market is through the direct provision of goods and services. Although a government could intervene in a market to discourage the production of goods and services, such as through the use of taxation, or to encourage the production of goods and services, such as through the use of subsidies, it could also intervene in a market by directly providing goods and services itself, often alongside the provision of such goods and services by the private sector.

Such direct provision in a market would increase the size of the public sector and reduce the size of the private sector in an economy. It could have a number of advantages, such as saving an industry from collapse, but it could also have a number of disadvantages, such as being less efficient.

> **Key term**
>
> **Direct provision of goods and services**: a situation where a government decides to provide particular goods and services itself.

> **💡 Remember**
>
> Make sure you understand that the direct provision of goods and services in a market can have both advantages and disadvantages.

3.6 Nationalisation and privatisation
AS 3 (f)

This topic is concerned with:

➤ the meaning of nationalisation and privatisation and their effect on the market.

Nationalisation

Nationalisation refers to the process of transferring firms and/or industries from the private sector to the public sector. Therefore, ownership becomes public ownership and these nationalised firms and/or industries will be controlled in some way by the government.

The effect on the market can be positive, such as avoiding a wasteful duplication of resources, or negative, such as when decisions are taken for political, rather than for economic, reasons.

> **Key term**
>
> **Nationalisation**: the process whereby private sector firms and/or industries become part of the public sector of an economy, with the government or state owning and controlling these resources.

Privatisation

Whereas nationalisation refers to the process of transferring the ownership of assets from the private sector to the public sector, privatisation refers to the process of transferring ownership in the opposite direction, i.e. from the public sector to the private sector. It is also known as denationalisation.

The effect on the market can be positive, such as bringing about an improvement in efficiency, or negative, such as an increase in negative externalities.

> **Key term**
>
> Privatisation: the process whereby public sector firms and/or industries become part of the private sector of an economy, with the government no longer owning or controlling these resources.

> ✓ **What you need to know**
>
> You need to understand that the process of privatisation can take different forms, including the creation of a public limited company in the private sector, deregulation in the form of removing legal restrictions and controls, and contracting out or outsourcing where the responsibility of providing particular services is transferred from the public to the private sector.

> **Key terms**
>
> Deregulation: the removal of legal restrictions and controls on economic activity, usually to allow a greater degree of competition in a market.
>
> Contracting out: the transfer of responsibility for providing a particular service from the public to the private sector. This can also be known as outsourcing.

> X **Common error**
>
> Make sure you don't confuse the creation of a public limited company, as a result of privatisation, with the public sector or public enterprise. A public limited company is in the private sector, not the public sector.

I can:

- ➤ understand what is meant by a maximum price and how it can affect a market ☐
- ➤ understand the meaning of a minimum price and how it has a different effect on a market compared to a maximum price ☐
- ➤ be clear about where a maximum price and a minimum price shown be shown in a diagram ☐
- ➤ understand the factors affecting the likely effectiveness of maximum and minimum prices in a market ☐
- ➤ understand the distinction between the impact and the incidence of a tax ☐
- ➤ be clear about the distinction between a direct and an indirect tax ☐
- ➤ be able to give appropriate examples of direct and indirect taxes ☐
- ➤ understand the difference between a specific tax and an *ad valorem* tax ☐
- ➤ be clear about the distinction between average and marginal rates of taxation ☐
- ➤ understand the differences between proportional, progressive and regressive taxes and are able to give appropriate examples of each type of tax ☐
- ➤ understand the principles or canons of taxation ☐
- ➤ understand what is meant by a subsidy and that the impact of a subsidy depends on the price elasticity of demand and supply ☐
- ➤ understand what is meant by a transfer payment and that you understand the effect a transfer payment could have on a market ☐
- ➤ be clear about what is meant by the direct provision of goods and services in a market and about the effect this could have on a market ☐
- ➤ understand what is meant by nationalisation ☐
- ➤ be clear about the possible advantages and disadvantages of nationalisation in an economy ☐
- ➤ understand what is meant by privatisation ☐
- ➤ be clear about the possible advantages and disadvantages of privatisation in an economy ☐
- ➤ be sure you understand that privatisation can take different forms. ☐

? Exam-style questions

1 A maximum price control in a market will establish a price:

    A above the equilibrium price

    B at the equilibrium price

    C below the equilibrium price

    D that creates a price floor. [1]

2 A minimum price control in a market will establish a price:

    A above the equilibrium price

    B at the equilibrium price

    C below the equilibrium price

    D that creates a price ceiling. [1]

3 The incidence of a tax refers to the:

    A eventual burden of a tax

    B person on which a tax is levied

    C rate at which the average rate of tax increases

    D rate at which the marginal rate of tax increases. [1]

4 A tax which involves a particular amount of money to be paid on a product is known as:

    A a marginal tax

    B a specific tax

    C an *ad valorem* tax

    D an average tax. [1]

5 A sales tax of a fixed percentage is an example of a:

    A progressive tax

    B proportional tax

    C regressive tax

    D transfer tax. [1]

6 The average rate of tax and the marginal rate of tax are the same in the case of a:

    A progressive tax

    B proportional tax

    C regressive tax

    D transport tax. [1]

7 Which of the following is not a canon of taxation?

    A Certainty.

    B Convenience.

    C Disincentive.

    D Equity. [1]

8 A subsidy will:

    A lead to a higher price in a market

    B lead to a lower quantity in a market

    C shift the supply curve to the left

    D shift the supply curve to the right. [1]

9 The transfer of ownership of assets from the private sector to the public sector is known as:

    A deregulation

    B nationalisation

    C outsourcing

    D privatisation. [1]

10 Which of the following is an advantage of privatisation?

    A A reduction in the number of people employed in an industry.

    B The creation of a private sector monopoly.

    C The establishment of greater efficiency in a market.

    D The duplication of resources. [1]

11 **(a)** Explain why the average rate of tax and the marginal rate of tax are different in the case of income tax. [8]

    (b) Discuss whether the provision of a subsidy is likely to be effective in substantially reducing the price of a product charged to consumers. [12]

12 **(a)** Explain what is meant by a transfer payment and why some such payments can have a distorting effect on a market. [8]

    (b) Discuss whether the privatisation of an industry is always in the public interest. [12]

Key topics

➤ aggregate demand (AD) and aggregate supply (AS) analysis

➤ inflation

➤ the balance of payments

➤ exchange rates

➤ the terms of trade

➤ the principles of absolute and comparative advantage

➤ protectionism.

4.1 Aggregate demand (AD) and aggregate supply (AS) analysis

AS 4(a)

This topic is concerned with:

➤ the shape and determinants of AD and AS curves;
AD = C + I + G + (X − M)

➤ the distinction between a movement along and a shift in AD and AS

➤ the interaction of AD and AS and the determination of the level of output, prices and employment.

The shape and determinants of AD and AS curves; AD = C + I + G + (X − M)

Aggregate demand (AD)

Aggregate demand (AD) refers to the total demand for all the goods and services in an economy. It is made up of four elements:

➤ C: consumer spending

➤ I: investment by firms, such as expenditure on machinery and equipment

➤ G: government expenditure

➤ X − M: the net effect of trade, i.e. exports minus imports.

The AD curve therefore reflects these four determinants. It slopes downwards from left to right. This is shown in Figure 4.1. If the price level rises from $0P_1$ to $0P_2$, real output falls from $0Y_1$ to $0Y_2$.

> **Key term**
>
> Aggregate demand (AD): the total value of demand in an economy, consisting of consumption (C), investment (I), government expenditure (G) and net exports (X-M).

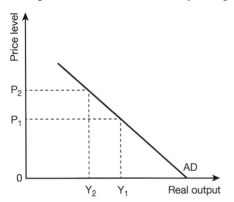

▲ **Figure 4.1** The AD curve

Aggregate supply (AS)

Aggregate supply (AS) refers to the total output that the firms in an economy are able and willing to supply at different price levels in a given period of time. The AS curve slopes upwards from left to right. This is shown in Figure 4.2. If the price level rises from $0P_1$ to $0P_2$, real output rises from $0Y_1$ to $0Y_2$.

Key term

Aggregate supply (AS): the total value of goods and services produced in an economy.

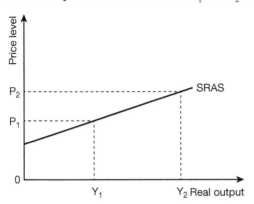

▲ **Figure 4.2** The AS curve in the short run

However, this is essentially the situation in the short run and it is important to distinguish between aggregate supply in the short run and in the long run. In the long run it is possible that the AS curve becomes vertical, i.e. supply is perfectly inelastic. This is shown in Figure 4.3 where at the full employment level of real output, the AS curve is vertical.

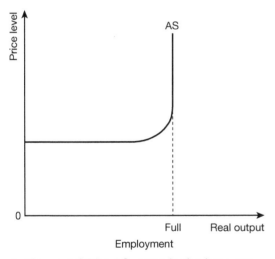

▲ **Figure 4.3** The AS curve in the long run

What you need to know

It is important that you are able to distinguish between AS in the short run and AS in the long run. At relatively low levels of real output, supply is likely to be relatively elastic. It could even be perfectly elastic, in which case it would be shown as a horizontal line. However, as real output increases, and gets closer to the full employment level of real output, aggregate supply will become increasingly inelastic, i.e. the AS curve will become closer to vertical. When the full employment level of real output is reached, the AS curve will be perfectly inelastic and vertical.

Remember

In the determination of aggregate demand in an economy, it is the net effect of international trade that needs to be taken into account, i.e. exports minus imports.

The distinction between a movement along and a shift in AD and AS

In the diagrams above, in relation to both AD and AS, a movement along the curve will be determined by a change in the price level. However, if there is a change in AD or AS other than as a result of a change in the price level, then there will be a shift of the AD or AS curve.

A shift of the AD curve, from AD_1 to AD_2, is shown in Figure 4.4, causing an increase in the price level from $0P_1$ to $0P_2$ and an increase in real output from $0Y_1$ to $0Y_2$. There is a movement along, but not a shift of, the AS curve.

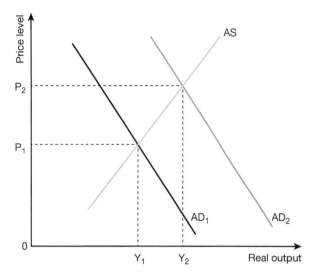

▲ **Figure 4.4** A shift of the AD curve to the right

A shift of the AS curve, from AS_1 to AS_2, is shown in Figure 4.5, causing an increase in price from $0P_1$ to $0P_2$ and a decrease in real output from $0Y_1$ to $0Y_2$. There is a movement along, but not a shift of, the AD curve.

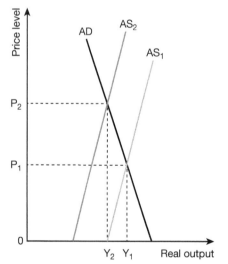

▲ **Figure 4.5** A shift of the AS curve to the left

✓ What you need to know

It is important to be able to distinguish between a movement along an AD or an AS curve, and a shift of an AD or an AS curve. The important difference is that movements along an AD or an AS curve can only be caused by a change in the price level, whereas shifts of an AD or an AS curve can be caused by any other factor affecting AD or AS apart from price. For example, in Figure 4.5, the shift of the AS curve to the left could have been caused by an increase in the price of imported materials, a decline in technology, less incentives to work, higher money wages, less capital, higher rates of interest or a smaller population of working age.

The interaction of AD and AS and the determination of the level of output, prices and employment

Levels of output, prices and employment in an economy are determined by the interaction of AD and AS. For example, in Figure 4.6, there has been a shift of the AD curve to the right.

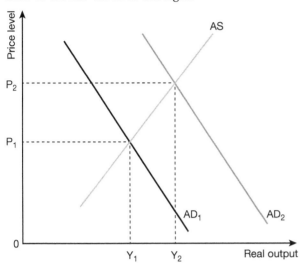

▲ **Figure 4.6** Changes in the level of output, prices and employment in an economy

The effect on the level of output, prices and employment in this economy is as follows:

Effect on the level of output	There is a rise in the level of output from $0Y_1$ to $0Y_2$
Effect on the level of employment	There is a rise in the level of employment as more workers will be required to produce this increased level of output
Effect on the level of prices	There is a rise in the level of prices from $0P_1$ to $0P_2$

Common errors

Be careful not to label the axes on an AD/AS diagram the same as on a demand and supply diagram, i.e. P and Q. In an AD/AS diagram, the vertical axis should be labelled 'price level' and the horizontal axis 'real output'.

4.2 Inflation

AS 4(b)

This topic is concerned with:

➤ the definition of inflation; degrees of inflation and the measurement of inflation; deflation and disinflation

➤ the distinction between money values and real data

➤ the causes of inflation (cost-push and demand-pull inflation)

➤ the consequences of inflation.

The definition of inflation; degrees of inflation and the measurement of inflation; deflation and disinflation

The definition of inflation

Inflation can be defined as a sustained increase in the general or average level of prices in an economy over a given period of time.

Key term

Inflation: a persistent rise in the general price level of an economy leading to a fall in the value of money.

Degrees of inflation

There are varying degrees of inflation, both in one economy at different times and in various economies at the same time. It is possible to distinguish between:

➤ creeping inflation, where the rate of inflation is relatively low and relatively stable over a period of time and so is not a major problem in an economy

➤ accelerating inflation, where the rate of inflation is getting significantly higher and is becoming a major problem in an economy

➤ hyperinflation, where the rate of inflation has reached such a high level that it affects confidence in an economy and may even lead to the collapse of the country's currency. This happened in Germany in 1923 and in Zimbabwe in 2008.

The measurement of inflation

The level of inflation in an economy is measured through the use of a prices index, such as the retail prices index or the consumer prices index. Different goods and services are included in a basket that would be bought by people in an economy and each of these products is given a weight in relation to the proportion of total expenditure spent on particular products. A base year is chosen, which is given a value of 100, and the general level of prices is compared with that base year.

Deflation

Deflation can be defined as a general decrease in the average level of prices in an economy over a period of time.

Disinflation

Disinflation can be defined as a general increase in the level of prices in an economy over a period of time, but where the rate of increase of these prices is slowing down.

✓ What you need to know

To calculate a price index, it is necessary to compare the price of a representative basket of goods and services today compared to the base year using the following equation:

$$\frac{\text{Present cost of a basket of goods and services}}{\text{Cost of the basket of goods and services in the base year}} \times 100$$

You need to remember that the various goods and services in the representative basket are given weights to reflect their relative importance in relation to total expenditure.

💡 Remember

There are a number of potential problems in the use of price indices.

The base year (=100) needs to be one in which there are not particularly wide fluctuations in prices.

Any particular basket of goods and services may not be representative of the spending patterns of all people in an economy.

The basket of goods and services will need to be updated on a regular basis, leaving out some products and bringing in others so as to reflect changes in spending patterns.

The relative importance of different goods and services may change and so the weights will need to change to reflect these changes in spending patterns.

There are different examples of price indices that could be used, such as the Consumer Prices Index (CPI) and the Retail Prices Index (RPI).

Key terms

Creeping inflation: a situation where the rate of inflation is relatively low, say 3-4%.

Accelerating inflation: a situation where the rate of inflation is rising and is beginning to become a serious problem in an economy.

Hyperinflation: a situation where the rate of inflation in an economy is becoming so high, e.g. over 100% or 1000%, that confidence in the currency is decreasing.

Deflation: a general decrease in the average level of prices in an economy over a period of time.

Disinflation: a situation where there is a fall in the rate of inflation in an economy.

Basket: a selection of goods and services that would be purchased by a representative sample of people in an economy.

Weights: values that is given to products in a basket to reflect the proportion of income spent on such products by people in an economy.

Consumer Prices Index (CPI): a method of measuring changes in the prices of a number of products in an economy over a given period of time.

Retail Prices Index (RPI): another form of prices index used in an economy, different from the consumer prices index in that it includes the costs of housing.

70

It is sometimes thought that hyperinflation is determined when inflation reaches a certain level in an economy, but this is not so. There is no precise point at which inflation becomes hyperinflation.

The distinction between the consumer prices index and the retail prices index can be confusing. The main difference between them is that the retail prices index includes the cost of housing, whereas the consumer prices index excludes such costs.

Deflation is a term that can be confusing because it actually has two meanings. It can refer to a general decrease in the average level of prices in an economy over a period of time, but it can also refer to a reduction in the level of aggregate demand in an economy.

Make sure you don't think that disinflation refers to a situation of a decrease in the general level of prices in an economy, as this is not the case. When an economy is experiencing disinflation, there is still inflation, i.e. the general level of prices is still increasing, but it is increasing at a lower rate of increase than was previously the case.

Make sure you understand that if there is a fall in the rate of inflation in an economy, it does not mean that the general level of prices is falling. It simply means that prices are still rising, but at a slower rate than previously.

The distinction between money values and real data

Money values

It is important to be able to distinguish between money values and real data. A money value is one that does not take into account the effects of inflation. It can also be known as the nominal value of a given amount of money.

Real data

Real data refers to the value of something that has taken the effects of inflation into account. The real value of a given sum of money is one where it is assumed that the prices of goods and services in an economy have remained constant over a period of time, i.e. the effect of inflation has been eliminated.

Remember to make the distinction between a money value, which has not taken the effects of inflation into account, and a real value, which has taken the effects of inflation into account.

The contrast between a nominal or money value and a real value can be seen in terms of a person obtaining a wage increase. If a person receives a nominal increase in their wage of 10%, and the rate of inflation in the country is 6%, then the real increase in the wage, i.e. what it can actually buy in terms of its purchasing power after taking into account the effects of inflation, is 10% − 6% = 4%.

The causes of inflation (cost-push and demand-pull inflation)

Cost-push inflation

Cost-push inflation in an economy arises as a result of an increase in the costs of production, such as the cost of labour, and these increased costs are passed on to consumers in the form of higher prices. Where the increase in costs is largely due to the increase in the cost of imported raw materials or component parts, it is called imported inflation.

Money value: this refers to the value of a given sum of money that has not taken into account the effects of inflation.

Real data: this refers to the value of a given sum of money after taking into account the effects of inflation, i.e. the effects of inflation have been removed.

Cost-push inflation: a rise in the general level of prices in an economy that is primarily caused by a significant rise in the costs of production.

Imported inflation: a rise in the general level of prices in an economy that is primarily caused by a significant rise in the cost of imported raw materials and component parts and/or in the price of imported finished goods.

Cost-push inflation can be seen in Figure 4.7 where the price level has increased from $0P_0$ to $0P_1$ as a result of changes in the costs of production.

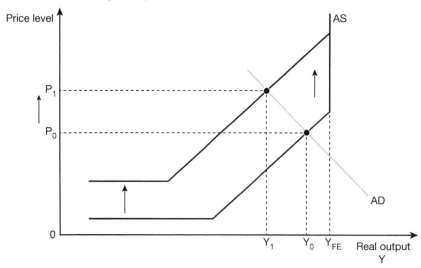

▲ **Figure 4.7** Cost-push inflation

Demand-pull inflation

Another possible cause of inflation in an economy is where there is too much demand in an economy, i.e. aggregate demand is greater than aggregate supply. This is termed demand-pull inflation This is likely to be the case when an economy is at a situation of full employment, and in this case prices are pulled upwards as a result of the excess demand. This emphasis on the demand side of an economy is often linked with monetary explanations, i.e. it is the increase in the money supply, making the increase in demand possible, which is important. This situation is known as monetary inflation.

Demand-pull inflation can be seen in Figure 4.8 where the price level has increased from $0P_0$ to $0P_1$ as a result of changes in demand.

> **Key terms**
>
> **Demand-pull inflation**: a rise in the general level of prices in an economy that is primarily caused by too much demand for goods and services, i.e. aggregate demand is greater than aggregate supply causing excess demand.
>
> **Monetary inflation**: a rise in the general level of prices in an economy that is primarily caused by too much money chasing too few goods.

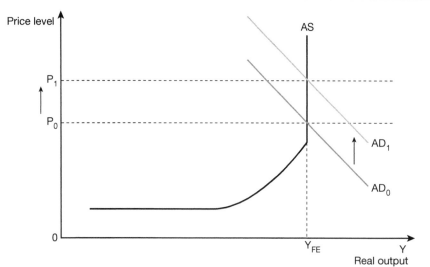

▲ **Figure 4.8** Demand-pull inflation

The consequences of inflation

Inflation is regarded as potentially a serious economic problem as there are a number of negative consequences, including the following:

➤ the purchasing power of a nominal sum of money will fall in real terms

➤ a country's exports could become uncompetitive

➤ there will be a redistribution of income in an economy, with some people adversely affected, such as those on fixed incomes and savers

➤ menu costs, i.e. the need to keep changing the advertised products, can be expensive

➤ shoe leather costs, i.e. the need to continually search for the best returns, involving time and effort

➤ a greater degree of uncertainty in an economy, making planning more of a problem

➤ a situation of fiscal drag could occur, with more people caught in the 'tax net' if tax allowances do not rise in line with inflation.

However, inflation can have a number of positive consequences in an economy, including the following:

➤ the profits of firms could increase if prices rise by more than costs, and in this situation they could be encouraged to expand, reducing the level of unemployment in an economy

➤ the redistribution of income in an economy could be advantageous to some people, such as borrowers, as their debt will be less in real terms.

✓ What you need to know
You need to understand that the effects of inflation will depend on a number of possible factors, including whether the inflation is anticipated or not, what the extent of the increase in prices is, whether the inflation rate is accelerating, stable or falling and the extent to which other countries are experiencing inflation.

Key terms

Menu costs: the costs of continually having to change the prices of products.

Shoe leather costs: the costs of continually having to search for the best returns, involving time and effort.

Fiscal drag: a situation where more people are dragged into the 'tax net' as a result of tax allowances not increasing in line with inflation.

★ Exam tip

If an exam question requires you to discuss the consequences of a relatively high rate of inflation, remember to include both the positive consequences and the negative consequences in your answer.

Raise your grade

Explain the differences between demand-pull and cost-push inflation in an economy. [8]

It is important to distinguish between demand-pull and cost-push inflation. Demand-pull inflation occurs where there is too much demand in an economy[1]. It is sometimes described as a situation where too much money is chasing too few products[2].

Cost-push inflation occurs where higher prices are caused by higher costs of production, such as when there is a wage-price spiral[3].

The key difference between these two explanations of inflation is related to the source of the price increases, i.e. whether they originate from the demand or the supply side[4].

4.3 The balance of payments

AS 4(c)

This topic is concerned with:

➤ the components of the balance of payments accounts (using the IMF/OECD definition): current account; capital and financial account; balancing item

➤ the meaning of balance of payments equilibrium and disequilibrium

➤ the causes of balance of payments disequilibrium in each component of the accounts

➤ the consequences of balance of payments disequilibrium on a domestic and external economy.

The components of the balance of payments accounts

The balance of payments is a record of the transactions that one country has with the rest of the world. It shows all the various payments and receipts arising from a country's involvement in international trade. It consists of the following four components:

➤ the current account

➤ the capital account

➤ the financial account

➤ the balancing item.

Key terms

Balance of payments: a set of accounts that shows the payments and receipts arising from the transactions of one country with the rest of the world. It consists of the current account, the capital account, the financial account and a balancing item.

Current account: this account is made up of four parts: the trade in goods, the trade in services, net primary income and net secondary income.

Current account

The current account of the balance of payments consists of the following four parts:

➤ the trade in goods, i.e. the balance of trade in relation to the exports and imports of goods

➤ the trade in services, i.e. the balance of trade in relation to the exports and imports of services

➤ net primary income, i.e. incomes from interest, profits, dividends resulting from investment and migrant remittances

➤ net secondary income, i.e. contributions to international organisations and overseas development aid.

Capital account

The capital account is the part of the balance of payments accounts that records capital movements, in terms of various assets and liabilities, into and out of a particular country, such as money brought into and taken out of a country by migrants.

Financial account

A financial account records the movement of funds into and out of a country, such as direct investment in the form of building a factory or portfolio investment in the form of the buying or selling of government bonds.

Balancing item

The balance of payments should eventually balance when all of the various accounts are included. However, it is possible that statistical discrepancies may prevent this from happening and so a balancing item is used to ensure that the accounts, when added together, equal zero.

The meaning of balance of payments equilibrium and disequilibrium

Balance of payments equilibrium

A balance of payments equilibrium refers to a situation where the account as a whole is balanced, either in a given year or over a period of time, and there is neither a deficit nor a surplus.

Balance of payments disequilibrium

A balance of payments disequilibrium refers to a situation where the account as a whole is not balanced, either in a given year or over a period of time, where there is either a deficit or a surplus. It usually means that a country is experiencing a persistent deficit or surplus over a period of time.

Key terms

Trade in goods: the balance of trade in relation to the export and import of goods.

Trade in services: the balance of trade in relation to the export and import of services.

Exports: goods and/or services that are sold to other countries.

Imports: goods and/or services that are brought into a country.

Capital account: this account records capital movements, in the form of assets and liabilities, when these are transferred from one country to another.

Financial account: this account records the inflows and outflows that result from different forms of investment.

Balancing item: this is a way of ensuring that the balance of payments, when all of the different component accounts are added together, does actually balance, i.e. it equals zero.

Deficit: a negative balance in the balance of payments of a country when outflows exceed inflows.

Surplus: a positive balance in the balance of payments of a country when inflows exceed outflows.

✗ Common error

Be careful not to confuse a deficit or a surplus in the balance of payments, with a deficit or a surplus in the budgetary position of a country, e.g. when a deficit occurs as a result of public expenditure exceeding government revenue. To avoid this confusion, it is better to refer to the balance of payments as an external balance to distinguish it from a government's fiscal situation.

The causes of balance of payments disequilibrium in each component of the accounts

The current account of the balance of payments could be negative, i.e. there is a deficit, as a result of the value of imports exceeding the value of imports. This could apply to the balance of trade in goods account and/or the balance of trade in services account.

The capital account of the balance of payments could be positive, i.e. there is a surplus, as a result of the money brought into a country by an increase in the number of immigrants.

The financial account of the balance of payments could be negative, i.e. there is a deficit, as a result of a greater value of outflows of portfolio investment than inflows.

The consequences of balance of payments disequilibrium on the domestic and external economy

It is important to be able to distinguish between the consequences of a balance of payments disequilibrium on the domestic economy and on the external economy.

Domestic economy

A balance of payments disequilibrium could have various consequences for a domestic economy. For example, if a deficit in the balance of trade in goods account has come about as a result of a decrease in the demand for exports and an increase in the demand for imports, this could lead to an increase in the level of unemployment in an economy. Such a situation could also lead to a fall in business confidence, possibly leading to a reduction in the level of investment in an economy.

External economy

In addition to the possible effects of a balance of payments disequilibrium on a domestic economy, there are also possible consequences for the external economy. For instance, if a country is experiencing a deficit in the balance of trade in goods account, it may be tempted to consider protectionism as a way of reducing imports into a country, but if it decided to take such a policy, it is likely that there would be a reduction in world trade negatively affecting all economies in the world.

> **★ Exam tip**
>
> Be sure that you understand that a balance of payments disequilibrium can have consequences for both a domestic economy and an external economy.

4.4 Exchange rates `AS 4(d)`

This topic is concerned with:

➤ definitions and measurement of exchange rates – nominal, real, trade-weighted exchange rates

➤ the determination of exchange rates-floating, fixed, managed float

➤ the factors underlying changes in exchange rates

➤ the effects of changing exchange rates on the domestic and external economy using AD, Marshall–Lerner and J-curve analysis

➤ depreciation/appreciation

➤ devaluation/revaluation.

> **★ Exam tip**
>
> Make sure you appreciate the various components that go to make up the balance of payments and how they are different. The composition of the current account of the balance of payments has changed in recent years and now comprises the balance of trade in goods, the balance of trade in services, net primary income and net secondary income.

> **★ Exam tip**
>
> Make sure you understand that a persistent disequilibrium in a country's balance of payments can arise from either a deficit or a surplus. It is easy to think that a state of disequilibrium only applies to deficits, but it can refer to either deficits or surpluses.

Definitions and measurement of exchange rates – nominal, real and trade-weighted exchange rates

Definitions of exchange rate

An exchange rate refers to the value of one currency in relation to the value of another, i.e. it is the price of one currency expressed in terms of another.

Measurement of exchange rates

It is possible to measure exchange rates in three different ways:

➤ nominal exchange rate

➤ real exchange rate

➤ trade-weighted exchange rate.

Nominal exchange rate

This is usually the most common way of measuring an exchange rate. It is expressed in money terms, but does not take the effects of inflation into account.

Real exchange rate

This way of measuring an exchange rate does take the effects of inflation into account. In this sense, it will give an indication of the purchasing power of one currency compared to another. When real exchange rates are used, they are expressed in terms of purchasing power parity by taking into account price levels in different countries.

Trade-weighted exchange rate

This is where the exchange rates of currencies are considered by weighting the different currencies being compared according to their importance in international trade. This method of measurement is sometimes called the effective exchange rate.

Key terms

Exchange rate: the value of one currency in relation to another.

Nominal exchange rate: an exchange rate that is expressed in money terms, without taking into account the possible effects of inflation.

Real exchange rate: an exchange rate that does take into account the effects of inflation in different countries.

Trade-weighted exchange rate: an exchange rate that takes into account the importance of a currency in international trade by giving it a weighting to reflect this importance.

Purchasing power parity: the value of a currency in terms of what it is able to buy in other countries.

★ **Exam tip**

When writing about exchange rates in an examination, make sure you make it clear what method of measurement of the value of a currency is being used, i.e. nominal, real or trade-weighted.

✗ **Common error**

Be careful not to confuse the internal value of money with the external value of a currency. Exchange rates are concerned with the external value of a currency, i.e. what it is worth when compared with other currencies.

The determination of exchange rates – floating, fixed and managed float exchange rates

It is important to distinguish between the different ways in which an exchange rate is determined.

Floating exchange rates

A floating exchange rate is a type of exchange rate system where the external value of a currency is determined through a market, the foreign exchange market. The value of a currency is determined, like any other price in a market, through the forces of demand and supply.

Key term

Floating exchange rate: an exchange rate system where the value of a currency is allowed to float up or down, determined by the market forces of the demand for, and supply of, the currency.

Figure 4.9 shows an increase in the value of a currency as a result of a shift in the demand curve to the right. The value of the currency has gone up from 0P to 0P₁.

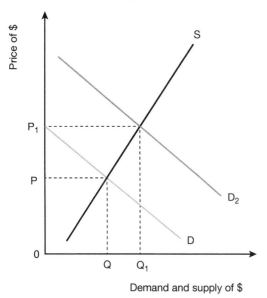

▲ **Figure 4.9** A floating exchange rate

Fixed exchange rates

A fixed exchange rate is a type of exchange rate system where the external value of a currency is determined by the government of the country, i.e. the government decides to fix the exchange rate at a particular level, rather than leaving the rate to be decided by market forces.

Managed float

A managed float is an exchange rate system which involves a combination of floating and fixed exchange rates. A government may decide to allow the exchange rate of a currency to be determined by market forces, but only to an extent. The government will decide the minimum and maximum rates between which the value will range. If market forces determine the rate above or below those maximum or minimum values, the government will intervene to buy or sell the currency to ensure that its value stays within the predetermined limits.

> 💡 **Remember**
>
> A managed float can also be referred to as a dirty float because of the fact that a government will only allow the exchange rate to move between predetermined limits. If the value goes above or below those limits, the government will intervene by buying or selling the currency.

The factors underlying changes in exchange rates

There are a number of possible factors that can cause changes in exchange rates. These include the following:

➤ the demand for a country's exports from other countries

➤ the demand for imports into a country from other countries

➤ relative inflation rates in different countries, affecting the international competitiveness of goods and services that are traded between different countries

➤ the quality and reliability of products that are traded internationally

➤ relative interest rates in different countries, which can be a major factor in the movement of hot money from one country to another

➤ changes in the costs of production in different countries

➤ changes in the levels of productivity in different countries

➤ differences in the state of technology in different countries.

The effects of changing exchange rates on the domestic and external economy using AD, Marshall–Lerner and J-curve analysis

AD analysis

It has already been stated that AD = C + I + G + (X − M). Exports and imports are therefore a part of AD and so any change in exports and/or imports is likely to have an effect on AD. If a country's currency rises so that exports are more expensive and imports are less expensive, and demand for both is elastic, the value of net exports, i.e. the value of exports after allowing for the value of imports, is likely to fall in an economy, and this will shift AD to the left. This can be seen in Figure 4.10 where real output will fall from $0Y_2$ to $0Y_1$, causing a fall in employment.

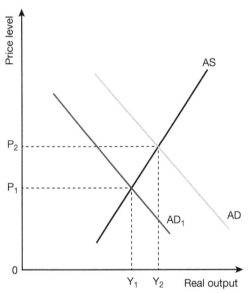

▲ **Figure 4.10** The effect of a changing exchange rate on an economy

Marshall–Lerner analysis

In the example above, it was assumed that the demand for both exports and imports was elastic, with the result that a rise in the exchange rate caused a fall in net exports. The Marshall–Lerner condition, in relation to the price elasticity of demand for a country's exports and imports, is useful here in terms of judging whether a reduction in the value of a country's exchange rate is likely to be successful in improving a country's balance of payments situation. The Marshall–Lerner condition states for a reduction in the external value of a currency to be successful, the sum of the price elasticity of demand for exports and the price elasticity of demand for imports needs to be greater than one.

J-curve analysis

A country's exchange rate could be lowered to encourage an increase in exports and a decrease in imports. This aim, however, might not happen immediately and it is possible that there may be a period of time when the situation becomes worse before it gets better. This situation is known as the

Key term

Marshall–Lerner condition: this states that the sum of the price elasticities of demand for both exports and imports must be greater than one if a reduction in the value of a currency is to lead to an improvement in the current account of a country.

J-curve effect. It can be seen in Figure 4.11. Initially the current account situation worsens as a result of the reduction in the external value of the currency, and the situation only improves after a certain period of time has elapsed.

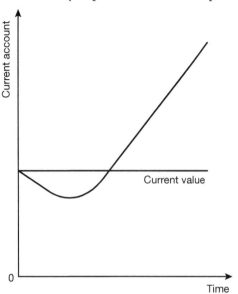

▲ **Figure 4.11** The J-curve effect

Depreciation/appreciation

There are different terms that need to be used when the external value of a currency changes, depending on whether there is a floating or a fixed exchange rate system.

If an exchange rate falls in a floating exchange rate system, it is called a depreciation. If the rate rises in a floating exchange rate system, it is called an appreciation.

Devaluation/revaluation

If an exchange rate is lowered in a fixed exchange rate system, it is called a devaluation. If the rate is increased in a fixed exchange rate system, it is called a revaluation.

> ★ **Exam tip**
>
> Make sure that you clearly understand the difference between a depreciation and a devaluation and between an appreciation and a revaluation.

Raise your grade

Discuss to what extent the depreciation of a currency is likely to be effective in reducing a balance of trade deficit. [12]

The depreciation of a currency refers to the fact that its value has been reduced[1]. This is often done to reduce a balance of trade deficit[2] because the effect of a depreciation is to make a country's exports cheaper and the imports into the country more expensive.

This is likely to be effective as long as price elasticity of demand is elastic[3] because the lower price of the exports will be likely to increase the demand for them and the higher price of the imports is likely to decrease the demand for them[4]. However, although the depreciation is likely to be effective over a period of time, it could lead to a worsening of the situation immediately after the depreciation[5].

In conclusion, the depreciation of a currency is very likely[6] to be effective in reducing a balance of trade deficit[7].

How to improve this answer

1 The candidate has referred to the fact that a depreciation means a reduction in the value of an exchange rate, but this could have been developed more fully by making it clear that a depreciation has to be seen in the context of a floating exchange rate system, in contrast to a devaluation which would only occur in a fixed exchange rate system.

2 The concept of a balance of trade deficit could have been explained more fully in terms of the value of the outflows being greater than the value of the inflows, with the result that the net effect is negative.

3 The candidate has referred to the fact that the depreciation will only be effective if the price elasticity of demand is elastic, but this point needed to be developed more fully in relation to the need for both the price elasticity of demand for exports and the price elasticity of demand for imports to be elastic.

4 The candidate should have referred to the Marshall–Lerner condition which states that a depreciation will only be effective in reducing a balance of trade deficit if the sum of the price elasticity of demand for exports and the price elasticity of demand for imports is greater than one.

5 The candidate recognises that although a depreciation may be effective in time, there may be a worsening of the balance of trade immediately after the depreciation, but it would have been helpful if there had been an explicit reference to the J-curve effect. It would also have been useful if the candidate had included a diagram to show the J-curve effect over time.

6   The candidate has made an attempt to address the 'to what extent' aspect of the question by stating that the depreciation is 'very likely' to be effective in reducing a balance of trade deficit.

7   The candidate's conclusion would have been improved if the likely effectiveness of the depreciation had been linked to the Marshall–Lerner condition and the J-curve effect.

Analysis:	3/8
Evaluation:	2/4
Total:	5/12

4.5 The terms of trade

AS 4(e)

This topic is concerned with:

➤ the measurement of the terms of trade

➤ the causes of changes in the terms of trade

➤ the impact of changes in the terms of trade.

The measurement of the terms of trade

The terms of trade refer to the relative changes of export prices and import prices. They are calculated by:

$$\frac{\text{Index of export prices}}{\text{Index of import prices}} \times 100$$

> **Key term**
>
> **Terms of trade**: the ratio of export prices to import prices.

> ✓ **What you need to know**
>
> An increase in the terms of trade index indicates that more imports can be purchased with a given quantity of exports. In this situation, the terms of trade are said to have improved or to have become more favourable. On the other hand, a decrease in the terms of trade indicates that fewer imports can be purchased with a given quantity of exports. In this situation, the terms of trade are said to have deteriorated or worsened.

> ✗ **Common error**
>
> Be careful not to confuse the terms of trade with the balance of trade. The terms of trade simply show the relationship between changes in the prices of exports and changes in the price of imports. They do not indicate changes in the quantity or value of exports and imports traded between different countries.

> 💡 **Remember**
>
> The terms of trade and the balance of trade are not the same. The terms of trade show changes in the relative prices of exports and imports. The balance of trade shows a country's trading position with other countries in the world.

The causes of changes in the terms of trade

Changes in the terms of trade can be caused by a number of different factors, including the following:

➤ a fall in the price of manufactured goods will cause the terms of trade of those countries producing such goods to worsen

➤ the increased demand for natural resources has pushed up their prices, benefiting those countries exporting such products

➤ if the prices of a country's exports rise significantly more than the price of imports into the country, then the terms of trade will increase

➤ if a country's exchange rate depreciates or is devalued, its terms of trade will have worsened because export prices will have fallen and import prices will have risen

➤ if a country has a monopoly in the production of a good, it will be better able to raise the prices of such goods, causing an improvement in its terms of trade.

The impact of changes in the terms of trade

When there is a worsening in a country's terms of trade, this is regarded as an unfavourable change because more exports will need to be sold to buy the same number of imports. However, if exports have become relatively cheaper than imports, this will help to improve a country's balance of trade situation as long as the price elasticity of demand for both exports and imports is elastic.

When there is an improvement in a country's terms of trade, this is regarded as a favourable change because fewer exports will need to be sold to buy the same number of imports. However, if exports have become relatively more expensive than imports, this is likely to worsen a country's balance of trade situation, assuming that the price elasticity of demand for both exports and imports is elastic.

> **X Common error**
>
> Be careful not to regard a fall in the terms of trade index as being unhelpful in terms of a country's trading position, whereas a fall in the terms of trade means that export prices have become relatively cheaper, and if the price elasticity of demand for both exports and imports is elastic, this will help to improve, not worsen, a country's balance of trade position.

4.6 Principles of absolute and comparative advantage

`AS 4(f)`

This topic is concerned with:

➤ the distinction between absolute and comparative advantage

➤ free trade area, customs union, monetary union, full economic union

➤ trade creation and trade diversion

➤ the benefits of free trade, including the trading possibility curve.

The distinction between absolute and comparative advantage

International trade between countries is based on the concept of specialisation, where one country is more efficient at producing a product than another country. This gives rise to two different types of advantage: absolute and comparative advantage.

Absolute advantage

An absolute advantage is a situation of absolute advantage occurs where one country is able to produce a particular good with fewer resources than another country. As a result of this absolute efficiency, the country will enjoy a cost advantage.

> **Key term**
>
> Absolute advantage: the ability to produce more of a product than another country can produce that has the same amount of resources.

Comparative advantage

Whereas absolute advantage is based on the idea that one country has an absolute efficiency in the production of a good, comparative advantage is based on the relative efficiency of one country compared to another. In this way, a country could produce a good in which it does not have an absolute advantage, but it could be relatively more efficient in producing this good than another good.

✓ What you need to know

You need to understand that the concept of comparative or relative advantage can best be explained by stating that this occurs where a product is produced at a lower opportunity cost. This means that a country will concentrate on producing a good where it has to give up less production of another good. This is another example of the importance of opportunity cost in economic analysis. Two countries will trade at a ratio somewhere between their two opportunity costs. It is important you understand that specialisation and trade will only take place if the opportunity cost ratios are different. If this was not the case, there would be no advantage in specialising and trading.

💡 Remember

There are a number of assumptions that have to be made in relation to the principle of comparative advantage. It is assumed that there are only two goods involved, that there is perfect competition in both factor and product markets, that there are no transport costs, that no capital movements take place which could affect the exchange rate, that production is subject to constant returns to scale and that there are no restrictions on trade.

Free trade area, customs union, monetary union, full economic union

It is important to be able to distinguish between different forms of economic integration.

Free trade area

A free trade area is where countries come together to trade freely with each other, but each of these member countries will retain their own trade barriers with other countries outside the free trade area, i.e. there is no common external tariff in existence.

Examples include:

➤ the European Free Trade Area (Iceland, Liechtenstein, Norway and Switzerland)

➤ the North American Free Trade Area (USA, Canada and Mexico).

Customs union

A customs union is where countries come together to trade freely with each other and they also have a common external tariff with other countries outside the customs union.

Examples include:

➤ the Caribbean Community (CARICOM) (15 full member countries including Jamaica, Barbados and Trinidad and Tobago).

Monetary union

A monetary union is where countries come together and adopt a single currency. Certain policies may also be adopted to support the operation of the currency and there is usually one single central bank.

Examples include:

➤ the eurozone (19 member countries of the European Union have adopted the euro as their currency, including France, Italy and Germany).

Full economic union

A full economic union is where countries come together and adopt a number of common economic policies that apply to all member countries. Full economic union usually involves the countries adopting a single currency, but this is not absolutely essential.

Examples include:

➤ the European Union (19 of the member countries have adopted the single currency)

➤ the Eurasian Economic Union (Russia, Belarus, Armenia and Kazakhstan, but each of the four countries have retained their own currency).

> **X Common error**
>
> Make sure you don't assume that all countries in an economic union will adopt a single currency. This is not always the case. For example, in the European Union, only 19 of the member countries have adopted the euro as their currency.

Trade creation and trade diversion

It is important to distinguish between trade creation and trade diversion.

Trade creation

If there is some form of economic integration between a group of countries, there will be fewer trade barriers between them. This is likely to lead to trade creation as new markets are opened up within the member countries and businesses take advantage of new opportunities. There is therefore likely to be increased specialisation and more trade between the countries.

However, it is also possible that economic integration may lead to a degree of trade diversion. For example, the member countries are likely to focus more on trade between themselves and less on trade with non-member countries.

> **★ Exam tip**
>
> Remember that in a 'discuss' question on economic integration, there are potential benefits in the form of trade creation as well as potential drawbacks in the form of trade diversion.

> **★ Exam tip**
>
> It is important that you can distinguish between the different forms of economic integration that can exist between countries in different parts of the world.

> **Key terms**
>
> **Monetary union:** a situation where a group of countries come together and adopt a single currency. The member countries are likely to have a number of common monetary policies to support the operation of the single currency.
>
> **Full economic union:** a situation where a group of countries come together and agree to integrate their economies as much as possible through a variety of laws, regulations and policies. They may or may not have a single currency.
>
> **Trade creation:** the creation of new trade resulting from the reduction or elimination of trade barriers between member countries of a trading bloc.
>
> **Trade diversion:** the loss of some existing trade between a trading bloc and non-member countries as a result of the imposition of trade barriers.

The benefits of free trade, including the trading possibility curve

The benefits of free trade

There are a number of potential benefits of free trade, including the following:

➤ an increase in world output

➤ the more efficient allocation of resources

➤ a wider range of products for consumers to choose from

➤ an increase in a country's economic growth

➤ an improvement in the standard of living and quality of life of people

➤ the possibility of economies of scale resulting from increased output through specialisation

➤ lower prices resulting from increased efficiency and economies of scale.

The trading possibility curve

A trading possibility curve can be used to show the gains from trade. A trading possibility curve shows the maximum possible quantities of each good that each country could produce, given the terms of trade between the two countries following specialisation. If two countries specialise in the production of goods in which they have a comparative advantage, i.e. a lower opportunity cost, it is possible for both countries to produce outside of their production possibility curve.

In Figure 4.12, Country A has a comparative advantage in the production of cars and Country B has a comparative advantage in the production of toys. The opportunity cost ratio is one car for five toys in Country B, and one car for one toy in Country A. Trade takes place at one car for three toys. If each country specialised in what it what was most efficient at producing, both countries would produce on their trading possibility curve(tpc) rather than on their production possibility curve(ppc). This can be seen in the diagram where the tpc is to the right of the ppc for both countries.

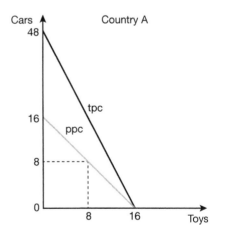 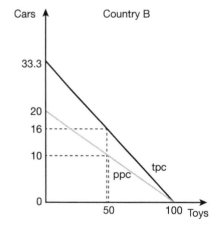

▲ **Figure 4.12** The trading possibility curve showing the gains from trade

⬆ Raise your grade

Explain how economic integration can lead to both trade creation and trade diversion. [8]

Economic integration, whether in the form of a free trade area or a customs union[1], can lead to both trade creation and trade diversion.

Trade creation can take place when countries form a trading bloc, which has the effect of reducing[2] the trade barriers between the member countries. Free trade will be encouraged and there will be more opportunities to conduct business between the countries[3].

However, at the same time, although increased trade between the member countries is encouraged, trade with non-member countries may be discouraged[4]. The member countries will tend to look inwards towards the trading bloc, possibly reducing or cutting off trade with countries that they previously traded with.

How to improve this answer

1   The candidate has referred to two types of economic integration, but could also have referred to the two other types of economic integration, a monetary union and a full economic union.

2   It is not simply that the trade barriers have been reduced; it is also possible that such barriers have been eliminated entirely, increasing the scope for trade creation.

3   The candidate could perhaps have included an example to support the point being made. This could have included an example of a free trade area, such as the North American Free Trade Area, or of an economic union, such as the European Union.

4   The candidate has referred to the discouragement of trade with non-member countries, but this point needed to be developed more fully, such as in relation to the existence of a Common External Tariff which the European Union has with all non-member countries.

Knowledge and understanding:	2/4
Application:	2/4
Total:	4/8

4.7 Protectionism

AS 4(g)

This topic is concerned with:

➤ the meaning of protectionism in the context of international trade

➤ the different methods of protection and their impact, e.g. tariffs, import duties, quotas, export subsidies, embargoes, voluntary export restraints (VERs) and excessive administrative burdens ('red tape')

➤ the arguments in favour of protectionism.

The meaning of protectionism in the context of international trade

Protectionism refers to those policies taken by countries to protect domestic producers from international competition, or to give support to them. It is the opposite of free trade and comes about because countries are worried that without trade barriers, domestic firms will not be able to compete effectively with firms in other countries.

The different methods of protectionism and their impact

Tariffs

A tariff is a tax that is imposed on products that are imported into a country. They are designed to make the imported products more expensive, leading to a reduction in the demand for them. The impact of a tariff, however, will depend on the price elasticity of demand for the imported goods.

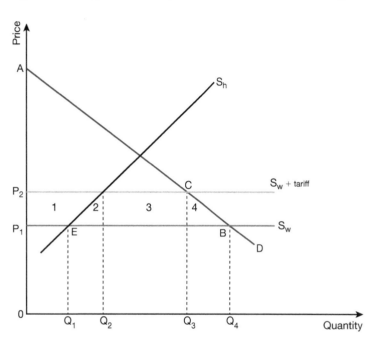

▲ **Figure 4.13** The impact of a tariff

The impact of the imposition of a tariff on an imported good can be seen in Figure 4.13. S_w shows the world supply of a product before the imposition of a tariff and S_w + tariff shows the world supply of a product after the imposition of a tariff. The vertical distance between P_1 and P_2 shows the size of the specific tariff. Sh shows the home or domestic supply of the product. The quantity of imports coming into the country has been reduced from Q_1Q_4 to Q_2Q_3.

Import duties

Import duties operate in the same way as a tariff, raising the price of the imported goods on which a duty has been imposed. This is likely to reduce the demand for them compared with alternative products produced in the domestic economy. The impact of an import duty will depend on the price elasticity of demand for the imported product and the extent to which there are alternative products available within the domestic economy of a comparable quality.

Quotas

Whereas tariffs and import duties involve trying to reduce the demand for imported goods by making them more expensive, a quota is a restriction on imports into a country. A quota can be expressed in one of three ways: a limit on the quantity of goods that can be imported into a country, a limit on the value of goods that can be imported into a country or a limit on the proportion of market share that they represent.

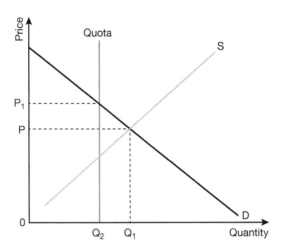

▲ **Figure 4.14** The imposition of a quota

Figure 4.14 shows the impact of a quota in a market. The original quantity demanded and supplied in the market was $0Q_1$, but once a quota has been established, the quantity available is only $0Q_2$. This amount is priced at $0P_1$.

Export subsidies

As already indicated in Unit 3, a subsidy is a payment by a government to firms to keep down the costs of production, enabling a lower price to be charged to consumers. If such subsidies are given to firms that are intending to export their goods, these are export subsidies. These should increase the demand for such products, assuming that demand is price elastic.

Embargoes

Embargoes are a complete ban on the imports of certain products from particular countries. An embargo is usually imposed largely for political, rather than economic, reasons.

Voluntary Export Restraints (VERs)

If a country imposes trade barriers on another country, there is always the possibility that this could lead to retaliation. Therefore, in an attempt to avoid this happening, a country could decide on export restraints that are entirely voluntary, i.e. it limits the amount of goods that it will export. These are voluntary export restraints (VERs).

Excessive Administrative Burdens

Excessive Administrative Burdens are often described as 'red tape'. The paperwork that is involved in the importation of goods into a country is made particularly difficult. The aim of such a measure is to discourage imports by making the process of importation much more time consuming and complex.

 Exam tip

Make sure that you understand the various benefits and drawbacks of the different methods of protectionism. For example, a tariff or import duty will provide government revenue, but this will not be the case with a quota.

Key term

Export subsidies: a payment by a government to domestic firms to keep down the costs of production and therefore the prices of the products, making their exports more competitive in international markets.

Key terms

Embargoes: a ban on imports from particular countries, either in relation to certain products imported from those countries or, in some cases, on all products.

Voluntary export restraints (VERs): a decision taken voluntarily by an exporting country to limit its exports as a way of avoiding importing countries imposing import barriers on such exports.

Excessive administrative burdens: this is often referred to as 'red tape' and it occurs when paperwork is made excessive in an attempt to make the importing process so complex and time-consuming that imports will be discouraged.

Make sure you understand that the imposition of a tariff has an effect on the size of the consumer surplus and producer surplus. In Figure 4.13 (on page 88), the original consumer surplus, before the tariff was introduced, was represented by the area P_1AB. After the imposition of the tariff, this has fallen to P_2AC. Some of this has been lost to producers in the form of an increased producer surplus and some to the government as revenue from the tariff. There has therefore been a redistribution of welfare from consumers to producers. Similarly, the imposition of a quota will involve a welfare loss to consumers.

The impact of a tariff, an import duty or an export subsidy will depend on the price elasticity of demand for the products being traded.

The arguments in favour of protectionism

Although the benefits of free trade have already been considered, it is also the case that a number of arguments can be put forward in favour of protectionism. These include the following:

➤ specific protection for infant or sunrise industries to enable such firms to compete with more established firms from other countries

➤ specific protection for sunset or declining industries to give sufficient time for factors of production to be transferred to other uses

➤ a strategic industry may need to be protected, such as military equipment, to provide a country with an appropriate defence

➤ to provide protection against firms that are dumping products in another country, i.e. they are selling below the cost of production

➤ protectionism may be necessary to help a country reduce a deficit on the current account of the balance of payments

➤ certain protectionist methods, such as tariffs and duties, are a form of raising government revenue.

Infant or sunrise industry: a newly established industry that will need protection, at least temporarily.

Sunset or declining industry: an industry that is declining and which will need protection, at least temporarily, to enable factors of production to be reallocated.

Dumping: the practice of selling a product that is below the cost of producing it.

Make sure you understand that although a case can be made for the protection of infant/sunrise industries and/or declining/sunset industries, these should only be temporary, otherwise it is possible that protectionist methods are used to support inefficient industries, especially in the case of declining/sunset industries. You also need to realise that protectionism to reduce a deficit in a country's current account will not overcome the underlying reasons for that deficit.

Make sure you appreciate that although there are certain arguments in favour of protectionism, these do go against the principle of free trade.

Revision checklist

I can:

➤ understand the shape and determinants of AD and AS curves ☐

➤ list the four components of aggregate demand ☐

➤ be clear about the distinction between a movement along, and a shift of, AD and AS curves ☐

➤ understand the link between the interaction of AD and AS and the determination of the level of real output, employment and the price level in an economy ☐

➤ be clear about what is meant by inflation ☐

- ➤ appreciate the different degrees of inflation in an economy ☐

- ➤ understand how the rate of inflation in an economy is measured ☐

- ➤ be clear about the distinction between deflation and disinflation ☐

- ➤ understand the distinction between money values and real data ☐

- ➤ distinguish between different possible causes of inflation, such as cost-push inflation and demand-pull inflation ☐

- ➤ be clear about the possible consequences of inflation, both positive and negative ☐

- ➤ understand the components of the balance of payments accounts, including the current account, the capital account, the financial account and the balancing item ☐

- ➤ understand the meaning of a balance of payments equilibrium and a balance of payments disequilibrium ☐

- ➤ understand the possible causes of balance of payments disequilibrium in each component of the accounts ☐

- ➤ understand the consequences of balance of payments disequilibrium on both the domestic and the external economy ☐

- ➤ be clear about the definitions and measurement of exchange rates, including nominal, real and trade-weighted exchange rates ☐

- ➤ understand the determination of exchange rates, including floating, fixed and managed float exchange rate systems ☐

- ➤ be clear about the factors underlying changes in exchange rates ☐

- ➤ understand the effects of changing exchange rates on the domestic and external economy using AD, Marshall–Lerner and J-curve analysis ☐

- ➤ distinguish between depreciation and appreciation ☐

- ➤ distinguish between devaluation and revaluation ☐

- ➤ understand the measurement of the terms of trade ☐

- ➤ understand the causes of changes in the terms of trade ☐

- ➤ be clear about the impact of changes in the terms of trade ☐

- ➤ understand the distinction between absolute and comparative advantage ☐

- ➤ understand the differences between a free trade area, a customs union, a monetary union and a full economic union ☐

- ➤ distinguish between trade creation and trade diversion ☐

- ➤ understand the benefits of free trade, including the trading possibility curve ☐

- ➤ understand the meaning of protectionism in the context of international trade ☐

- ➤ understand the different methods of protection and their impact, e.g. tariffs, import duties, quotas, export subsidies, embargoes, voluntary export restraints (VERs) and excessive administrative burdens ('red tape') ☐

- ➤ understand the arguments in favour of protectionism. ☐

1   Aggregate demand consists of:

   A consumption, government and net exports

   B consumption, investment, government and exports

   C consumption, investment, government and net exports

   D investment, government and imports.

2   Disinflation refers to a situation of:

   A a fall in the general level of prices

   B an annual inflation rate of over 10%

   C the price level neither rising or falling

   D the price level rising at a decreasing rate.

3   A wage increase that has been adjusted to take into account the effects of inflation is known as a:

   A fair wage

   B money wage

   C nominal wage

   D real wage.

4   When the money inflows into a country are greater than the money outflows out of a country, as shown in the balance of payments accounts, this is known as:

   A a balancing item

   B a deficit

   C an equilibrium

   D a surplus.

5   When an exchange rate is determined by the forces of demand and supply, it is known as a:

   A fixed exchange rate system

   B floating exchange rate system

   C managed float exchange rate system

   D weighted exchange rate system.

6   When the value of an exchange rate is lowered in a fixed exchange rate system, it is known as:

   A a depreciation

   B a devaluation

   C a revaluation

   D an appreciation.

7   The terms of trade shows the relationship between changes in the:

   A prices of exports and imports

   B quality of exports and imports

   C quantity of exports and imports

   D value of exports and imports.

8   The increase in trade between member countries of a trading bloc is known as trade:

   A creation

   B diversion

   C establishment

   D tariff.

9   A ban on imports from a particular country is known as:

   A a duty

   B a quota

   C a tariff

   D an embargo.

10 Which of the following methods is a country likely to use to avoid having import controls imposed against it?

   A A tariff.

   B A voluntary export restraint.

   C An export subsidy.

   D An import duty.

11 **(a)** Explain the distinction between a movement along and a shift of an AD curve.   [8]

   (b) Discuss whether the consequences of inflation will always be negative.   [12]

12 **(a)** Explain the difference between a tariff and a quota as a method of protection.   [8]

   (b) Discuss whether the arguments in favour of protectionism are always stronger than the arguments against.   [12]

Key topics

- ➤ types of policy: fiscal, monetary and supply side policy
- ➤ policies to correct a balance of payments equilibrium
- ➤ policies to correct inflation and deflation.

5.1 Types of policy: fiscal policy, monetary policy and supply side policy *AS 5(a)*

This topic is concerned with:

- ➤ instruments of fiscal policy
- ➤ instruments of monetary policy
- ➤ instruments of supply side policy.

Instruments of fiscal policy

Fiscal policy refers to the use of revenue and expenditure decisions by a government to influence economic activity in a country. In particular, these decisions are taken to influence the level of aggregate demand in an economy. Slight changes in policy in relation to revenue and/or expenditure can have significant economic effects and so the term fine-tuning has been used to describe what is happening when a government takes policy decisions on revenue and/or expenditure.

It might be thought that a government would deliberately aim to achieve a balanced budget by ensuring that revenue was equal to expenditure. This can happen, but governments frequently decide to aim for a budget deficit or a budget surplus. If an economy is facing a relatively high level of unemployment and a relatively low rate of economic growth, a government may decide to stimulate the economy by deliberately aiming to achieve a budget deficit, i.e. more money will go into the economy than goes out. Examples of instruments to bring such a situation about include reductions in taxation and increases in public expenditure.

On the other hand, if an economy is facing a relatively high rate of inflation, a government may decide to deflate the economy by deliberately aiming to achieve a budget surplus, i.e. more money will go out of an economy than goes in. Examples of instruments to bring such a situation about include increases in taxation and decreases in public expenditure.

Key terms

Fiscal policy: the use of public revenue and/or public expenditure to influence the level of economic activity in a country.

Fine-tuning: the use of relatively small adjustments in taxation and expenditure to influence the level of economic activity in a country.

Balanced budget: a budget where revenue is equal to expenditure.

Budget deficit: a budget where expenditure is greater than revenue.

Budget surplus: a budget where revenue is greater than expenditure.

Instruments of monetary policy

Monetary policy refers to use of decisions by a government to influence economic activity in a country in relation to the price of money and the quantity of money. If an economy is facing a relatively high rate of unemployment and a relatively low rate of economic growth, a government may decide to stimulate the economy by reducing the interest rate and/or increasing the money supply. Slight changes in policy in relation to the price or the supply of money can have significant economic effects and so the term 'fine-tuning' has been used to describe what is happening when a government takes policy decisions on interest rates and/or the money supply.

On the other hand, if an economy is facing a relatively high rate of inflation, a government may decide to deflate the economy by increasing the rate of interest and/or decreasing the money supply.

Instruments of supply side policy

Supply side policy is a general term that refers to a number of different policies that a government could take to influence economic activity in a country. In particular, such policies are often taken in an attempt to improve the efficiency of markets.

Examples of supply side policies include the following:

➤ increasing incentives to work through the lowering of income tax and unemployment benefits, the idea being that this will encourage more people to seek employment

➤ increasing expenditure on education and training to improve the quality of the labour force, the idea being that this will improve the productivity and flexibility of the labour force

➤ reforming trade unions so that their power is reduced, the idea being that fewer working days will be lost as a result of industrial action, such as strikes

➤ encouraging privatisation so that the size of the private sector in an economy increases and the size of the public sector decreases, the idea being that firms in the private sector are likely to be more efficient than those in the public sector, especially when there is intense competition in an industry

➤ encouraging deregulation which will allow greater competition, the idea being that a reduction of barriers into an industry will enable more firms to enter

➤ providing more information about job vacancies, the idea being that greater knowledge of what is available in the labour market could encourage a greater degree of occupational and geographical mobility of labour in an economy.

> **Key terms**
>
> **Monetary policy**: the use of interest rates and/or the money supply to influence the level of economic activity in a country.
>
> **Interest rate**: the cost of borrowing money or the reward for parting with liquidity.
>
> **Money supply**: the amount of money that is available to the banking system and the public in an economy.
>
> **Supply side policy**: policies that are designed to allow markets to work more efficiently and flexibly.

In terms of fiscal policy, it is important to distinguish between discretionary fiscal policy and automatic stabilisers. When a government deliberately decides to change taxation and/or public expenditure to bring about a particular change in an economy, this is known as discretionary fiscal policy. However, with automatic stabilisers, this is where changes in an economy take place without deliberate government action.

In terms of supply side policy, it is important to distinguish between market-orientated supply side policies and interventionist supply side policies. Examples of market-orientated supply side policies include privatisation and deregulation. Examples of interventionist supply side policies include the direct provision of infrastructure and funding for training schemes.

Make sure you understand that a government will deliberately aim for a budget deficit or a budget surplus due to the prevailing economic conditions in a country at any one time. It is not the case that a budget deficit or a budget surplus accidentally happens and that all governments ought to aim for a balanced budget all of the time.

Similarly, it is incorrect to think that monetary policy only works through changes in the price of money, i.e. through changes in interest rates. Monetary policy can also operate through the changes in the quantity, as well as the price, of money.

5.2 Policies to correct a balance of payments disequilibrium

`AS 5(b)`

This topic is concerned with:

➤ the assessment of the effectiveness of fiscal, monetary and supply side policies to correct a balance of payments disequilibrium

➤ expenditure-reducing and expenditure-switching.

The assessment of the effectiveness of fiscal, monetary and supply side policies to correct a balance of payments disequilibrium

Fiscal policy

If a country is experiencing a deficit on the current account of its balance of payments, it may use fiscal policy instruments to try to reduce this deficit. For example, to reduce the demand for imports, a government could increase income tax and/or reduce government spending. This will reduce aggregate demand in an economy, reducing expenditure on imports. A government could also use fiscal policy to discourage the consumption of imported goods by imposing a tariff on the imports, making them more expensive.

The effectiveness of fiscal policy to correct a balance of payments disequilibrium will depend on a number of factors. For instance, the effect of imposing a tariff on imported goods will depend on the price elasticity of demand for imports. If demand is price elastic, consumers will be likely to reduce the demand for the imports and buy domestically produced goods instead, but if demand is price inelastic, it will not have a very significant effect in reducing the demand for imports. There is also the danger that the imposition of tariffs on imports into a country could lead to retaliation by the country producing those goods and this could lead to a decrease in a country's exports to that country. Also, an increase in income tax and/or a decrease in government spending may have negative effects on other parts of an economy, e.g. it may lead to an increase in the level of unemployment.

Monetary policy

If a country is experiencing a deficit on the current account of its balance of payments, it may use monetary policy instruments to try to reduce this deficit. For example, to reduce the demand for imports, a government could increase interest rates and/or reduce the money supply. Either of these policies is likely to reduce aggregate demand in an economy and make it less likely that consumers will buy imported goods.

The effectiveness of monetary policy to correct a balance of payments disequilibrium will depend on a number of factors. For instance, the effect of an increase in interest rates on demand in an economy will depend on the extent to which the demand is interest-elastic. If demand is relatively interest-inelastic, an increase in interest rates will be unlikely to have much of an impact on the demand for imports. Also, the effect of a change in interest rates in an economy can take a while because of a time lag between a change in interest rates and the full consequences of such an action being seen.

Supply side policies

If a country is experiencing a deficit on the current account of its balance of payments, it may use supply side policy instruments to try to reduce this deficit. For example, if a domestic market was made more efficient and more flexible, such as through a policy of privatisation or deregulation, this would be likely to make a country's exports more competitive in international markets, encouraging the demand for them to increase. This would be as a result of increased quality and/or a more competitive price.

The effectiveness of supply side policy to correct a balance of payments disequilibrium will depend on a number of factors. For instance, increased spending on education and training is only likely to have a significant effect over a relatively long period of time. Privatisation may not necessarily lead to greater efficiency if a public sector monopoly is replaced by a private sector monopoly that does not take into account external costs.

Expenditure-reducing and expenditure-switching

It is important to be able to distinguish between expenditure-reducing and expenditure-switching.

Expenditure-reducing

Expenditure-reducing policies are those which are designed to reduce the demand for all products in an economy, i.e. they are intended to reduce the demand for imported goods, but the effect is that the demand for all goods, including domestically produced goods, will be reduced.

Deflationary fiscal policy, to reduce expenditure, can include an increase in taxation and/or a reduction in government expenditure. Deflationary monetary policy, to reduce expenditure, can include an increase in interest rates and/or a reduction in the money supply.

Expenditure-switching

Whereas expenditure-reducing policies are designed to reduce the demand for all products in an economy, expenditure-switching policies are designed to switch demand away from some products and towards others. For example, they could intend to decrease the demand for imports and increase the demand for exports.

There are a number of protectionist methods that can be used to decrease the demand for imports and increase the demand for exports, including the following:

➤ tariffs

➤ quotas

➤ subsidies

➤ exchange controls

➤ embargoes

➤ administrative restrictions.

> **Remember**
>
> A balance of payments disequilibrium can refer to a persistent surplus as well as a persistent deficit.

> ★ **Exam tip**
>
> Make sure that you are able to explain the distinction between expenditure-reducing policies, which are designed to bring about a fall in demand for all products in an economy, and expenditure-switching policies, which are designed to bring about a change in the pattern of demand for different products in an economy, e.g. reducing the demand for imported products and increasing the demand for exported products.

> ✗ **Common error**
>
> Be careful not to get confused between the idea of deflation, i.e. a period of falling prices in an economy, and deflationary policies which are designed to reduce the level of aggregate demand in an economy.

> ⬆ **Raise your grade**
>
> Explain the difference between expenditure-reducing and expenditure-switching policies in an economy. [8]
>
> It is important to be able to distinguish between expenditure-reducing policies and expenditure-switching policies in an economy.
>
> Expenditure-reducing policies refer to those policies which are intended to reduce the demand for certain products in an economy[1]. Examples of such policies include deflationary fiscal policy, such as an increase in taxation[2], and deflationary monetary policy, such as an increase in interest rates[3].
>
> Expenditure-switching policies refer to those policies which are designed to change the pattern of demand for different products in an economy, e.g. to reduce the demand for imports[4]. Examples of such policies include tariffs, quotas and subsidies[5].

How to improve this answer

1   The candidate appears somewhat confused at this point. Expenditure-reducing policies are intended to reduce the demand for all products in an economy, not just certain products, i.e. there is a deliberate attempt to reduce the level of aggregate demand in an economy.

2   The candidate has given the example of an increase in taxation, but fiscal policy includes expenditure as well as revenue, and so the candidate could also have given as an example a reduction in government expenditure.

3   The candidate has given the example of an increase in interest rates, but monetary policy includes the quantity, as well as the price, of money. So, the candidate could also have given as an example a reduction in the money supply.

4   The candidate has referred to the reduced demand for imports as an example of the change in the pattern of demand, but they could also have referred to an increased demand for exports.

5   The candidate has referred to three possible policies designed to switch expenditure from some products to others, but more could have been written about each of these policies. For example, it would have been useful if the candidate had distinguished between tariffs and quotas as methods to reduce the demand for imports and subsidies as a method to increase the demand for domestically produced goods.

Knowledge and understanding:	2/4
Application:	2/4
Total:	4/8

5.3 Policies to correct inflation and deflation   AS 5(c)

This topic is concerned with:

➤ the assessment of the effectiveness of fiscal, monetary and supply side policies to correct inflation and deflation.

Fiscal policy to correct inflation

Inflation can be corrected by fiscal policy. For example, if the inflation is caused by demand-pull factors, a government may decide to reduce the level of aggregate demand in an economy by reducing the level of government expenditure and/or increasing the level of taxation.

The effectiveness of fiscal policy to correct inflation will depend on a number of factors. Higher rates of income tax could reduce aggregate demand, but this could create a disincentive effect, with workers only prepared to work fewer hours. Also, higher rates of income tax may lead trade unions to demand significant wage increases to at least maintain the disposable incomes of their members, and increased wages will lead to increased costs for firms, generating cost-push inflation.

Monetary policy to correct inflation

Inflation can be corrected by monetary policy. For example, if the inflation is caused by demand-pull factors, a government may decide to reduce the level of aggregate demand in an economy by reducing the money supply and/or increasing the interest rate.

The effectiveness of monetary policy to correct inflation will depend on a number of factors. The impact of a rise in the rate of interest will depend on how interest-elastic the demand is for products, but if demand is interest-elastic, borrowing will be discouraged as it is now more expensive. Saving will be encouraged by a higher rate of interest, if demand for savings accounts is interest-elastic.

Supply side policy to correct inflation

Inflation can be corrected by supply side policies. For example, if such policies are used to reduce the power of trade unions and make the labour market more competitive, this is likely to increase aggregate supply. If inflation was caused by an excess of aggregate demand over aggregate supply, this will have the effect of reducing the imbalance and so reducing inflationary pressures. Privatisation might also help to increase aggregate supply in an economy if the privatised firms are more efficient.

The effectiveness of supply side policy to correct inflation will depend on a number of factors. The main factor is that supply side measures usually take quite a while to have any significant effect. For instance, making markets more competitive and flexible is something that can take quite a lot of time and so the impact on inflation may not be immediate.

Fiscal policy to correct deflation

Whereas inflation refers to a persistent and sustained increase in the general level of prices in an economy over a period of time, deflation refers to a persistent and sustained decrease in the general level of prices in an economy over a period of time. Deflation can be corrected by reflationary fiscal policy. For example, if the deflation is caused by demand-pull factors, a government may decide to increase the level of aggregate demand in an economy by increasing the level of government expenditure and/or decreasing the level of taxation.

The effectiveness of fiscal policy to correct deflation will depend on a number of factors. One of these is taking decisions on the basis of correct information, e.g. if the information on which decisions are taken is inaccurate, a government may cure the deflation, but replace it with a relatively high rate of inflation which, if above the inflation target rate, will not be helpful.

Monetary policy to correct deflation

Deflation can be corrected by reflationary monetary policy. For example, if the deflation is caused by demand-pull factors, a government may decide to increase the level of aggregate demand in an economy by increasing the money supply and/or decreasing the interest rate.

The effectiveness of monetary policy to correct deflation will depend on a number of factors. For example, the interest rate may already be so low that when there are further reductions, they have very little, if any, effect in stimulating increased borrowing and spending.

Supply side policy to correct deflation

Deflation can be corrected by supply side policies, especially where the deflation has been caused by a high level of supply relative to aggregate demand. For instance, a government could reduce the financial support it gives to training and education schemes.

The effectiveness of supply side policy to correct deflation will depend on a number of factors. For example, it has already been stressed that it often takes supply side policies quite a long time to have any effect, and the same point would apply if any of the policies were reversed in an attempt to reduce the level of aggregate supply in an economy.

> **Remember**
>
> It is important to differentiate between inflation, i.e. a persistent and sustained rise in the general level of prices in an economy over a period of time, and deflation, i.e. a persistent and sustained fall in the general level of prices in an economy over a period of time.

Revision checklist

I can:

- ➤ understand fiscal policy and the instruments that can be used as part of this policy ☐
- ➤ understand monetary policy and the instruments that can be used as part of this policy ☐
- ➤ understand supply side policy and the instruments that can be used as part of this policy ☐
- ➤ understand the difference between a balanced budget, a budget deficit and a budget surplus ☐
- ➤ understand, and can explain, what is meant by the 'fine-tuning' of an economy ☐
- ➤ appreciate the difference between the price of money and the quantity or supply of money ☐
- ➤ refer to examples of supply side policies ☐
- ➤ be clear about the distinction between discretionary fiscal policy and automatic stabilisers ☐
- ➤ understand the difference between market-orientated supply side measures and interventionist supply side measures ☐
- ➤ understand the different policies that could be taken to correct a balance of payments disequilibrium ☐
- ➤ assess the effectiveness of different policies that could be taken to correct a balance of payments disequilibrium ☐
- ➤ understand that a balance of payments disequilibrium can either refer to a deficit or a surplus ☐
- ➤ understand the difference between expenditure-reducing policies and expenditure-switching policies ☐
- ➤ understand the different policies that could be taken to correct inflation ☐
- ➤ assess the effectiveness of different policies that could be taken to correct inflation ☐
- ➤ understand the difference between inflation and deflation ☐
- ➤ understand the different policies that could be taken to correct deflation ☐
- ➤ assess the effectiveness of different policies that could be taken to correct deflation ☐
- ➤ understand the difference between deflationary and reflationary policies ☐
- ➤ understand that a time lag can apply to the period between the implementation of a policy and the impact that such a policy can have in an economy. ☐

? Exam-style questions

1 Which of the following would stimulate demand in an economy?

   A Decrease in the money supply.

   B Increase in government expenditure.

   C Increase in taxation.

   D Increase in the interest rate. [1]

2 Slight changes in fiscal or monetary policies to affect the level of economic activity in a country are known as:

   A balanced

   B deregulation

   C fine-tuning

   D targeting. [1]

3 When a government deliberately decides to change public revenue and/or public expenditure to achieve an objective, it is known as:

   A automatic fiscal policy

   B automatic monetary policy

   C discretionary fiscal policy

   D discretionary monetary policy. [1]

4 Which of the following is an example of a market-orientated supply side policy?

   A Direct provision of infrastructure.

   B Funding for training.

   C Grants for research and development.

   D Privatisation. [1]

5 The effectiveness of a tariff to correct a balance of payments deficit will depend on:

   A the money supply in an economy

   B the price elasticity of demand for the exported products

   C the price elasticity of demand for the imported products

   D the rate of interest in an economy. [1]

6 Which of the following is an example of deflationary monetary policy?

   A Reduction in public expenditure.

   B Increase in the interest rate.

   C Increase in the money supply.

   D Increase in taxation. [1]

7 A policy to encourage spending in an economy is called:

   A deflationary

   B disinflationary

   C reflationary

   D regulatory. [1]

8 Providing more information about job vacancies is likely to:

   A contribute to a lower rate of inflation in an economy

   B encourage greater occupational and geographical mobility of labour

   C increase the amount of money paid out through unemployment benefits

   D lead to the privatisation of industries in an economy. [1]

9 **(a)** Explain the distinction between fiscal policy and monetary policy. [8]

   (b) Discuss whether fiscal policy or monetary policy is more likely to correct a balance of payments deficit. [12]

10 **(a)** Explain the difference between market-orientated and interventionist supply side policies. [8]

   (b) Discuss whether supply sides policies are guaranteed to correct inflation. [12]

6 Basic economic ideas and resource allocation AL 1(a)–(c)

Key topics

➤ efficient resource allocation

➤ externalities and market failure

➤ social costs and benefits; cost-benefit analysis.

6.1 Efficient resource allocation AL 1(a)

This topic is concerned with:

➤ productive and allocative efficiency

➤ Pareto optimality

➤ dynamic efficiency.

Productive and allocative efficiency

Economic efficiency can be divided into two types – productive efficiency and allocative efficiency.

Productive efficiency

One way of measuring productive efficiency is at the micro level in terms of the minimum average cost at which a given output can be produced. In this sense, productive efficiency involves two elements. Technical efficiency is where the best possible combination of factors of production is used in the production process, i.e. the greatest amount of output is produced that is possible from a given set of inputs. Cost efficiency is where the production is influenced by the relative costs of different inputs. Figure 6.1 shows productive efficiency in a firm.

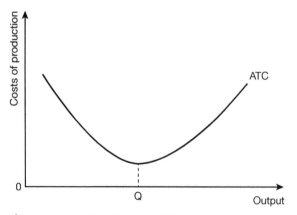

▲ **Figure 6.1** Productive efficiency in a firm

> **Key terms**
>
> **Productive efficiency**: a situation where there is both technical efficiency and cost efficiency in a firm, or where an economy is operating on its production possibility curve.
>
> **Technical efficiency**: a situation where a firm is able to produce the maximum output possible from the given inputs.
>
> **Cost efficiency**: a situation where a firm uses the most appropriate combination of inputs, given the relative costs of those inputs.

Another way of measuring productive efficiency is at the macro level in terms of the production possibility curve of an economy. The PPC in Figure 6.2 shows the possible combinations of production of two products. Point X, inside the PPC, indicates productive inefficiency because there are unused resources that could be used to produce more of both products. Any point on the PPC, however, such as point Y, shows that all of the available resources in an economy are being fully used in the production of the two products, i.e. productive efficiency is being maximised.

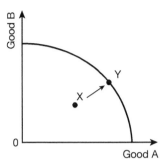

▲ **Figure 6.2** Productive efficiency in an economy

Allocative efficiency

Another element in economic efficiency is allocative efficiency. This allocation of resources is the one which fits the wishes of the consumers and producers most closely. It occurs where price is equal to marginal cost. This is because the value that is put on a product by a consumer, i.e. the price, is equal to the value put on a product by a producer, i.e. the marginal cost of producing one more unit of the product.

> ✗ **Common error**
>
> Productive efficiency can occur at the lowest point on any average cost curve and not only at the lowest point on the average total cost curve.

Pareto optimality

An optimal resource allocation refers to a situation where there is the best possible allocation of scarce resources. The Italian economist, Vilfredo Pareto (1848-1923), stated that such a situation existed when it was impossible to make one person better off without making another person worse off. This situation is therefore known as Pareto optimality. In this situation, there needs to be both productive efficiency and allocative efficiency.

Dynamic efficiency

Whereas productive and allocative efficiency are examples of static efficiency, i.e. they are concerned with the allocation of resources at a given moment in time, dynamic efficiency is concerned with changes in the allocation of resources over time. For example, new products may appear as a result of invention and innovation. There may be new methods of production that can be used as a result of technological progress. There could also be changes in the management of resources.

> 💡 **Remember**
>
> Productive and allocative efficiency are both examples of static efficiency, i.e. they refer to the most efficient allocation of resources in a given period of time. Dynamic efficiency, however, is the result of changes over time, such as in relation to the products that are produced or the way that they are produced.

Efficient resource allocation refers to both productive and allocative efficiency, but each of these is a static concept, i.e. that level of efficiency is the best that can be achieved at a given moment in time. Over a period of time, however, dynamic efficiency can occur, leading to changes in the allocation of resources.

 Raise your grade

Explain why dynamic efficiency is important in an economy. [12]

Productive and allocative efficiency are examples of static efficiency[1], but dynamic efficiency is different in that it is concerned with changes in the allocation of scarce resources over a period of time.

It is important in an economy for a number of reasons. For example, new products may appear as a result of invention and innovation[2]. There may be new methods of production that can be used as a result of technological progress[3]. There could also be changes in the management of resources[4].

The existence of dynamic efficiency in an economy will enable it to compete effectively with other countries in international trade. This would be likely to enhance the rate of economic growth in the country[5].

How to improve this answer

1   The candidate could have explained more fully what is meant by a static concept in relation to efficiency, such as the fact that they are concerned with the allocation of resources at a given moment in time.

2   It is good that the candidate has referred to invention and innovation, which are crucial in dynamic efficiency, but examples of new products could have been included to develop the answer, such as in relation to mobile phones and televisions.

3   Again, the candidate has usefully referred to new methods of production that could be used as a result of technological progress, but the answer could have been developed more fully by reference to appropriate examples, such as the use of robots in the mass production of cars.

4   Changes in the management of resources are relevant to dynamic efficiency and again it would have been useful to have included some examples, such as the use of a more effective stock control system.

5   This is a useful point to have made, stressing the link between dynamic efficiency and economic growth, but this final sentence could have been taken further, such as by a reference to the shifting outwards of a country's production possibility curve.

Level 2 – 5/12

6.2 Externalities and market failure `AL 1(b)`

This topic is concerned with:

➤ reasons for market failure

➤ positive and negative externalities for both consumers and firms

➤ inefficient resource allocation.

Reasons for market failure

Market failure refers to a market imperfection which gives rise to an allocation of resources which is not as efficient as might otherwise have been the case.

There are many possible reasons for market failure, including the following:

➤ the under-production and under-consumption of merit goods

➤ the over-production and over-consumption of demerit goods

➤ the non-provision of public goods

➤ the existence of externalities which are costs or benefits which affect third parties, sometimes referred to as spillover effects

➤ information failure leading to a sub-optimal allocation of resources

➤ government failure where a government intervenes to try to overcome a failure in a market, only to create further distortions

➤ imperfect competition, such as the existence of a monopoly

➤ an inequality in the distribution of income and wealth in an economy, giving some individuals more influence in a market than others

➤ the existence of geographical and/or occupational immobility of factors of production, making it difficult to reallocate them to alternative uses

➤ price instability in markets, especially in agricultural markets.

> ⭐ **Exam tip**
>
> Make sure you understand what is meant by a third party and a spillover effect. This is where someone who is not directly involved in the consumption and/or production of a product can still be affected in some way.

> ✗ **Common error**
>
> Don't get confused by what is meant by a third party. Make sure you understand that although a third party can be affected by a decision in some way, the third party is not directly involved in the taking of the decision.

Positive and negative externalities for both consumers and firms

An externality refers to an action that results in either external costs or external benefits in relation to either production or consumption.

Positive externalities

Figure 6.3 on the next page shows a situation where there is a positive externality, i.e. social benefits are greater than private benefits. The original equilibrium position is where the supply curve, S, representing

Key terms

Market failure: a market imperfection which gives rise to an allocation of resources which is not as efficient as might otherwise have been the case.

Third parties: individuals or groups that are in some way affected by a decision, even though they are not the main parties in such a decision.

Spillover effect: a situation where a certain decision has an impact on third parties, i.e. those who are nether the producers or the consumers of a certain product.

Key terms

Externality: an action that results in either external benefits or external costs in relation to either production or consumption.

External cost: a cost which arises from any activity which is not paid for by the firm or the consumer carrying out the activity.

External benefit: a benefit to a third party which arises from an activity carried out by a firm or a consumer.

marginal social cost (MSC), intersects with the demand curve, D_1, representing marginal private benefit (MPB). However, if all of the benefits are taken into account, this will be shown by the demand curve D_2, representing marginal social benefit (MSB) which is made up of both marginal private benefit (MPB) and marginal external benefit (MEB). The effect of taking all benefits and costs into account is that the equilibrium price rises from $0P_1$ to $0P_2$ and the equilibrium quantity rises from $0Q_1$ to $0Q_2$.

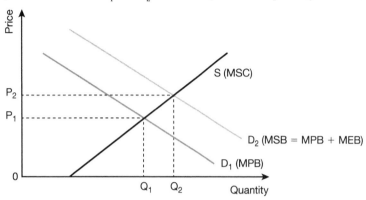

▲ **Figure 6.3** A positive externality

Negative externalities

Figure 6.4 shows a situation where there is a negative externality, i.e. social costs are greater than private costs. The original equilibrium position is where the supply curve, S_1, representing marginal private cost (MPC), intersects with the demand curve, D, representing marginal social benefit (MSB). However, if all of the costs are taken into account, this will be shown by the supply curve S_2, representing marginal social cost (MSC) which is made up of both marginal private cost (MPC) and marginal external cost (MEC). The effect of taking all costs and benefits into account is that the equilibrium price rises from $0P_1$ to $0P_2$ and the equilibrium quantity falls from $0Q_1$ to $0Q_2$.

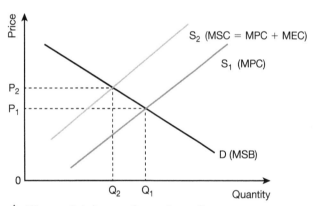

▲ **Figure 6.4** A negative externality

★ Exam tip

You need to remember that an externality can be either positive or negative and can refer to either consumption or production benefits or costs or to both.

Remember

Marginal social benefit includes both marginal private benefit and marginal external benefit. Marginal social cost includes both marginal private cost and marginal external cost.

Inefficient resource allocation

The existence of market failure gives rise to inefficient resource allocation in an economy. For example, information failure on the part of consumers means that they do not fully appreciate the potential advantages of the consumption of merit goods such as education and health care, not only to themselves but to the wider society. As a result, merit goods are under-consumed and under-produced.

On the other hand, information failure on the part of consumers means that they do not fully appreciate the potential disadvantages of the consumption of demerit goods such as alcohol and tobacco, not only to themselves but to the wider society. As a result, demerit goods are over-consumed and over-produced.

The existence of positive and negative externalities also gives rise to an inefficient resource allocation. In a market economy, without any government intervention, too much may be produced and/or consumed of one product and too little produced and/or consumed of another, giving rise to inefficient resource allocation.

> **Remember**
>
> The existence of market failure, such as in relation to positive and negative externalities for both consumers and firms, gives rise to inefficient resource allocation in an economy.

6.3 Social costs and benefits; cost-benefit analysis

AL 1(c)

This topic is concerned with:

➤ social costs as the sum of private costs and external costs

➤ social benefits as the sum of private benefits and external benefits

➤ use of cost-benefit analysis in decision-making.

Social costs as the sum of private costs and external costs

It is important to understand that social costs represent the true cost of something to society, i.e. they include not only private costs, but also the external costs imposed on a society as the result of an economic action.

> **Key term**
>
> Social costs: the sum of private costs and external costs.

> **✗ Common error**
>
> It is easy to confuse social costs and external costs. An external cost is a cost that arises from any activity which is not paid for by the firm or the consumer carrying out the activity, but a social cost includes **both** external costs and private costs.

Social benefits as the sum of private benefits and external benefits

Just as social costs represent the true cost of something to society, social benefits represent the true benefit of something to society, i.e. they include not only private benefits, but also the external benefits that are of benefit to the whole society as the result of an economic action.

> **Key term**
>
> Social benefits: the sum of private benefits and external benefits.

> **✗ Common error**
>
> It is easy to frequently confuse social benefits and external benefits. An external benefit is a benefit to a third party which arises from an activity carried out by a firm or a consumer, but a social benefit includes **both** external benefits and private benefits.

The use of cost-benefit analysis in decision-making

Cost-benefit analysis refers to a process that includes all the costs and benefits that relate to an investment project and which need to be considered before a decision is taken whether or not to go ahead with the project.

There are a number of advantages associated with cost-benefit analysis, including the following:

➤ it takes into account all of the various costs and benefits resulting from a proposed investment project

➤ many of the various costs and benefits will have market prices attached to them, making it relatively easy to calculate monetary values

➤ it can analyse not only costs and benefits today, but also future costs and benefits, enabling the long-term consequences of an investment project to be considered and not only the short-term ones

➤ it helps to make it more likely that the correct decision will be taken.

However, cost-benefit analysis does have a number of potential drawbacks and limitations, including the following:

➤ it may be difficult to identify all of the relevant external costs and benefits to include in the analysis

➤ not all of the costs and benefits will have market prices and this will make it more difficult to calculate their monetary value

➤ shadow prices can be used where market prices do not apply, but these can be very difficult to estimate

➤ the estimation of costs and benefits in the future can be a problem and this gives rise to the issue of time value of money

➤ future values can be discounted to give present values, but this may not always be easy to calculate accurately

➤ cost-benefit analysis usually relates to investment projects in the public sector, but even if the analysis suggests that there will be a net benefit to a community, there may be political reasons why the project does not go ahead.

Key term

Cost-benefit analysis: a method used to evaluate large-scale investment projects which take into account all relevant costs and benefits, including both private and external costs and benefits.

> ★ **Exam tip**
>
> Make sure that you are able to support answers on cost-benefit analysis with appropriate examples of investment projects, such as the building of an airport, a motorway or a railway line.

> **Remember**
>
> Remember that although cost-benefit analysis has many potential advantages, there are also a number of limitations in the use of such an analysis.

> ✓ **What you need to know**
>
> Cost-benefit analysis can be extremely useful in decision-making, but you need to understand that there are some important limitations to its use.

Revision checklist

I can:

- ➤ understand the distinction between productive efficiency and allocative efficiency ☐

- ➤ understand that Pareto optimality refers to a situation where it is impossible to make one person better off without making another person worse off ☐

- ➤ understand that Pareto optimality requires both productive efficiency and allocative efficiency to be in existence ☐

- ➤ understand how dynamic efficiency is different from productive and allocative efficiency in relating to changes over a period of time ☐

- ➤ understand the various reasons for market failure in an economy ☐

- ➤ understand what is meant by a third party ☐

- ➤ be clear about what is meant by a spillover effect ☐

- ➤ understand what is meant by positive and negative externalities for both consumers and firms ☐

- ➤ appreciate what is meant by inefficient resource allocation in an economy ☐

- ➤ understand that social costs are the sum of private costs and external costs ☐

- ➤ understand that social benefits are the sum of private benefits and external benefits ☐

- ➤ understand what is meant by cost-benefit analysis ☐

- ➤ understand the potential benefits of cost-benefit analysis as an aid to decision-making in relation to public sector investment projects ☐

- ➤ understand the potential limitations of cost-benefit analysis as an aid to decision-making in relation to public sector investment projects. ☐

? Exam-style questions

1 Productive efficiency occurs where:

   A average cost is at its lowest

   B average cost is equal to marginal cost

   C average variable cost is at its lowest

   D production is inside a production possibility curve. [1]

2 Pareto optimality includes:

   A allocative efficiency only

   B neither productive or allocative efficiency

   C productive efficiency and allocative efficiency

   D productive efficiency only. [1]

3 A third party interrupted by loud music from a neighbour is an example of a:

   A negative externality in relation to consumption

   B negative externality in relation to production

   C positive externality in relation to consumption

   D positive externality in relation to production. [1]

4 An example of a market failure is the:

   A non-provision of a public good

   B optimal allocation of resources

   C over-production of a merit good

   D under-production of a demit good. [1]

5 Marginal social benefit is the addition of:

   A marginal external benefit and marginal cost

   B marginal private benefit and marginal cost

   C marginal private benefit and marginal external benefit.

   D marginal private benefit and marginal social benefit. [1]

6 What does cost-benefit analysis use when it is not possible to use market prices?

   A Discounted prices.

   B Shadow prices.

   C Transitional prices.

   D Underground prices. [1]

7 (a) Explain the distinction between productive and allocative efficiency. [12]

   (b) Discuss to what extent market failure can undermine the efficiency of an economy. [13]

8 Discuss whether cost-benefit analysis will guarantee that a decision about whether to build a new airport is the correct one. [25]

Key topics

- ➤ the law of diminishing marginal utility
- ➤ indifference curves and budget lines
- ➤ types of cost, revenue and profit, short-run and long-run production
- ➤ different market structures
- ➤ the growth and survival of firms
- ➤ differing objectives of a firm.

7.1 The law of diminishing marginal utility AL 2(a)

This topic is concerned with:

- ➤ the relationship of the law of diminishing marginal utility to the derivation of an individual demand schedule
- ➤ the equi-marginal principle
- ➤ the limitations of marginal utility theory; rational behaviour versus behavioural economic models.

The relationship of the law of diminishing marginal utility to the derivation of an individual demand schedule

Utility refers to the benefit or satisfaction that is derived from the consumption of a product. Marginal utility is the extra satisfaction that can be gained from consuming one additional unit of a product. This is in contrast to total utility, which refers to the total satisfaction obtained from consuming a particular number of units of a product.

The law of diminishing marginal utility refers to the situation where the consumption of successive units of a product will eventually lead to a fall in marginal utility, i.e. as someone consumes more units of a product, the satisfaction provided by each unit will be progressively less.

There is an important relationship between the law of diminishing marginal utility and the derivation of an individual demand schedule. If the marginal utility of consuming extra units of a product continually diminishes, a consumer will be unwilling to pay as much for each successive unit consumed, i.e. as the utility falls, so will the price that a consumer is willing to pay. This can be shown in an individual demand schedule and explains why a demand curve for a product is downward sloping from left to right.

✗ Common error

Be careful not to confuse the concepts of marginal utility and total utility. Total utility refers to the satisfaction gained from the consumption of all of the units of a product whereas marginal utility refers to the satisfaction gained from the consumption of just one more additional unit of a product.

Key terms

Utility: the satisfaction gained from the consumption of a product.

Marginal utility: the satisfaction gained from the last unit of a product consumed over a particular time period.

Total utility: the satisfaction gained from the consumption of all units of a product over a particular time period.

Law of diminishing marginal utility: a situation where as the quantity consumed of a product by an individual increases, the additional or extra satisfaction gained from each unit (the marginal utility) will eventually decline.

The fact that marginal utility diminishes with the consumption of additional units of a product means that consumers are only willing to pay a lower price for these additional units. This explains why a demand curve is downward sloping from left to right, i.e. as quantity increases, price falls. It is assumed that the marginal utility of a product can be measured by the price an individual is prepared to pay for it. This is why an individual's demand curve for a product will be the same as their marginal utility curve and an individual will purchase a product up to the point where P = MU.

Make sure that you are able to clearly differentiate between the concepts of marginal utility and total utility.

Total utility increases up to a certain quantity of units of a product consumed, but at a decreasing rate. This is because the marginal utility of consuming additional units of a product is decreasing. At the point where total utility is at the maximum, marginal utility is equal to zero. When total utility begins to decline, marginal utility becomes negative. This can be seen in Figure 7.1 below.

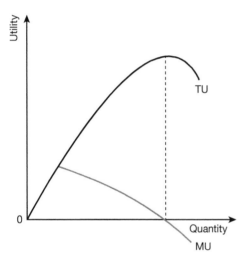

▲ **Figure 7.1** Total utility and marginal utility

The equi-marginal principle

The equi-marginal principle shows the relationship between the marginal utility obtained from the consumption of different products and the prices paid for those products. It can be represented as follows: $\dfrac{MUa}{Pa} = \dfrac{MUb}{Pb} = \dfrac{MUc}{Pc}$

To maximise their utility or satisfaction, a consumer will be at the situation shown above for the three products a, b and c. The extra satisfaction produced by the last unit of a consumed, in relation to the money spent to buy this last unit, will be equal to the extra satisfaction produced by the last unit of b consumed, in relation to the money spent to buy this last unit and this will be equal to the extra satisfaction produced by the last unit of c consumed, in relation to the money spent to buy this last unit.

Make sure you understand the principle *and* the static principle. The consumption of the different products will change if there is a change in the price of any of them.

The limitations of marginal utility theory

The law of diminishing marginal utility is based on a number of assumptions, but if these assumptions do not actually apply, there will be limitations to the theory. These assumptions include the following:

➤ the idea that the utility or satisfaction that an individual gains from the consumption of a product can be easily measured, but this may not necessarily be so

➤ the idea that consumers behave in a rational way, but this may not always be the case

➤ the idea that consumers have limited incomes, but it is possible that incomes may rise over a period of time

➤ the idea that consumers can be expected to maximise their total utility, but this may not always be so

➤ the idea that prices are constant, but the prices of products are likely to be continually changing

➤ the idea that consumer tastes and preferences remain constant, but these may change over time, perhaps as a result of advertising campaigns

➤ the idea that the consideration of marginal utility is vitally important, but this may not always be the case, especially where consumption is habit forming or made on impulse

➤ the idea that all units of a product available for consumption are identical, but if quality control in the production process is not very efficient, this may not always be so.

Rational behaviour versus behavioural economic models

The rational behaviour of consumers is based on the idea that they will maximise their utility, given the following constraints: limited income, a given set of prices and constant tastes and preferences.

Rational behaviour essentially means the following:

➤ individual consumers will take decisions to maximise their utility and satisfaction

➤ individual consumers will have access to all the information that they require to make a decision at zero cost

➤ individuals take decisions that are based on a very careful comparison of the benefits and costs to achieve the optimal outcome

➤ these decisions will be taken by individuals based on changes at the margin, stressing the importance of the margin as a key economic concept

➤ the tastes and preferences of individuals and their attitude to risk are assumed to be fixed.

However, behavioural economic models have been developed to offer a contrast to the idea of rational behaviour. Behavioural economics attempts to explain the decisions taken by individuals in practice, particularly when they are opposed to those predicted by traditional economic theory, i.e. it attempts to explain what might appear apparently 'irrational' behaviour.

The key elements of behavioural economic models include the following:

➤ instead of attempting to achieve optimal outcomes as a result of taking decisions, individuals take decisions based on the potential gains and losses that might arise

➤ individuals may not always possess all the relevant information that they require, possibly because of reasons of time and/or cost, giving rise to the existence of an opportunity cost in terms of possible alternative uses of this time and/or money

➤ there may be just too much information available, making decision taking more difficult; an individual's ability to act rationally is therefore restricted or 'bounded', and so they may engage in satisficing rather than optimising behaviour (this is known as bounded rationality)

➤ individuals may take decisions based on rules of thumb (known as heuristics), simplifying what is involved in the decision-making process, or on the first piece of information received (known as anchoring)

➤ decisions can be based on assumptions, even though this could lead to irrational decisions

➤ the way that information is presented can influence behaviour (this is known as framing)

➤ individuals can be 'nudged' to take particular decisions, such as through government advertising.

Raise your grade

Explain why the idea of rational behaviour is being increasingly challenged by behavioural economic models. [12]

The rational behaviour of consumers is based on the idea that they will maximise their utility.[1] Rational behaviour assumes that individual consumers will have access to all the information that they require to make a decision[2] and that individuals take decisions that are based on a very careful comparison of the benefits and costs to achieve the optimal outcome.[3]

However, it has often been pointed out that many economic decisions are not rational and so behavioural economic models have been developed to offer a contrast to the idea of rational behaviour.

Behavioural economics explains the decisions taken by individuals in practice, particularly when they are opposed to those predicted by traditional economic theory. There are a number of key elements of behavioural economic models. It is argued, for example, that individuals may not always possess all the relevant information that they require to take decisions.[4] Alternatively, it could be that there is too much information available, making decision making more difficult.[5] It is possible that individuals may take decisions based on rules of thumb (known as 'heuristics'), simplifying what is involved in the decision-making process.[6] The way that information is presented can influence behaviour.[7] Individuals can be persuaded to take particular decisions, such as through government advertising.[8]

This increasing challenge to the idea of rational behaviour by behavioural economists has attempted to address the criticisms made about rational behaviour and it has succeeded in offering an alternative, and perhaps more realistic, analysis and explanation of consumer behaviour.

How to improve this answer

1 There is no mention here of the constraints that are assumed to exist, such as a limited income and constant tastes and preferences.

2 There could have been reference to the assumption that this information can be obtained at zero cost.

3 The candidate could have stressed that these decisions are taken at the margin.

4 The concept of opportunity cost could have been brought in, e.g. alternative uses of the time taken to obtain the information.

5 The candidate could have brought in the idea of 'bounded rationality' here.

6 There could have been reference here to 'anchoring', where the first information obtained is regarded as the most important.

7.2 **Indifference curves and budget lines**   AL 2(b)

This topic is concerned with:

➤ income, substitution and price effects for various types of goods.

Indifference curves

An indifference curve shows the possible combinations of two products between which a consumer is indifferent. It slopes downwards from left to right and is convex to the origin. The slope of an indifference curve shows the marginal rate of substitution between two products, i.e. the number of units of one product that an individual is prepared to give up in order to obtain additional units of the other product.

An indifference curve is shown in Figure 7.2. This indicates the possible combinations of apples and pears between which a consumer is indifferent.

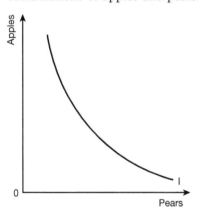

▲ **Figure 7.2** Indifference curve

A series of indifference curves can be shown in an indifference map, as in Figure 7.3. These indifference curves indicate higher levels of total utility as there is movement away from the origin, i.e. I_3 permits an individual to increase consumption of at least one of the two products.

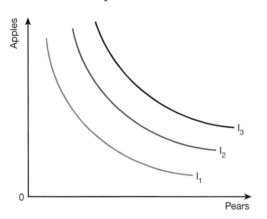

▲ **Figure 7.3** Indifference map

> **Key terms**
>
> **Indifference curve:** a curve showing all possible combinations of two products between which an individual consumer is indifferent.
>
> **Marginal rate of substitution:** the quantity of one product that an individual is prepared to give up in order to obtain an additional unit of another product while leaving the individual at the same level of utility.

✓ **What you need to know**

It is important that you understand the properties of indifference curves:

➤ they identify different combinations of two products between which an individual has no preference, i.e. the individual is indifferent as to which combination of products they consume

➤ all points on an indifference curve represent combinations of two products which give an individual equal satisfaction

➤ there is an infinite number of indifference curves for each consumer, each one associated with a particular level of total utility

➤ they slope downwards from left to right

➤ they are convex to the origin

➤ the slope of an indifference curve indicates the marginal rate of substitution between two products

➤ an indifference curve becomes shallower as there is movement down the curve, reflecting an individual consumer's diminishing marginal rate of substitution of one product for another, i.e. as an individual obtains more and more of one product, they are prepared to sacrifice fewer and fewer units of the other product

➤ indifference curves can never intersect each other.

★ **Exam tip**

Make sure you are able to demonstrate you understand that an indifference curve is downward sloping from left to right because of the marginal rate of substitution between two products.

Budget lines

A budget line shows the possible combinations of two products that an individual consumer is able to purchase with a given income and fixed prices. Each of the combinations of two products along a budget line would cost the consumer the same total amount of money. Any point along a budget line will indicate the maximisation of consumption at a given level of income.

Key term

Budget line: a line that shows all possible combinations of two products that an individual is able to purchase at particular prices and with a given level of income.

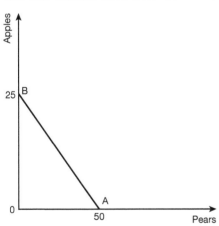

▲ **Figure 7.4** Budget line

A budget line is shown in Figure 7.4. This shows an individual's budget line for two products, apples and pears. If all income is spent on apples, it is possible to buy 0B apples and no pears. If all income is pent on pears, it is possible to buy 0A pears and no apples. The budget line is AB. Any combination of apples or pears inside the budget line, or on the budget line, can be consumed by the individual. However, the individual cannot consume beyond the budget line.

If there is a change in an individual's income, they will be able to consume more apples and more pears. This can be seen in Figure 7.5 on the next page. The effect of an increase in an individual's income will be to shift the budget line upwards to the right, parallel to the original budget line. This can be seen in the diagram where the new budget line is CD. If an individual's income was reduced, this would have the effect of shifting the budget line inwards towards the origin, parallel to the original budget line.

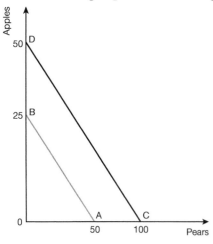

▲ **Figure 7.5** The effect of a change in income on a budget line

A budget line will be affected not only by a change in an individual's income, but also by changes in the prices of the different products. If the price of one of the two products changes, then the slope of the budget line will also change. Figure 7.6 shows the effect of a fall in the prices of apples with the price of pears remaining the same. The budget line will now pivot outwards and is now AC.

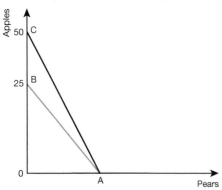

▲ **Figure 7.6** The effect of a change in price on a budget line

The optimum consumption point for a rational consumer can be shown by combining indifference curves and a budget line in one diagram. A rational consumer will wish to maximise their total utility by achieving the highest indifference curve that their income permits. This is shown by X in Figure 7.7. At this point, an individual consumer's budget line, VZ, is tangential to the highest attainable indifference curve, I_3. At this point, the individual will consume $0A_1$ apples and $0P_1$ pears.

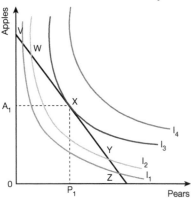

▲ **Figure 7.7** The optimum consumption point for an individual

118

It is important that you understand the properties of budget lines:

➤ they show the combinations of two products that an individual is able to consume

➤ these combinations are limited by an individual consumer's level of income

➤ these combinations are limited by fixed prices for the two products

➤ a budget line can also be known as a consumption possibility line

➤ any combination of two products inside a budget line, or on a budget line, can be consumed

➤ an individual cannot consume beyond a budget line

➤ if there is a change in the income of an individual, there will be a parallel shift of a budget line; if income rises, there will be a parallel shift to the right and if income falls, there will be a parallel shift to the left

➤ if the price of one of the products changes, the slope of the budget line will change, pivoting outwards if there is a fall in price of one of the products and pivoting inwards if there is a rise in price of one of the products.

Income, substitution and price effects for various types of goods

A price effect includes both an income and a substitution effect.

If the price of a product falls, it means that it is now cheaper relative to other products. This means that a consumer is likely to purchase more of the product. The consumer is therefore likely to substitute purchases of products whose price has fallen for other more expensive products. This is known as the substitution effect.

The fall in the price of a product will also mean that a consumer's real income has effectively risen so that more of all products, including the one whose price has fallen, can now be purchased. This is known as the income effect.

Key terms

Price effect: the sum of the substitution effect and the income effect of the change in the price of a product on the quantity demanded of that product.

Income effect: the change in the quantity demanded of a product as a result of the fact that a change in its price has brought about a change in a consumer's real income.

If the product is a normal good, the income effect will operate so that consumption of the product whose price has fallen will increase. If the product is an inferior good, the income effect will operate so that consumption of the product whose price has fallen will decrease, but with an inferior good the substitution effect will be greater than the income effect and so overall there will be an increase in the quantity consumed of the good whose price has fallen.

If the product is a Giffen good, the income effect will be greater than the substitution effect and so a fall in the price of a good will lead to a decrease in the quantity consumed.

Indifference curves and budget lines can be used to show the effects of a fall in the price of a product. Figure 7.8 shows the income and substitution effects of a fall in the price of a normal good.

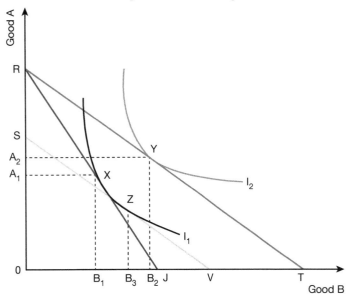

▲ **Figure 7.8** The income and substitution effects of a fall in the price of a normal good

When there is a fall in the price of good B, the movement from X to Z, along the original indifference curve I_1, shows the substitution effect and the movement from Z to Y, on a new indifference curve I_2, shows the income effect. On the horizontal axis, the substitution effect is shown by the movement from $0B_1$ to $0B_3$ and the income effect is shown by the movement from $0B_3$ to $0B_2$. It is clear that with a normal good, the substitution and the income effects of the price fall have worked in the same direction causing an increase in the quantity of B demanded.

Figure 7.9 shows the income and substitution effects of a fall in the price of an inferior good.

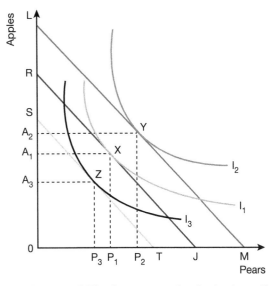

▲ **Figure 7.9** The income and substitution effects of a fall in the price of an inferior good

When there is fall in the price of good B, the movement from X to Z, along the original indifference curve I$_1$, shows the substitution effect and the movement from Z to Y, on a new indifference curve I$_2$, shows the income effect. On the horizontal axis, the substitution effect is shown by the movement from 0B$_1$ to 0B$_3$ and the income effect is shown by the movement from 0B$_3$ to 0B$_2$. It is clear that with an inferior good, the substitution and income effects of the price fall have worked in opposite directions, but the positive substitution effect is greater than the negative income effect so that there is still an increase in the quantity of B demanded.

> **Key term**
>
> **Substitution effect**: the change in the quantity demanded of a product as a result of a change in its relative price.

Figure 7.10 shows the income and substitution effects of a fall in the price of a Giffen good. When there is fall in the price of good B, the movement from X to Z, along the original indifference curve I$_1$, shows the substitution effect and the movement from Z to Y, on a new indifference curve I$_2$, shows the income effect. On the horizontal axis, the substitution effect is shown by the movement from 0B$_1$ to 0B$_3$ and the income effect is shown by the movement from 0B$_3$ to 0B$_2$. It is clear that with a Giffen good, the substitution and income effects of the price fall have worked in opposite directions, but the negative income effect is greater than the positive substitution effect so that there is now a decrease in the quantity of B demanded.

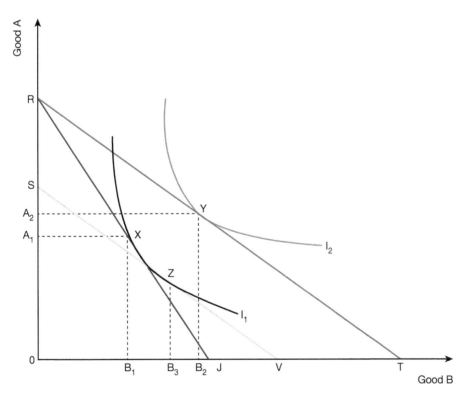

▲ **Figure 7.10** The income and substitution effects of a fall in the price of a Giffen good

It is important that you understand the key features of using indifference curves and budget lines to show the effects in the price of various types of good:

➤ a price effect includes both an income effect and a substitution effect

➤ a substitution effect always leads to an increase in the consumption of the good whose relative price has fallen, i.e. the substitution effect will always be positive

➤ the income effect will depend on the type of good: if it is a normal good, the income effect will be positive, but if it is an inferior good or a Giffen good, the income effect will be negative

➤ with a normal good, both the substitution effect and the income effect are positive and so both effects move in the same direction, meaning that a fall in the price of a good will lead to an increase in its demand

➤ with an inferior good, the positive substitution effect and the negative income effect move in opposite directions, but the substitution effect will be greater than the income effect, meaning that a fall in the price of a good will lead to an increase in its demand

➤ with a Giffen good, the positive substitution effect and negative income effect move in opposite directions, but the income effect will be greater than the substitution effect, meaning that a fall in the price of a good will lead to a decrease in its demand.

💡 **Remember**

The substitution effect of a fall in the price of a good will always be positive, but the income effect can be either positive or negative depending on what type of good it is.

★ **Exam tip**

Make sure that you clearly understand the different effects of a fall in the price of a product, depending on what type of product it is. With a normal good, both the income and substitution effects are positive and so there will be an increase in the demand for such a product. With an inferior good, the positive substitution effect will be greater than the negative income effect and so there will be an increase in the demand for such a product. With a Giffen good, the negative income effect will be greater than the positive substitution effect and so there will be a decrease in the demand for such a product.

✗ **Common error**

Make sure you don't confuse the income and substitution effects of a price change. If there is a fall in the price of a product, the substitution effect will always be positive, but the income effect can either be positive, in the case of a normal good, or negative, in the case of an inferior good or a Giffen good.

7.3 Types of cost, revenue and profit, short-run and long-run production

AL 2(c)

This topic is concerned with:

➤ the long-run production function

➤ revenue: total, average and marginal

➤ profit: normal and abnormal (supernormal).

The short-run production function

Production function

The production function indicates the relationship between inputs and output over a particular time period. It shows how a given output is produced as a result of using the different factors of production involved in the production process.

Key term

Production function: the relationship between quantity of inputs of factors of production and the resulting output.

Fixed and variable factors of production

In the short run, there will be at least one fixed factor of production, e.g. machinery. However, it will be possible to change the quantity of variable factors of production in the short run, e.g. raw materials.

> **Key terms**
>
> Fixed factor of production: a resource input that exists in the short run when the quantity of factors used in the production process cannot be changed, e.g. capital equipment.
>
> Variable factor of production: a resource input that can be varied in the short run, e.g. raw materials.
>
> Short run: a period of time in the production process when at least one factor of production is fixed.

Total product, average product and marginal product

It is important to be able to distinguish between these three different concepts. Total product is the total output that is produced from using the factors of production. Average product is the output per unit of the variable factor, e.g. the output per worker per period of time (also known as productivity). Marginal product is the additional output that is produced as a result of employing one more variable factor, e.g. an extra worker.

> **Key terms**
>
> Total product: the total output produced from a combination of factors of production (also known as total physical product).
>
> Average product: total product divided by the quantity of the variable factor of production, e.g. labour (also known as average physical product).
>
> Marginal product: the addition to total product resulting from the employment of an additional unit of the variable factor of production (also known as marginal physical product).

The law of diminishing returns (or law of variable proportions)

In the short run, the process of production involves a combination of fixed and variable factors of production. Extra units of a variable factor, such as labour, can be combined with a fixed factor, such as capital equipment. As more and more units of the variable factor are employed, total output or total physical product (TPP) will continue to increase, but at a diminishing rate. This is because the marginal output or marginal physical product (MPP) and the average output or average physical product (APP), resulting from the employment of one more worker, will eventually diminish. This is known as the law of diminishing returns or the law of variable proportions. The relationship between APP and MPP can be seen in Figure 7.11 on the next page.

> **Key term**
>
> Law of diminishing returns: a situation where as increasing quantities of a variable factor of production are added to fixed quantities of other factors of production, the return to the variable factor will eventually diminish (also known as the law of variable proportions).

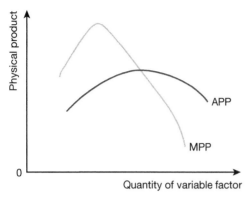

▲ **Figure 7.11** Average and marginal physical product

Marginal cost and average cost

Marginal cost refers to the increase in total cost when output is increased by one additional unit. Average cost refers to the cost per unit of production.

Short-run cost function: fixed costs versus variable costs

It has already been pointed out that it is important to be able to distinguish between fixed and variable factors of production. It is also important to distinguish between fixed and variable costs of production. Variable costs are costs that vary with changes in output. If output is zero, there will be no need to pay for any variable costs, such as raw materials, but as output is expanded, the variable costs of production will increase. However, even if output is zero, there are still likely to be some costs of production, such as rent or interest, and these are known as fixed costs of production. They will stay constant at all levels of output.

Figure 7.12 shows the relationship between marginal cost, average total cost, average variable cost and average fixed cost.

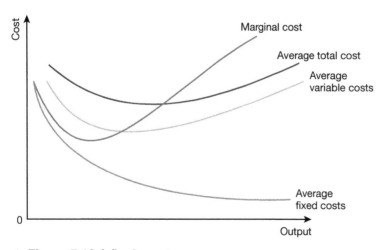

▲ **Figure 7.12** A firm's cost curves

Explanation of the shape of the short-run average cost (SRAC) curve

In Figure 7.12 on previous page, you can see that the shape of a firm's short-run average cost (SRAC) curve is U-shaped. At lower levels of output, both average variable costs and average fixed costs are falling and so average total cost falls. However, although average fixed costs are continually falling, average variable costs, beyond a certain level of output, will stop falling and start rising. This will cause average total cost to also rise as output is increased.

✓ What you need to know

- ➤ in the short run, at least one factor of production is fixed
- ➤ the production function shows the relationship between the factor inputs required to produce a product and the final output
- ➤ the law of diminishing returns shows that as increasing quantities of a variable factor are added to fixed quantities of other factors, the return to the variable factor will eventually diminish
- ➤ the average total cost curve, the average variable cost curve and the marginal cost curve all fall to begin with and then rise
- ➤ the average fixed cost curve continually falls.

✗ Common error

It is important to be able to draw the diagrams accurately, avoiding common errors:

- ➤ when drawing APP and MPP curves, make sure that the two curves intersect at the maximum point of the APP curve
- ➤ when drawing the marginal cost curve, make sure that it crosses the average total cost curve at the minimum point; this is because when marginal cost is less than average cost, average cost will be falling, whereas when marginal cost is more than average cost, average cost will be rising
- ➤ the marginal cost curve will also cross the average variable cost curve at its minimum point.

The long-run production function

Returns to scale

The short-run production function, and the corresponding short-run costs of production, is based on the fact that there is at least one fixed factor of production. In the long run, however, all factors of production are variable. This means that it is possible for a firm to increase output by increasing the factors of produced used in the production process.

Returns to scale refer to the relationship between a firm's level of output and the quantity of inputs needed to produce that output. Increasing returns to scale are where output is increased by a greater increase than the increase in the factors of production, e.g. factor inputs are increased by 10% and output is increased by 20%. Constant returns to scale are where the output is increased by the same percentage as the increase in the factors of production, e.g. factor inputs are increased by 10% and output is increased by 10%. Decreasing returns to scale are where the output is increased by a smaller increase than the increase in the factors of production, e.g. factor inputs are increased by 10% and output is increased by 5%.

Key terms

Short-run average cost (SRAC) curve: a curve that shows how average costs change as output changes in the period when at least one factor of production is fixed in supply.

Fixed costs: costs that do not vary with output.

Variable costs: costs that do vary with output.

Average fixed costs: the fixed costs of production divided by the output produced.

Average variable costs: the variable costs of production divided by the output produced.

Key terms

Long run: a period of time in the production process when all factors of production are variable.

Returns to scale: the relationship between a firm's level of output and the quantity of inputs needed to produce that output.

Increasing returns to scale: a situation in which a given increase in the quantity of factor inputs leads to a greater proportionate increase in output.

Constant returns to scale: a situation in which a given increase in the quantity of factor inputs leads to an equal proportionate increase in output.

Decreasing returns to scale: a situation in which a given increase in the quantity of factor inputs leads to a smaller proportionate increase in output.

Long-run cost function

In the long run, all factors of production are variable and so as a firm expands, it is able to increase the quantity of factors that were previously fixed in supply. This means that as it expands its output in the long run, it will move to a new SRAC curve. In the long run, there are potentially an infinite number of SRAC curves.

Explanation of the shape of the long-run average cost (LRAC) curve

The long-run average cost (LRAC) curve will actually be a combination of a series of short-run average cost curves, as can be seen in Figure 7.13 below. The LRAC curve joins all the points where the cost of producing a given output is at its lowest and so it is drawn as a smooth envelope curve.

> **Key term**
>
> Long-run average cost (LRAC) curve: a curve that shows how average costs change as output changes in the period when the supply of all factors of production can be increased.

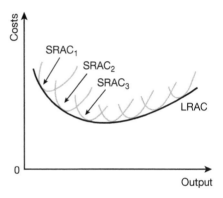

▲ **Figure 7.13** The LRAC envelope curve

The relationship between economies of scale and decreasing costs

Declining long-run average costs are the result of economies of scale, i.e. as the level of output increases, the long-run average cost of production decreases. This can be seen in Figure 7.14 below.

> **Key term**
>
> Economies of scale: reductions in long-run average cost (LRAC) as the scale of production increases. There can be both internal and external economies of scale.

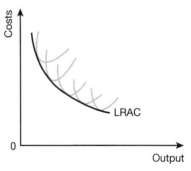

▲ **Figure 7.14** The relationship between economies of scale and decreasing costs

Internal and external economies of scale

It is possible to distinguish between internal and external economies of scale. Internal economies of scale include the following:

➤ financial

➤ purchasing/bulk buying

➤ managerial

➤ technical/economies of increased or large dimensions/division of labour/ large capital equipment

➤ research and development

➤ marketing

➤ risk-bearing/diversification

➤ economies of scope.

Whereas internal economies of scale refer to the potential advantages of a firm growing in size, external economies of scale refer to the potential advantages to all firms in an industry, including the following:

➤ concentration/development of support or ancillary firms in a particular area

➤ transport and infrastructure

➤ specialised labour/specialist skills

➤ knowledge/specialist research and marketing agencies/specific courses in colleges and universities.

Diseconomies of scale

Figure 7.14 on the previous page shows the relationship between economies of scale and decreasing costs of production. However, if a firm increases output beyond a certain level, costs may stop decreasing and may even to start to rise. Such a situation is known as diseconomies of scale and can be seen in Figure 7.15, where the U-shaped LRAC curve can be seen as first decreasing and then, beyond a certain level of output, increasing.

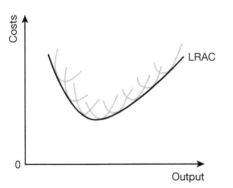

▲ **Figure 7.15** The U-shaped LRAC curve showing decreasing and increasing costs

As with economies of scale, it is possible to distinguish between internal and external diseconomies of scale. Internal diseconomies of scale include the following:

➤ poor communication/slower communication

➤ lower levels of efficiency/productivity

- lower levels of motivation/alienation/boredom/workers distanced from management
- greater frequency of industrial disputes
- poor management/greater complexity of organisation/difficulties of co-ordination and monitoring of performance
- less flexibility/slow response to changing market conditions.

External diseconomies of scale refer to situations where all firms in an industry may be negatively affected, including the following:

- greater competition for limited inputs/higher cost of inputs
- greater congestion/increase in costs/reduced efficiency.

Revenue: total, average and marginal

It is important to be able to distinguish between the three different forms of revenue. Total revenue refers to all the money received from the sales of a product. Average revenue refers to the total revenue obtained from selling a product divided by the number of units sold. Marginal revenue refers to the extra or additional revenue received when one more unit of a product is sold.

Profit: normal and abnormal (supernormal)

It is possible to distinguish between normal profit and abnormal profit (also known as supernormal profit). Profit is defined as the difference between the total revenue (TR) received by a firm and the total costs (TC) involved in producing what is sold, i.e. it is equal to total revenue minus total costs.

Normal profit refers to the amount of profit that needs to be made by a firm to stay in a particular market and to carry on doing what it is already doing. It represents the opportunity cost of a particular line of business, i.e. the profit that can be earned in the next most profitable enterprise. It is included in the average cost curve of a firm.

Abnormal, or supernormal, profit is where a firm makes a profit that is over and above normal profit. Whereas normal profit is included in the average cost curve of a firm, abnormal or supernormal profit can be explicitly shown in diagrams as a particular area.

> ### 💡 Remember
>
> Normal profit is included in the average cost of a firm and so cannot be shown in a diagram. Abnormal or supernormal profit, on the other hand, can be explicitly shown in a diagram.

> ### ★ Exam tip
>
> Make sure you can show you understand that the normal profit earned by a firm in a particular line of business is actually the opportunity cost, i.e. it is the profit that can be earned in the next most profitable enterprise.

⬆ Raise your grade

Discuss whether firms always benefit from an increase in the level of output that they produce [13]

It is likely to be the case that firms will always benefit from an increase in the level of output that they produce because as output increases, the long-run average cost curve falls,[1] giving rise to economies of scale.[2]

There are a number of internal economies of scale that a firm can benefit from. For example, financial economies could lead to a reduction in the rate of interest paid on a loan by a firm. Purchasing economies could be made by negotiating discounts as a result of bulk buying. Managerial economies may be in the form of a larger firm employing specialist managers who can operate more efficiently.[3] There are a number of potential technical economies of scale, such as through the use of large capital equipment. Economies of scale could be in the form of benefits gained from research and development.[4] Risk-bearing economies could exist through diversification where a firm is able to be involved in different markets.[5]

The existence of economies of scale therefore shows that firms always benefit from an increase in the level of output that they produce.[6,7]

How to improve this answer

1   The candidate points out that the long-run average cost curve falls as output increases, but doesn't state that beyond a certain level of output, the long-run average cost curve can begin to rise.

2   The candidate refers to economies of scale, but there is no reference to diseconomies of scale.

3   This point could have been linked to a reduction in the average cost of production.

4   An example could have been included here to support this point.

5   The candidate has included a number of internal economies of scale in the answer, but there is no reference at all to possible external economies of scale that could affect all firms in an industry, such as the availability of support or ancillary firms in a particular area, various potential benefits of transport and infrastructure, the availability of specialised labour possessing specialist skills or the availability of specific courses in colleges and universities.

6   The answer is very unbalanced, taking no account of the possibility of diseconomies of scale as a firm produces beyond a certain level of output. The candidate could have referred to a range of internal diseconomies of scale, including slower communication, lower levels of efficiency and productivity, lower levels of motivation leading to employees becoming alienated, bored and distanced from management, the possibility of a greater frequency of industrial disputes, poor management and difficulties of co-ordination and a slow response to changing market conditions.

7   The candidate could also have referred to possible external diseconomies of scale, including greater competition for limited inputs leading to a higher cost of inputs and the possibility of greater congestion leading to reduced efficiency and an increase in costs.

Level 2 – 6/13

7.4 Different market structures   AL 2(d)

This topic is concerned with:

➤ perfect competition, imperfect competition (monopoly, monopolist competition, oligopoly, natural monopoly)

➤ the structure of markets as explained by the number of buyers and sellers, the nature of the product, the degree of freedom of entry and the nature of information

➤ contestable markets and their implications

➤ concentration ratio.

Perfect competition and imperfect competition

Perfect competition

The characteristics of perfect competition include the following:

➤ there are many buyers and sellers

➤ the buyers and sellers are price takers, i.e. they have to accept the price prevailing in a market (the price is determined through the interaction of demand for, and supply of, the product) and cannot influence it in any way

➤ there is perfect knowledge among the producers and consumers, so that they know what is for sale and at what price

➤ the product is homogeneous, i.e. all products are identical and there is no product differentiation

➤ there are no barriers to entry or exit, so that firms can enter or leave the industry in the long run

➤ there is perfect mobility of factors of production in the long run, i.e. there is a perfectly elastic supply of all factors of production

➤ there are no transport costs

➤ all producers have access to the same technology

➤ each firm in the industry faces a perfectly elastic demand curve for its product, although the demand curve for the industry is downward sloping from left to right

➤ it is assumed that firms in the industry aim to maximise their profits

➤ only normal profit can be earned in the long run, although abnormal or supernormal profit can be earned in the short run

➤ consumers are indifferent as to which firm they buy a product from, i.e. there is no brand loyalty

➤ both consumer surplus and producer surplus are at a maximum

➤ the industry is allocatively efficient.

Although a firm can make normal profit in a perfectly competitive industry in the short run, it is also possible that it could make abnormal or supernormal profit, or less than normal profit (sometimes known as sub-normal profit), in the short run.

Figure 7.16 below shows a firm in perfect competition that has made abnormal or supernormal profit in the short run.

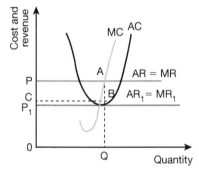

▲ **Figure 7.16** A firm making abnormal or supernormal profit in the short run

The abnormal or supernormal profit is shown by the area CPAB. This will attract new firms into the industry, reducing the market price from 0P to $0P_1$, and the abnormal or supernormal profit will be eliminated so that only normal profit will exist.

Figure 7.17 shows a firm in perfect competition that has made less than normal profit in the short run.

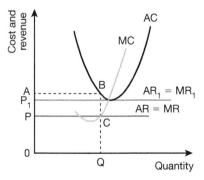

▲ **Figure 7.17** A firm making less than normal profit in the short run

The less than normal profit is shown by the area PABC. This will cause firms to exit the industry, increasing the price from 0P to 0P$_1$, and the less than normal profit will be eliminated so that only normal profit will exist.

Figure 7.18 shows a firm in perfect competition that is making normal profit.

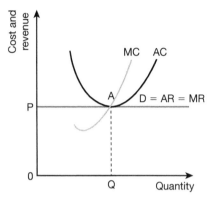

▲ **Figure 7.18** A firm making normal profit in a perfectly competitive industry

Figure 7.18 also shows the long-run equilibrium for the firm and the industry in perfect competition where all firms in the industry are making normal profit.

✓ **What you need to know**

➤ the long-run equilibrium for the firm in perfect competition is MC = MR = AC = AR.
The firms in the industry are both productively efficient (P = minimum AC) and allocatively efficient (P = MC).

➤ the long-run equilibrium for the industry in perfect competition is that there is no tendency for the number of firms in the industry to change.

💡 **Remember**

Although perfect competition does not exist in the real world, it provides a very useful 'ideal type' model which can be used to compare firms and industries that do exist in the real world.

Imperfect competition

Imperfect competition includes a number of different types of market structure: monopoly, monopolistic competition, oligopoly and natural monopoly.

Monopoly

The characteristics of monopoly include the following:

➤ there is one firm in an industry, i.e. one single seller

➤ legally, a monopoly can also be defined in terms of a particular percentage of market share, e.g. 25%

➤ a monopoly is a price maker, not a price taker

➤ there are no substitutes for the product being sold by the monopolist

➤ strong barriers to entry make it very difficult, if not impossible, for new firms to enter the industry

Key terms

Imperfect competition: a type of market that lacks some, or all, of the features of perfect competition.

Monopoly: the sole supplier of a product in a market.

➤ abnormal or supernormal profits can be made in both the short run and long run

➤ the demand for the firm's product is also the market or industry demand, so the demand curve for both the firm and the industry is downward sloping from left to right

➤ marginal revenue is always less than average revenue

➤ it is assumed that the firm aims to maximise its profits.

Figure 7.19 shows the equilibrium price and equilibrium quantity for a profit maximising monopoly firm. The monopolist is a price maker and so faces downward sloping demand (AR) and marginal revenue (MR) curves. The profit maximising output is at 0Q where marginal cost (MC) is equal to marginal revenue (MR). The price is 0P, but the cost is 0C, so the firm is able to make abnormal or supernormal profits of CPAB. These can exist in the long run as well as the short run due to the very strong barriers that make it difficult for new firms to enter the industry.

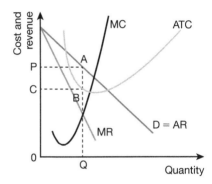

▲ **Figure 7.19** Equilibrium price and equilibrium quantity for a profit maximising monopoly firm

X Common error

The monopoly diagram is often drawn incorrectly. Make sure that you realise that the equilibrium price and equilibrium quantity positions are determined by where MC and MR intersect. This is the profit maximisation position. The MC curve crosses the ATC curve at its minimum point. The cost of production is determined where the ATC curve is directly below where the horizontal price line meets the AR curve.

Monopolistic competition

The characteristics of monopolistic competition include the following:

➤ there are a large number of firms in the industry

➤ there are a large number of consumers

➤ products are differentiated and not homogeneous or identical

➤ each firm in the industry faces a downward sloping demand curve

➤ demand for a product is relatively, but not perfectly, price elastic (much more elastic than is the case in monopoly)

➤ there is a great deal of advertising of products in the industry to develop brand loyalty

➤ there are no barriers to entry or exit, so firms can enter or leave the industry in the long run

✓ What you need to know

Barriers to entry into a market can include the following:

➤ high start-up costs

➤ control of sources of supply

➤ copyrights and patents

➤ legal protection

➤ economies of scale

➤ brand loyalty

➤ mergers and takeovers

➤ location.

Key term

Monopolistic competition: a market with many firms producing similar, but differentiated, products.

➤ only normal profits can be earned in the industry in the long run

➤ it is assumed that firms in the industry aim to maximise their profits.

In the short run, a firm in monopolistic competition can make abnormal or supernormal profit, but as there are no barriers to entry, this will attract new firms into the industry so the abnormal or supernormal profits are competed away. In the long-run, only normal profits will be earned as can be seen in Figure 7.20.

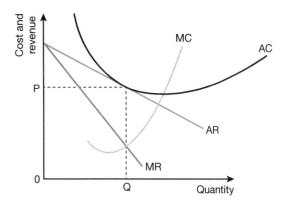

▲ **Figure 7.20** Long-run equilibrium for a firm in monopolistic competition

<table>
<tr><td>X</td><td>Common error</td></tr>
</table>

The demand or AR curves in monopoly and in monopolistic competition are often drawn the same, but the D or AR curve in monopolistic competition should show that the demand curve is significantly more elastic in monopolistic competition than in monopoly.

Oligopoly

The characteristics of oligopoly include the following:

➤ there are only a small number of firms in the market (sometimes there might be only two firms, in which case it is called a duopoly)

➤ there are differentiated, not homogeneous, products

➤ great use is made of advertising to create and maintain brand loyalty

➤ barriers to entry make it very difficult for new firms to enter the industry

➤ firms can make abnormal or supernormal profits in both the short run and the long run

➤ there could be a mixture of price makers and price takers

➤ the firms are mutually interdependent

➤ there could be a degree of collusion between firms operating in a cartel

➤ there is a kinked demand curve

➤ there is a great deal of price stability/rigidity.

One characteristic of a firm in oligopoly is that it faces a kinked demand curve. This occurs because in oligopoly, firms try to anticipate the reactions of rival firms to their actions. It is assumed that if an oligopolistic firm increases its price, other firms in the market will not follow and so demand above the kink is elastic. However, it can also be assumed that if an oligopolistic firm reduces its price, other firms in the market will follow and so demand below the kink is inelastic.

Key term

Oligopoly: a market that is dominated by a few firms which are mutually interdependent.

The kinked demand curve can be seen in Figure 7.21. It is a characteristic of a non-collusive oligopoly. One key feature of the diagram is that there is a discontinuity in the marginal revenue (MR) curve. Changes in marginal cost (MC) between MC_1 and MC_3 do not change the profit maximising price and output, i.e. prices are likely to be relatively fixed despite changes in cost.

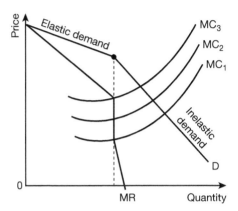

▲ **Figure 7.21** The kinked demand curve

In addition to the non-collusive model of monopoly, there is also a collusive model of oligopoly. Collusion between such oligopolistic firms can be formal or informal, and if it is formal, it can involve the creation of a cartel which is an agreement between firms to fix price and output in a market. This situation can be seen in Figure 7.22 where the profit maximising position is where MC = MR.

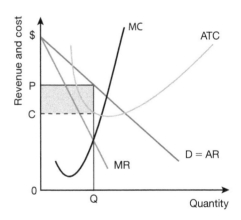

▲ **Figure 7.22** Collusive oligopoly

There are a number of conditions necessary for a cartel to operate successfully as a collusive oligopoly and these include the following:

➤ a limited number of firms in the industry, all of whom are members of the cartel, making it easier to share information and to keep a check on each other

➤ a similar cost structure for all firms

➤ relatively high barriers to entry to prevent new firms entering the industry

➤ all firms are expected to obey the rules of the cartel

➤ a relatively stable market

➤ the firms in the cartel produce identical, or very similar, products which will make price agreements easier to establish.

Natural monopoly

A natural monopoly exists when a single supplier has a very significant cost advantage as a result of being in a monopoly situation. If competition existed, there would be an increase in the costs of production. It is therefore advantageous for a natural monopoly to continue in existence because it will avoid the extra costs that will come about as the result of a duplication of resources. In a natural monopoly, it may well be that one firm will be able to benefit from sufficient economies of scale to satisfy the level of demand more efficiently than two or more firms. A natural monopoly will usually have relatively high start-up costs and because they experience economies of scale over most of their production, the minimum efficient scale of production is only achieved at an extremely high level of output.

Figure 7.23 shows the situation for a natural monopoly. The long-run average total cost (LRATC) curve is downward sloping throughout its length and the long-run marginal cost (LRMC) curve is always below it. The profit maximising output is at 0Q, but this output will not enable the full benefits of the economies of scale to be achieved. It would therefore be better if output was 0Q₁, which is allocatively efficient, but this would mean that the firm operated at a loss and so either the government would need to take the natural monopoly into state ownership or it would need to provide it with a subsidy.

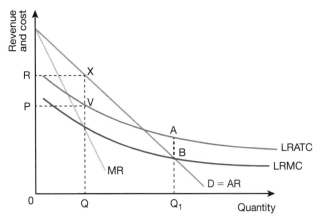

▲ **Figure 7.23** Natural monopoly

The structure of markets as explained by the number of sellers, the nature of the product, the degree of freedom of entry and the nature of information

It is possible to distinguish between the structure of markets according to:

➤ the number of sellers

➤ the nature of the product

➤ the degree of freedom of entry

➤ the nature of information.

	Perfect competition	Monopoly	Monopolistic competition	Oligopoly
Number of sellers	Many	One	Varied, but not too many	Few
Nature of the product	Homogenous	No close substitutes	Differentiated	Varied
Freedom of entry	Not restricted	High barriers to entry	Not restricted	Some barriers to entry
Nature of information	Perfect knowledge	Incomplete	Incomplete	Incomplete

Contestable markets and their implications

The characteristics and implications of contestable markets include:

➤ there are no barriers to entry or exit; entry into a contestable market is relatively easy (in a perfectly contestable market, the costs of entry and exit are zero)

➤ the product being produced in the market is relatively standardised and any new firms entering the market will have access to the same technology as firms already established in the market

➤ the low entry and exit barriers means that the market may suffer from hit and run competition where firms enter the market when profits are relatively high and leave when profits are relatively low.

> **Key terms**
>
> Contestable markets: markets in which there is the threat of potential competition in the future, in which case even though an existing firm may currently have a monopoly position, it may decide to act more like a perfectly competitive firm in order to deter such competition.
>
> Hit and run competition: a situation where firms enter a contestable market when profits are relatively high and leave it when profits are relatively low.

➤ firms already in a contestable market continually face the threat of competition, making them behave as if these potential firms were already operating in the market; this means that although there may only be a few firms in a contestable market, they act in a competitive way (therefore, it is not the number of firms in the market that is important, but the threat of potential competition from new firms possibly entering the market)

- this puts pressure on the firms to be efficient

- abnormal profits can be made in the short run, but only normal profits in the long run, as new firms are attracted by the abnormal profits to enter the market

- there will be no, or relatively low, sunk costs, i.e. costs that are already invested in a market and cannot be recovered

- there is no collusion between existing firms in the market.

> **Remember**
>
> The lower the entry and exit costs, the more contestable the market will be.

> ✓ **What you need to know**
>
> The key feature of a contestable market is not the number of firms that are operating in the market, but the threat of competition from new firms entering the market. This makes the firms behave in a competitive manner, even if there is very little competition in the market.

Concentration ratio

The concentration ratio in a market shows the percentage in a particular industry that is accounted for by a certain number of firms. For example, six firms in a particular market might have a 90% share of the market between them. The concentration ratio can be used in any market, but it is particularly associated with an oligopoly market structure.

> **Remember**
>
> A concentration ratio does not have to relate to a specific number of firms in a market. It can apply, for example, to four, five or six firms in a market. What it shows is that if it is related to a four firm concentration ratio, it measures the proportion of the output produced by the four largest firms in the market.

7.5 The growth and survival of firms   AL 2(e)

This topic is concerned with:

- reasons for small firms

- integration, diversification, mergers, cartels.

The reasons for small firms

Despite the potential advantages of large firms, a number of small firms continue to exist in many economies. The reasons for the continued existence of small firms include the following:

- the size of the market served by the firms is small

- the market may be highly localised

- the firm may operate in a very specific niche market, e.g. producing customised products

- the firm is providing customers with a service that requires personal attention

- the firm may only have recently started and so is relatively small at the moment, e.g. many large firms today started off relatively small before expanding

- the owners of the firm may have made a deliberate decision to keep it small, e.g. an individual's desire to be their own boss

- small firms may receive specific financial support from governments in some countries

- small firms may be relatively more flexible in responding to changes in demand and in changes in consumer tastes and preferences

- small firms may be more innovative and pioneering

- a small firm may be unable to grow because of the difficulties involved in raising the necessary funds to finance any expansion

- in some industries, the process of 'contracting out' may lead to an increase in the demand for small firms

- small ancillary firms may have a key role to play in some industries in supplying specialised component parts to larger firms

- a small firm may be more efficient than a large firm, e.g. labour relations may be better and so there is less likelihood of industrial disputes in a small firm

- the start-up costs for a small firm are likely to be significantly less than for a large firm, making them easier to start economic activity.

Integration, diversification, mergers, cartels

Integration

It is important to be able to distinguish between the internal growth and external growth of firms. The internal, or organic, growth of a firm comes about as a result of a firm increasing in size through producing and selling more products.

The extent of the growth of a firm can be measured through a number of ways, including the following:

- the volume of sales

- sales revenue (also known as sales turnover)

- the number of employees

- market share

- the amount of profit.

The external growth of a firm comes about as a result of a merger, takeover or acquisition where two or more firms combine together. This process is known as integration.

There are a number of possible reasons for the growth of firms, including the following:

- to benefit from possible economies of scale, leading to a decrease in the average costs of production of a firm

- to be a stronger economic entity and therefore safer from a hostile takeover proposal

- to take advantage of opportunities to benefit from a larger market share, such as increased profitability

- the possible desire of the owners and/or managers to expand.

Remember

The criteria that determines whether a particular firm should be described as small or not will vary from country to country.

Key terms

Internal growth: an increase in the size of a particular firm without involving any other firm; this process is also referred to as organic growth.

External growth: an increase in the size of a particular firm through a process of integration with other firms.

Integration: the joining together of two or more firms through a merger, a takeover or an acquisition; the integration can take a number of different forms.

One form of integration is horizontal integration. This is when two or more firms at the same stage of the production process join together. An example would be where two or more financial services providers integrate.

Another form of integration is vertical integration. This is when two or more firms at different stages of the production process join together. There are two types of vertical integration.

The first type is known as backward vertical integration. This is where the integration involves going back to an earlier stage in the production process, such as when it is necessary to secure sufficient supplies of raw materials. An example would be a tyre manufacturer taking over a rubber plantation.

The second type is known as forward vertical integration. This is where the integration involves going forward to a later stage in the production process, such as when it is necessary to secure sufficient distribution of the finished product. An example would be a car manufacturer taking over a garage that sells cars.

Key terms

Horizontal integration: the integration of two or more firms at the same stage of production.

Vertical integration: the integration of two or more firms at different stages of production. It can involve either backward vertical integration or forward vertical integration.

Backward vertical integration: this is where a firm joins with another firm at an earlier stage of the production process.

Forward vertical integration: this is where a firm joins with another firm at a later stage of the production process.

Conglomerate integration: the integration of two or more firms which are operating in completely different markets rather than at different stages of the same market.

Another form of integration is conglomerate integration. Whereas horizontal and vertical integration involve firms joining together that are operating in the same industry, conglomerate integration is where two or more firms that are operating in entirely different industries join together. The reason for this form of integration is to spread risk by operating in more than one industry, a process known as diversification.

Diversification

It has already been pointed out that conglomerate integration is different from horizontal and vertical integration in that it brings together firms that are operating in different industries and not simply at different stages of the production process in the same industry.

This form of integration gives rise to diversification. This has the advantage of allowing a firm to spread risk rather than focusing on just one industry. A strategy of diversification by a firm is designed to reduce risk by becoming involved in a number of industries which are unlikely to all change in the same direction. The aim of diversification is to reduce the risk that a firm is exposed to and this should produce a more consistent performance under a wide range of different economic conditions.

★ Exam tip

If there is a question in the exam about integration, make sure that you write about all three types of integration, i.e. horizontal integration, vertical integration (including both backward vertical integration and forward vertical integration) and conglomerate integration. It is also helpful to be able to include relevant examples of each type of integration to show that you clearly understand the differences between the various types of integration.

Key term

Diversification: a situation where a firm decides to operate in a number of different markets to spread risk.

Mergers

A merger is where two or more firms combine as a result of mutual agreement. This is in contrast to a takeover or acquisition which usually involves some form of hostile bid by one firm for another. A merger can give rise to horizontal, vertical or conglomerate integration.

Cartels

Cartels have already been referred to in the context of a collusive oligopoly market structure when it was pointed out that there could be a degree of collusion between firms in an oligopoly market, operating together through a cartel.

Key terms

Merger: a process whereby two or more firms come together under one management.

Takeover: a process whereby a firm makes a bid to assume control of another firm, often by purchasing a majority stake in the firm. It is possible to distinguish between a welcome takeover and a hostile takeover.

Acquisition: a process whereby a firm buys most, if not all, of another firm to assume control of it. It occurs when a firm buys more than 50% ownership in another firm.

Cartels: formal agreements between firms to collude to fix prices and output in a market.

7.6 The differing objectives of a firm   AL 2(f)

This topic is concerned with:

➤ the traditional profit maximising objective of a firm

➤ other objectives of a firm

➤ pricing policy

➤ comparisons of the performance of firms.

The traditional profit maximising objective of a firm

Profit maximisation has traditionally been regarded as the main objective of a firm. This will be at the output where marginal cost (MC) = marginal revenue (MR).

Normal and abnormal profit

The distinction between normal and abnormal, or supernormal, profit has already been referred to in this unit.

Key term

Profit maximisation: the situation where marginal cost (MC) is equal to marginal revenue (MR).

Although profit maximisation has traditionally been assumed to be the main objective of a firm, this assumption has been increasingly called into question for a number of reasons:

➤ the growth of modern public limited companies, particularly multinational companies, has shown that it may be difficult for them to maximise profits, even if they wanted to

➤ these companies have a large number of stakeholders who may pursue other goals instead of, or in addition to, profit maximisation

➤ the traditional aim of profit maximisation assumes that a firm can actually calculate its MC and MR, but this is not without difficulties

➤ in terms of MR, a firm needs to be able to accurately estimate the position and elasticity of its demand (AR) curve, which can be extremely difficult

➤ in terms of MC, this may also be difficult to calculate accurately; there is also the issue of whether a firm should use short-run or long-run marginal costs

➤ there is evidence to suggest that instead of using MC and MR to determine the price and output, a firm may adopt a different strategy, such as applying a percentage mark up to average costs; this is known as cost plus pricing.

In the exam, be willing to be critical of the idea that the objective of all firms is to maximise profits.

The relation between elasticity and revenue

The relationship between elasticity and revenue has already been referred to in Unit 2.

Other objectives of a firm

It is now increasingly recognised that a firm may have other possible objectives, apart from profit maximisation, and these could include the following:

➤ survival: one objective of a firm, especially in the first years of its existence, might be to survive; this would be particularly the case in markets where firms do not tend to survive for a long period of time

➤ strategic: a firm may decide to establish its aims and objectives within a broad strategic approach, such as in relation to 'corporate social responsibility' and the strategic objective of not causing any significant environmental problems. Game theory, which is covered later, offers scope for firms to behave in a strategic way

➤ satisficing: where there is a divorce of ownership from control, the managers of a firm may wish to deal with all the stakeholders of a firm in such a way that all stakeholders are satisfied; in this situation, satisfactory, rather than maximum, profits may be the objective of a firm

➤ sales revenue maximisation: in some firms, the objective may be to maximise the sales revenue of a firm rather than the profits; in this situation, the output would be higher and the price lower than the profit maximising position.

Game theory: the analysis of strategies and decision-making by rational players in any activity or situation in which those involved know that their decision will have an impact on other players and the way that these other players are expected to react will affect the original decision made.

Satisficing: a situation in which a firm aims for a minimum level of attainment of a number of objectives.

Sales revenue maximisation: an alternative theory of the objectives of a firm which assumes that managers aim to maximise sales revenue as opposed to profit; this is also sometimes known as sales maximisation.

The principal agent problem, such as the divorce of ownership from control

It is important to understand that there may be a divorce of ownership of a firm from control. For example, the shareholders own a firm, but they will not be able to exercise full day-to-day control of it.

This gives rise to the principal agent problem. The principal is the owner of a firm and the owners will employ an agent, or manager, to run the firm and take the everyday decisions affecting the firm. The problem that arises from this divorce is that the agent may not run the firm in exactly the way that the principal would like.

> **Remember**
>
> Although profit maximisation is traditionally assumed to be the main objective of a firm, it is now increasingly recognised that firms may have other possible objectives.

> **Key terms**
>
> **The divorce of ownership from control**: the situation that arises when a firm is owned by one group of people (the shareholders) and controlled and run by another group of people (the managers).
>
> **Principal agent problem**: the problem that can arise from the divorce of ownership from control in a firm, so that the principals (the shareholders) may have different aims and objectives from the agents (the managers).

> **Remember**
>
> The divorce of ownership from control in a firm, giving rise to the principal agent problem, means that the principals of a firm (the shareholders) are not able to guarantee that their agents (the managers) will operate the firm in the principals' best interests.

> **Exam tip**
>
> The existence of the principal agent problem means that the principal and the agent may have different objectives and it would be helpful if you could gives possible examples of such a problem. For example, the principal may have the objective of profit maximisation, but the agent may have the objective of salary maximisation.

The behavioural analysis approach to the decision-making of a firm

The behavioural analysis approach to the decision-making of a firm has introduced game theory to economic analysis, such as in relation to the prisoner's dilemma and the two-player pay-off matrix.

The Prisoner's Dilemma

The prisoner's dilemma is an example of game theory where there is a competitive situation in which attempts by two or more individuals or firms to find the best strategy for themselves by acting independently results in a final outcome that is worse than if they had colluded or worked co-operatively. The dilemma is that the best outcome would be to co-operate or collude, but if it is not possible to communicate, collusion becomes impossible. Even if collusion had been possible, two individuals would need to trust the other person to stick to any deal that had been agreed.

> **Key term**
>
> **Prisoner's dilemma**: in game theory, a competitive situation in which attempts by two or more individuals or firms to find the best strategy for themselves by acting independently results in a final outcome that is worse than if they had colluded or worked co-operatively.

The two-player pay-off matrix

In game theory, the possible strategies for each individual, or player in the game, can be shown in a matrix that show the possible outcomes (or pay-offs) for the two players of their respective strategies or decisions. This is known as the two-player pay-off matrix.

The kinked demand curve

The **kinked demand curve** has already been referred to in this unit in relation to the non-collusive oligopoly model. It can be used as an example of a behavioural analysis approach because it is based on assumptions about the behaviour of other firms in the market in response to decisions taken by a firm. If a firm reduces price, it is assumed that the behaviour of other firms will be to follow this decision and reduce their prices. However, if a firm increases price, it is assumed that the behaviour of other firms will be to not follow this decision and so their prices will remain constant. This behavioural analysis approach explains why the demand curve is kinked and it also helps to explain why there is a great deal of price stability in oligopoly.

> ★ **Exam tip**
>
> Game theory is an interesting aspect of the increasing importance given to the behavioural analysis approach to the decision-making of a firm and you should be prepared to include examples of it in any answers to questions on a firm's decision-making.

Pricing policy

Price discrimination

Price discrimination occurs when different prices are charged to different customers and when the different prices are not a reflection of differences in the costs of production. The differences in price occur because of differences in the price elasticity of demand for different products. Price discrimination occurs in monopoly where the firm is able to keep different markets separate. This separation of markets could involve different geographical regions, different times of the day or different ages.

Certain conditions must apply for price discrimination to exist and these include the following:

➤ the firm practising price discrimination must be able to exercise some monopoly power in the market

➤ it must be possible to separate the market

➤ it must not be possible to buy in one market and sell in another (this is known as arbitrage)

➤ the price elasticities of demand for a product must be different in the separate markets.

> **Key terms**
>
> Price discrimination: the practice of selling the same product in different markets at different prices for reasons that have nothing to do with the costs of production.
>
> Arbitrage: the ability to buy in one market and sell in another.

Key terms

Two-player pay-off matrix: in game theory, a table or matrix that shows the outcomes (pay-offs) for the players of their respective strategies or decisions.

It is possible to distinguish between three degrees of price discrimination. First-degree price discrimination occurs when the monopoly firm is able to charge each individual consumer the maximum amount that they are prepared to pay for a product. Second-degree price discrimination occurs where different prices are charged for successive blocks of consumption. Third-degree price discrimination refers to the selling of the same product in different markets to different consumers at different prices.

Limit pricing

Limit pricing refers to a situation where price is below the profit-maximising price. For example, a firm may decide to limit price in an attempt to discourage new firms from entering an industry and so protecting the position of the firm that adopts this pricing policy.

Price leadership

Price leadership is most likely to exist in an oligopoly market structure where there is some degree of collusion between the firms in the market. In this situation, firms in the market will follow the price leadership of one firm. The objective is to maximise the profits of all the firms by behaving as if they were one monopolistic firm. This agreement on price could be informal and there are three models of such price leadership: the dominant firm model, barometric price leadership and parallel pricing.

However, price leadership, although usually part of an informal agreement, could be part of a formal cartel arrangement.

Mutual interdependence

In the case of oligopoly, a pricing policy could be based on the idea of mutual interdependence. Firms in oligopoly take into account expectations about the behaviour of other firms in the market and it is this which gives rise to the existence of a kinked demand curve, as has already been explained. This helps to explain the existence of price rigidity in oligopolistic market structures. The consideration of the behaviour of other firms in the market is a useful example of how game theory can be applied to pricing policy in oligopoly.

> **Key terms**
>
> First-degree price discrimination: the practice of charging each consumer the maximum they are prepared to pay for a product.
>
> Second-degree price discrimination: the practice of charging consumers different prices for successive blocks of consumption of a product.
>
> Third-degree price discrimination: the practice of charging different consumers different prices for the same product.
>
> Limit pricing: a policy adopted by a firm in monopoly or oligopoly of setting price below that which would maximise profits in order to deter new entrants from entering the market.
>
> Price leadership: the practice in an oligopoly where one firm sets or changes price and other firms in the market follow this lead.
>
> Mutual interdependence: a pricing policy in oligopoly where some or all of the firms in the market formulate their decisions on price in the light of anticipated reactions and countermoves of rival firms.

 Exam tip

You need to be able to demonstrate an understanding of each of these different pricing policies in the exam.

Comparisons of the performance of firms

The performance of firms can be compared in the following ways:

➤ revenue: firms in perfect competition face a perfectly elastic horizontal average revenue (AR) and marginal revenue (MR) curve, whereas other firms face downward sloping AR and MR curves; in this situation, AR and MR are not the same, with MR sloping down more steeply than AR

➤ output: assuming that all firms are profit maximising, output will be determined where MC = MR

➤ profits: firms can make abnormal (or supernormal) profit, normal profit and less than normal profit, but in perfect competition, monopolistic competition and contestable markets only normal profit can be made in the long run, whereas in oligopoly and monopoly abnormal (or supernormal) profit can continue to be made in the long run

➤ efficiency: this will exist where P = MC (allocative efficiency) and where the ATC curve is at its minimum point (productive efficiency) and this situation applies to firms in perfect competition

➤ X-inefficiency: this can occur in a monopoly firm when production is not at the lowest point on the average total cost curve because of a lack of competition in an industry and a situation of organisational slack in a firm

➤ barriers to entry and exit: there are no barriers to entry or exit for firms in perfect competition, monopolistic competition or contestable markets, but there are some barriers to entry and exit and oligopoly and many barriers to entry and exit in monopoly

➤ price competition: there is price competition in perfect competition where buyers and sellers are price takers, but there is a greater degree of price rigidity in oligopoly and monopoly firms are price makers, subject to the demand curve, i.e. a monopoly firm can determine price, but not how much will be demanded at that price

➤ non-price competition: firms in monopolistic competition and oligopoly compete through various forms of non-price competition a great deal, such as through the use of advertising and product promotion, the creation and maintenance of brand loyalty, sales promotions, such as BOGOF ('buy one, get one free'), the control of the distribution of products to particular retail outlets, distinctive packaging and differences in quality or design

➤ collusion: collusion between firms is a particular characteristic of an oligopoly market structure and it can either be of a formal or an informal nature.

Key terms

Efficiency: the use of resources in the most economical or optimal way possible.

X-inefficiency: the inefficiency that can occur in a monopoly when production is not at the lowest point on the average total cost curve; it is where production takes place at a cost above the average cost curve and the marginal cost curve due to a lack of strong competition in an industry and because of organisational slack in a firm.

Non-price competition: alternatives to price reductions as methods used by firms to increase sales and market share, e.g. advertising, after-sales service.

 Exam tip

You need to be able to make comparisons of the performance of firms using a number of criteria.

Revision checklist

I can:

- ➤ understand what is meant by the law of diminishing marginal utility ☐
- ➤ understand the relationship between the law of diminishing marginal utility and the derivation of an individual demand schedule ☐
- ➤ understand and explain the equi-marginal principle ☐
- ➤ understand the limitations of marginal utility theory ☐
- ➤ be clear about the distinction between traditional ideas of rational behaviour and behavioural economic models ☐
- ➤ understand the essential features of indifference curves ☐
- ➤ understand the essential features of budget lines ☐
- ➤ be clear about the meaning of the marginal rate of substitution and of the diminishing marginal rate of substitution ☐
- ➤ understand that a price effect consists of both an income effect and a substitution effect ☐
- ➤ understand how these effects are different for normal goods, inferior goods and Giffen goods ☐
- ➤ understand what is involved in the short-run production function ☐
- ➤ distinguish between fixed and variable factors of production ☐
- ➤ explain the difference between total product, average product and marginal product ☐
- ➤ understand the law of diminishing returns (the law of variable proportions) ☐
- ➤ distinguish between marginal cost and average cost ☐
- ➤ understand the short-run cost function and the difference between fixed and variable costs ☐
- ➤ explain the shape of the short-run average cost (SRAC) curve ☐
- ➤ understand what is involved in the long-run production function ☐
- ➤ explain what is meant by returns to scale ☐
- ➤ be clear about the long-run cost function ☐
- ➤ explain the shape of the long-run average cost (LRAC) curve ☐
- ➤ understand the relationship between economies of scale and decreasing costs ☐
- ➤ understand the relationship between diseconomies of scale and increasing costs ☐
- ➤ be clear about the meaning of internal and external economies of scale ☐
- ➤ be clear about the meaning of internal and external diseconomies of scale ☐
- ➤ understand the difference between total revenue, average revenue and marginal revenue ☐
- ➤ distinguish between normal profit and abnormal (or supernormal) profit ☐
- ➤ be sure about the features and characteristics of perfect competition ☐
- ➤ be sure about the features and characteristics of monopolistic competition ☐
- ➤ be sure about the features and characteristics of oligopoly ☐
- ➤ be sure about the features and characteristics of monopoly ☐
- ➤ be sure about the features and characteristics of natural monopoly ☐

- ➤ be sure about the features and characteristics of contestable markets and about the implications of these features and characteristics ☐
- ➤ understand the meaning of the concentration ratio in an industry ☐
- ➤ understand the reasons for the continued existence of small firms ☐
- ➤ understand the possible reasons for the growth of firms ☐
- ➤ appreciate the different possible types of integration of firms ☐
- ➤ be clear about what is meant by diversification ☐
- ➤ be able to distinguish between mergers, takeovers and acquisitions ☐
- ➤ be clear about what is meant by cartels ☐
- ➤ understand the traditional profit maximisation objective of a firm ☐
- ➤ understand the relationship between elasticity and revenue ☐
- ➤ understand that a firm can have other objectives apart from profit maximisation, such as survival, strategic, satisficing and sales revenue maximisation ☐
- ➤ be clear about the meaning of the principal agent problem in terms of the divorce of ownership of a firm from its control ☐
- ➤ be sure about the behavioural analysis approach to the decision-making of a firm, such as through game theory, the prisoner's dilemma, the two player pay-off matrix and the kinked demand curve ☐
- ➤ understand the different types of pricing policy that can be used by a firm, including price discrimination, limit pricing, price leadership and mutual interdependence in the case of firms in oligopoly ☐
- ➤ compare the performance of different firms according to certain criteria ☐
- ➤ be clear about the distinction between efficiency and X-inefficiency ☐
- ➤ be clear about the distinction between price competition and non-price competition ☐
- ➤ understand when and how collusion between firms can take place. ☐

? Exam-style questions

1 Marginal utility refers to the satisfaction gained:

   A from all of the units of a product consumed

   B from the first unit of a product consumed

   C from the last unit of a product consumed

   D on average from all of the units of a product consumed.

2 The tendency to rely on the first piece of information obtained when making a decision is known as:

   A anchoring

   B bounded rationality

   C framing

   D heuristics.

3 The substitution effect will:

   A always be negative

   B always be positive

   C depend on whether the good is a Giffen good

   D depend on whether the good is an inferior good.

4 Which of the following is an example of a fixed cost of production?

   A Component parts.

   B Interest payments.

   C Manual labour.

   D Raw materials.

5 Which of the following is an example of an external economy of scale?

   A Bulk buying to obtain a discount.

   B Managerial specialisation.

   C Research and development by a firm.

   D The provision of specific courses at colleges.

6 Profit is defined as the difference between:

   A average revenue and average cost

   B marginal revenue and marginal cost

   C total revenue and average cost

   D total revenue and total cost.

7 Which of the following is a feature of perfect competition?

   A Supernormal profit can be made in both the short run and the long run.

   B The buyers and sellers are price takers.

   C The product is differentiated.

   D There are only a few producers in the market.

8 A kinked demand curve occurs in oligopoly because:

   A demand is elastic above the kink and inelastic below it

   B demand is inelastic above the kink and elastic below it

   C the marginal revenue curve is below the average revenue curve

   D the marginal revenue curve is discontinuous.

9 A manufacturer taking over a supplier of raw materials needed in the production of a product is an example of:

   A backward vertical integration

   B conglomerate integration

   C forward vertical integration

   D horizontal integration.

10 Which of the following is an example of a principal of a firm?

   A A consumer.

   B A manager.

   C A shareholder.

   D An employee.

11 (a) Explain the main features of perfect competition. [12]

   (b) Discuss to what extent monopolistic competition is a more realistic and useful model of a market structure than perfect competition. [13]

12 Discuss whether a monopoly will always operate against the interests of consumers. [25]

Key topics

- ➤ policies to achieve efficient resource allocation and correct market failure
- ➤ equity and policies towards income and wealth redistribution
- ➤ labour market forces and government intervention
- ➤ government failure in microeconomic intervention.

8.1 Policies to achieve efficient resource allocation and correct market failure   AL 3(a)

This topic is concerned with:

- ➤ the application of indirect taxes and subsidies
- ➤ price and output decisions under nationalisation and privatisation
- ➤ prohibitions and licences
- ➤ property rights
- ➤ information
- ➤ regulatory bodies, deregulation and the direct provision of goods and services
- ➤ pollution permits
- ➤ behavioural insights and 'nudge' theory.

The application of indirect taxes and subsidies

Indirect taxes and subsidies can be used to achieve the efficient allocation of resources and to correct market failure. The impact and incidence of indirect taxes and subsidies were covered in Unit 3.

An indirect tax can be used to discourage the consumption of demerit goods, such as alcohol and tobacco, by making them more expensive and as long as the demand for such products is relatively elastic, the consumption of them will fall in response to the higher price being charged.

A subsidy can be used to encourage the consumption of merit goods, such as education and health care, by making them less expensive and as long as the demand for such products is relatively elastic, the consumption of them will rise in response to the lower price being charged.

> **Key terms**
>
> **Indirect tax**: a tax levied on expenditure.
>
> **Subsidy**: an amount of money paid by a government to a producer so that the price to the consumer will be lower than it otherwise would have been.

✗ Common error

It is easy to confuse the application of indirect taxes and subsidies in a market. An indirect tax will be shown by a shift of the supply curve to the left, leading to an increase in price, and a subsidy will be shown by a shift of the supply curve to the right, leading to a decrease in price.

★ Exam tip

Make sure that you are able to both explain the effect of the introduction of indirect taxes and subsidies in a market and to illustrate the effect through the use of appropriate diagrams.

Price and output decisions under nationalisation and privatisation

Nationalisation and privatisation have already been referred to in Unit 3. Nationalisation involves the creation of a monopoly where there is just one firm in an industry and this firm can control the supply of a product in a market.

Monopoly can be regarded as an example of market failure. This is because the equilibrium price is likely to be higher and the equilibrium quantity is likely to be lower than would be the case in perfect competition. Unlike the situation in perfect competition, the abnormal or supernormal profits are not competed away in the long-run because there are barriers to entry which make it very difficult for new firms to enter the market.

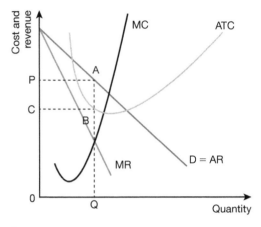

▲ **Figure 8.1** Price and output decisions under monopoly

Figure 8.1 above shows the price and output decisions that would be taken by a monopoly firm. The profit maximisation position is determined by where MC = MR and this will give an equilibrium price of 0P and an equilibrium quantity of 0Q. This is an example of market failure because there is a lack of both productive and allocative efficiency. The lack of competition in the industry also gives rise to X-inefficiency.

In such a situation, a government could decide to nationalise this monopoly firm, i.e. take it under state ownership. A price could be charged that would be lower than in a private sector monopoly and a quantity could be produced that would be higher than in a private sector monopoly, but the government would need to be able and willing to support the nationalised firm with public funds.

An alternative policy to correct market failure, instead of through nationalising the firm, would be through a process of privatisation. This would involve the transfer of ownership of an economic activity from the public sector to the private sector. With greater competition in the market, price is likely to be lower and output higher than would otherwise be the case.

X Common error

Make sure you don't confuse the terms nationalisation and privatisation. Nationalisation involves the transfer of ownership from the private sector to the public sector and privatisation involves the transfer of ownership from the public sector to the private sector.

Key terms

Nationalisation: the process whereby private sector firms and/or industries become part of the public sector of an economy, with the government or state owning and controlling these resources.

Privatisation: the process whereby public sector firms and/or industries become part of the private sector of an economy, with the government no longer owning or controlling these resources.

X-inefficiency: the inefficiency that can occur in a monopoly when production is not at the lowest point on the average total cost curve; it is where production takes place at a cost above the average cost curve and the marginal cost curve due to a lack of strong competition in an industry and because of organisational slack in a firm.

Prohibitions and licences

Another policy to achieve efficient resource allocation and to correct market failure in an economy is through the use of prohibitions and licences.

A prohibition refers to a ban on certain products being supplied in an economy. For example, a government could decide to make a product illegal and this would have the effect of prohibiting its consumption.

An alternative to a prohibition is the use of a licence to correct market failure. A licence involves a government giving permission to producers to sell a product. The impact of using licences is usually not as effective as prohibition, but it does give a government some control in a market, and it can decide to make the policy more effective by reducing the number of licences issued.

Property rights

Property rights refers to the rights of the owner of an economic good to decide how such a good should be used. Market failure can occur because of the absence of clear property rights, so one way to correct market failure is to bring about greater clarity in relation to property rights. A government could decide to extend property rights, such as through the establishment of voluntary agreements. An example might be in relation to the dumping of rubbish, creating an environmental problem. If such a voluntary agreement was unsuccessful, a government could decide to introduce a system of pollution permits.

✓ What you need to know

In most situations, property rights are private and so it is relatively easy to establish the rights of a person in relation to their property, i.e. the assets that they own. If there is a dispute about these private property rights, redress can be obtained through legal action. However, in some cases, property rights are not private, but relate to open spaces and to air and water. In these situations, there are common, rather than private, property rights. The existence of common property rights can give rise to market failure, such as in relation to pollution, and so a government might decide to extend property rights so that they cover open spaces, air and water.

Information

Market failure can be caused by inadequate or inaccurate information. It is assumed that consumers will always aim to maximise their utility or satisfaction, but this aim can only be achieved if they are in possession of the required information. If this information is not readily available, they will be less likely to make rational decisions. This is why information failure can be a major cause of market failure.

To correct this type of market failure, a government needs to try to increase the availability, accuracy and reliability of appropriate information to consumers in an attempt to influence their economic behaviour. This will help them to make rational decisions in relation to the consumption of merit goods and demerit goods and ensure that scarce resources are allocated as efficiently as possible. Nudge theory is an example of where a government could try to discourage consumers from consuming demerit goods.

> ✓ **What you need to know**
>
> A government could try to overcome the problem of information failure by improving the information that is made available to consumers. In the case of merit goods, a government would try to ensure that people were as well informed as possible about the potential advantages of consuming merit goods, such as education and health care. In the case of demerit goods, a government would try to ensure that people were as well informed as possible about the potential disadvantages of consuming demerit goods, such as alcohol and tobacco.

Regulatory bodies

A government could try to correct the existence of market failure in an economy through the use of regulations. A regulation refers to a rule or law that can be used to reduce the extent of market failure. There are many examples of such regulations in different countries, such as in relation to the following:

➤ the control of monopolies

➤ proposed mergers and acquisitions

➤ consumer protection

➤ protection of the environment

➤ control of the transportation system.

In each of these situations, there will usually be a regulatory body set up to enforce the regulations.

> **Key terms**
>
> **Regulations:** a variety of laws and rules which apply to firms in different circumstances.
>
> **Regulatory body:** an organisation that imposes requirements, restrictions and conditions, sets standards and secures compliance or enforcement.

> ✓ **What you need to know**
>
> Regulatory bodies perform the function of ensuring that regulations are adhered to. For example, regulations may exist to control monopolies and to ensure that any proposed merger is not against the public interest. If it is thought that a proposed merger would be against the public interest, it can be referred to a regulatory body.

Deregulation

Although regulations can be used as part of a policy to correct market failure, it is also possible that there are too many regulations in existence in an economy and that these regulations are making it impossible for efficient resource allocation to be achieved. In such situations, a government could decide to reduce the number of regulations that exist in an economy so that a greater degree of competition is allowed to exist in a market than would otherwise be the case. This process is known as deregulation. If greater competition did take place in a market, it is likely to lead to an increase in the level of efficiency of resource allocation and to a reduction in the extent of market failure.

> **Key term**
>
> **Deregulation:** a reduction in the number of regulations, laws and rules that operate in an industry or an economy.

The direct provision of goods and services

Another policy that can be used to correct market failure in an economy is through the direct provision of certain goods and services. This was covered in Unit 3.

In many countries, the government has decided to directly provide particular goods and services through the public sector which can exist alongside the private sector.

> **✓ What you need to know**
>
> A government may decide to directly provide certain goods and services if it was thought that the consumption of such products would be relatively low if only provided through the private sector. For example, a government could decide to directly provide certain merit goods, such as education and health care.

Pollution permits

A pollution permit, or tradable permit as it is also called, is a particular example of a licence that can be issued by a government. The permit allows a firm to pollute the environment in some way, but only up to a certain extent. This level of pollution will be less than when the permit was first issued. Each successive permit will allow a lower and lower level of pollution to exist.

> **✗ Common error**
>
> Try not to argue that pollution permits will entirely eradicate pollution in an economy. Instead, focus on the fact that a policy of using pollution permits is designed to reduce the extent of pollution that exists in an economy over a period of time.

Behavioural insights and 'nudge' theory

Behavioural economics was referred to in Unit 7. Behavioural economic models are designed to provide an insight into why consumers do not always act in a rational way. These insights stress the importance of understanding the actual behaviour of people in an economy rather than the traditional approach which stresses the idea that people are assumed to behave rationally.

The behavioural approach emphasises that it is possible to 'nudge' people to act in a particular way, different from how they would act if there was no government intervention. This is why it is also known as nudge theory. An example of this would be in relation to a government policy to discourage the consumption of certain demerit goods.

> **Key terms**
>
> Behavioural economics: the branch of economics that attempts to explain the decisions and choices that individuals make in practice, particularly when they are opposed to those predicted by traditional economic theory.
>
> Nudge theory: an attempt by a government to alter the economic behaviour of people in some particular way.

✓ **What you need to know**

A government can try to nudge consumers to change their economic behaviour in some way. For example, medical evidence is very clear about the damage that can be caused by the consumption of tobacco and yet millions of people still smoke. It is clear that the medical evidence has had no, or a very limited, effect on the consumption pattern of many people. A government could therefore adopt a policy of nudging people away from smoking, stressing how harmful such a product is to the health of people. For example, a government could insist that all packets of cigarettes sold in a country should carry a health warning.

★ **Exam tip**

It would be helpful if you were able to give examples to support an answer on nudge theory. For example, a government could start with a moderate nudge, such as when a packet of cigarettes contains the warning: 'smoking can damage your health'. If this nudge was not sufficient to substantially change the demand for cigarettes, packets of cigarettes could contain a stronger warning, such as: 'smoking can kill'.

 Raise your grade

Explain how 'nudge' theory can be used to inform government policies to correct market failure. [12]

Behavioural economics can offer insights into the economic behaviour of people.[1] For example, a government might decide to adopt a policy of nudging people in a particular direction, such as in relation to the consumption of demerit goods.[2]

The consumption of alcohol could be an example of where such a government policy might be successful. Medical evidence is very clear about the potential dangers to a person's health of excessive alcohol consumption. A government might therefore decide to intervene in a market to try to reduce the extent of alcohol consumption.[3]

The effectiveness of such a policy to change consumer behaviour will depend on a number of factors,[4] but it is likely that the behaviour of at least some consumers will be changed.

How to improve this answer

1   The candidate refers to the fact that behavioural economics is able to offer insights into the economic behaviour of people, but this point could have been developed more fully. For example, the candidate could have stressed how behavioural economic models are designed to provide an insight into why consumers do not always act in a rational way. These insights stress the importance of understanding the actual behaviour of people in an economy rather than the traditional approach which stresses the idea that people are assumed to behave rationally.

2 The behavioural approach emphasises that it is possible to 'nudge' people to act in a particular way, different from how they would act if there was no government intervention. It is appropriate that the candidate has referred to a government policy to discourage the consumption of demerit goods, but it would have been useful if they had explained the meaning of the term 'demerit goods' at this point.

3 The candidate has referred to the possibility of a government intervening in a market to try to reduce the extent of alcohol consumption, but has not given any indication of how this could actually be done. It would have been helpful if the candidate had referred to the idea of advertisements for alcohol containing certain warnings, such as 'drink sensibly'.

4 The candidate has referred to the fact that the effectiveness of such a policy to change consumer behaviour will depend on a number of factors, but has not indicated what any of these factors might be. For instance, it might depend on the strength of the wording of any health warnings, the extent to which consumers are aware of such warnings or the extent o which the warnings are part of a much wider information campaign, such as the decision of a government to launch a 'Drink Awareness' campaign to make as many people as possible aware of the possible health dangers of excessive alcohol consumption.

Level 2 – 6/12

8.2 Equity and policies towards income and wealth redistribution

AL 3(b)

This topic is concerned with:

➤ equity versus efficiency

➤ price stabilisation

➤ means-tested benefits

➤ transfer payments

➤ progressive income taxes, inheritance and capital taxes

➤ negative income tax

➤ poverty trap analysis

➤ Gini coefficient and the Lorenz curve

➤ inter-generational equity.

Equity versus efficiency

One objective of government microeconomic intervention is the achievement of efficiency. This involves the achievement of both productive and allocative efficiency. The attainment of this objective would ensure that the scarce resources in an economy were allocated in the best possible way.

Another objective of government microeconomic intervention is the achievement of equity. This is concerned with the ideas of fairness and justice, such as a government policy to bring about a more equitable distribution of income and wealth.

Key terms

Efficiency: the use of resources in the most economical or optimal way possible.

Equity: the idea of fairness or justice, such as in relation to the distribution of income and wealth in an economy.

★ Exam tip

It is important to be able to distinguish clearly between equity and efficiency. A certain allocation of resources in an economy may be efficient, but this does not necessarily mean that it will be equitable.

Price stabilisation

Without any government intervention, it is possible that prices in a particular market may fluctuate widely. This is likely to be particularly the case where supply can vary a great deal, such as in agricultural markets.

A government may decide to intervene in a market to stabilise prices. This is known as a buffer stock system. Figure 8.2 shows what happens with such a system. When supply is high, as with S_1, the government purchases some of the stock and prevents it from entering the market. The effect of this intervention is to prevent the price falling too low, i.e. it is kept at 0P rather than being allowed to fall to $0P_2$. When supply is low, as with S_2, the government releases some of the stock and allows it to enter the market. The effect of this intervention is to prevent the price rising too high, i.e. it is kept at 0P rather than being allowed to rise to $0P_1$. Government intervention through a buffer stock scheme brings about price stabilisation in a market, with price maintained at or close to 0P and quantity maintained at or close to 0Q.

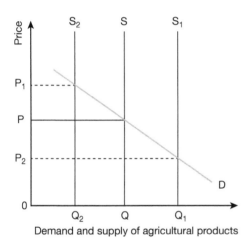

Demand and supply of agricultural products

▲ **Figure 8.2** Price stabilisation through a buffer stock scheme

✓ What you need to know

A buffer stock scheme can have a number of possible advantages:

➤ it can overcome the problem of wide fluctuations in the prices in a market from one year to another

➤ if price stabilisation can be brought about in a market, it will also help to bring about greater stability in the incomes received by the producers

➤ this greater stability of prices and incomes will make medium-term and long-term planning easier.

However, a buffer stock scheme can also have a number of possible disadvantages:

➤ it might not be easy for a government to decide what the stable price in a market should be and this will affect the amount of stock that is stored or released

➤ there will be a cost involved in running a buffer stock scheme, such as the cost of storage, and if a government pays for this, there will be an opportunity cost involved, i.e. the other goods or services that the money could have been spent on

➤ the scheme may become very difficult to operate if there is either a succession of good harvests or a succession of bad harvests.

Means-tested benefits

There are two types of benefit. A universal benefit is paid to every person who is entitled to such a benefit, irrespective of their income or wealth. A means-tested benefit is paid to a person depending on their income and wealth. Such a benefit has the advantage of targeting those people who are most in need of the money and so is more effective in bringing about income and wealth redistribution.

Remember

Means-tested benefits are better than universal benefits if the aim of a government is to redistribute income and wealth in an economy.

Transfer payments

Another example of government microeconomic intervention to bring about a redistribution of income and wealth is through the use of transfer payments. These were covered in Unit 3. Revenue that is received from taxation can be used to give financial support to those in need.

Progressive income taxes, inheritance and capital taxes

The concept of a progressive tax was covered in Unit 3. This means that a higher proportion of income can be taken in tax as the incomes of people rise above a certain level.

It is not only income tax that can be progressive. It can also apply to inheritance tax and capital tax.

Key terms

Progressive tax: a situation where the proportion of income paid in tax increases as income increases.

Income tax: this is a tax on earned incomes.

Inheritance tax: this is a tax on income in the form of property, money and possessions, also known as the 'estate', of someone who has died.

Capital tax: this is a tax, also called a capital gains tax, on income in the form of an increase in the value of possessions, such as a second home, antiques or shares, during the time that a person has owned them.

Negative income tax

Whereas an income tax involves people paying tax to a government, according to their earned income, a negative income tax involves people receiving money from a government. It is also a progressive system where people earning below a certain amount receive money from the government. In this way, people will be able to receive a minimum income. The key feature of a negative income tax is that it combines the payment of income tax and the receipt of benefits in one system. All people earning above a certain income level would pay income tax and receive no benefits, while all people earning below that income level would not pay any income tax, but would receive benefits.

Exam tip

Make sure you don't confuse universal and means-tested benefits. Universal benefits do not take into account a person's income or wealth whereas means-tested benefits do take this into account.

Key term

Transfer payments: a situation where revenue is received from one part of society, such as taxpayers, and paid to another part of society, such as pensioners.

Key term

Negative income tax: a system which brings together the payment of tax and the receipt of benefits.

Poverty trap analysis

A problem with an increase in earned income is that it is possible that as some people receive more money, they may no longer be entitled to as many benefits as before. The effect of this is that they can actually be worse off as a result of an increase in income. This situation is known as a poverty trap and creates a disincentive effect. For example, a person may not wish to work longer hours because the extra income received from this work may mean that they are no longer entitled to some benefits that they were originally entitled to before working the extra hours. The existence of the poverty trap means that a person may become worse off as a result of earning more money because they are no longer entitled to certain benefits.

The Lorenz curve and the Gini coefficient

The Lorenz curve is a graphical representation which shows the extent of inequality in the distribution of income in an economy. The more unequal the distribution of income, the more divergent the Lorenz curve will be from the diagonal line of total equality. This can be seen in Figure 8.3.

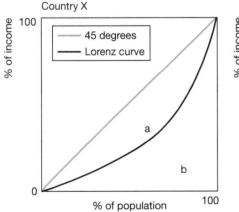 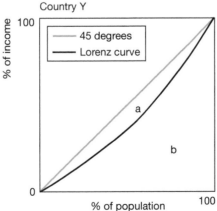

▲ **Figure 8.3** A comparison of income equality in two countries

In country Y, the Lorenz curve is quite close to the 45 degree line of absolute equality and so income is distributed relatively evenly. In country X, however, the Lorenz curve is further away from the 45 degree diagonal line and this shows that income is more unevenly distributed in country X than in country.

A Gini coefficient is a way of measuring the extent of inequality in the distribution of income in an economy. It is measured as the ratio of the area between the 45 degree diagonal line of total equality and the Lorenz curve to the total area under the diagonal. In Figure 8.3 on the previous page, it is area 'a' divided by area 'a' and 'b'. The lower the value of the Gini coefficient, the more even is the distribution of income, e.g. in many developed countries, the coefficient is about 0.3. The higher the value of the Gini coefficient, the less even is the distribution of income, e.g. in many developing countries, the coefficient is about 0.5.

> ✓ **What you need to know**
>
> A Gini coefficient figure of 0.5 or above is considered relatively high, e.g. Brazil. A Gini coefficient of between 0.3 and 0.5 is considered medium, e.g. Vietnam. A Gini coefficient of less than 0.3 is considered relatively low, e.g. Austria.

> ✗ **Common error**
>
> Make sure you don't mix up these two terms, referring to a Lorenz coefficient and a Gini curve. The correct terms are Gini coefficient and Lorenz curve.

Inter-generational equity

Inter-generational equity refers to the fairness or justice in the distribution of income of different generations over a period of time. It is concerned with the extent to which income distribution today can affect future generations.

> ✓ **What you need to know**
>
> Increasing inequality in the distribution of income of relatively high-income countries, such as the USA, could have the effect of limiting economic mobility for the next generation of young adults. In some countries, young people are experiencing, for the first time, a lower income than their parents.

8.3 Labour market forces and government intervention   AL 3(c)

This topic is concerned with:

➤ factors affecting the demand for labour

➤ the derivation of an individual firm's demand for labour, using marginal revenue product theory

➤ factors affecting the supply of labour

➤ net advantages and the long-run supply of labour

➤ competitive product and factor market forces determining wage differentials, transfer earnings and economic rent

➤ the influence of trades unions on wage determination

➤ the influence of government on wage determination

➤ monopsony.

The demand for, and the supply of, labour

Factors affecting the demand for labour

The factor of production, labour, is not demanded for its own sake, but for what it is able to contribute to the production process. This is known as derived demand.

The demand for labour is closely linked to the marginal physical product (MPP) of labour. This refers to the additional output produced if a firm increases the labour input by one unit.

Firms are interested not only in the extra output that is produced by employing one more unit of labour, but also in the revenue obtained from selling the additional output that has been produced. The marginal revenue product (MRP) of labour is obtained by multiplying the marginal physical product of labour by the marginal revenue (MR) received by a firm.

> **Remember**
>
> Labour is not demanded for its own sake, but for what it can contribute to the production process.

> **Common error**
>
> Make sure you don't confuse marginal physical product (MPP) and marginal revenue product (MRP). MPP refers to the extra output resulting from employing one more worker. MRP refers to the extra revenue received by a firm from selling the additional output that results from employing one more worker.

The derivation of an individual firm's demand for labour using marginal revenue product theory

It has already been pointed out in Unit 7 that a profit maximising firm will produce where marginal cost (MC) is equal to marginal revenue (MR). This situation also applies to a profit maximising employer of labour. This employer will employ labour up to the point where the extra cost of employing an additional worker is equal to the extra revenue earned by the firm from this output. If it is assumed that the product produced is sold in a perfectly competitive market and that all units of a product are sold at the same price, then the employer will employ workers up to the point where the wage rate equals the marginal revenue product of labour. The MRP curve shows the quantity of labour that is employed at each wage. Therefore the firm's demand curve for labour is the MRP curve.

Figure 8.4 shows the individual firm's demand curve for labour, which is also the MRP curve. Any change in the wage rate will bring about a movement along the firm's demand curve. A rise in the wage rate will lead to a fall in the quantity of labour demanded by a firm and a fall in the wage rate will lead to a rise in the quantity of labour demanded by a firm. However, there can also be a shift of the demand curve for labour as a result of a change in the MPP of labour and/or a change in the price of the product. Figure 8.4 shows a shift of the demand curve for labour to the right, from $D(MRP)_1$ to $D(MRP)_2$. This could be the result of an increase in labour productivity, increasing MPP, and/or an increase in the price of the product. Although the diagram shows an individual firm's demand curve for labour, the industry's demand curve for labour will be the sum of each of the individual firms' demand for labour at each wage.

Key terms

Derived demand: the situation where the demand by employers for labour is related to, or derived from, the demand for the product that the labour is helping to produce.

Marginal physical product (MPP): the amount of extra output that is produced if a firm increases its input of labour by one unit.

Marginal revenue product (MRP): the extra output produced by an additional worker (the marginal physical product or MPP) multiplied by the additional revenue earned by a firm from this output (the marginal revenue or MR), i.e. MRP = MPP x MR.

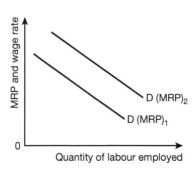

▲ **Figure 8.4** An individual firm's demand for labour

The slope of the individual firm's demand curve for labour will depend on the elasticity of demand for labour, i.e. the degree of responsiveness of the demand for labour in response to a change in the wage rate. Figure 8.5 shows differences in the elasticity of demand for labour. If the demand for labour is elastic, then a change in the wage rate will bring about a greater percentage change in the quantity of labour demanded. If the demand for labour is inelastic, then a change in the wage rate will bring about a smaller percentage change in the quantity of labour demanded.

Key term

Elasticity of demand for labour: a measure of the responsiveness of the demand for labour to a change in the wage rate.

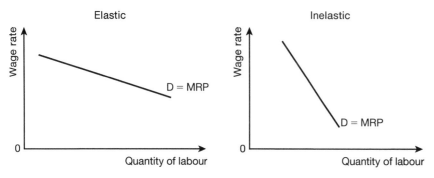

▲ **Figure 8.5** Differences in the elasticity of demand for labour

✓ What you need to know

The elasticity of demand for labour can be influenced by a number of possible factors:

➤ the proportion of labour costs to the total costs of production: if the proportion is relatively high, the elasticity of demand for labour is likely to be high and if the proportion is relatively low, the elasticity of demand for labour is likely to be low

➤ the ease of factor substitution: if labour can be easily replaced by another factor, e.g. capital, the demand for labour is likely to be relatively elastic and if labour cannot be easily replaced by another factor, the demand for labour is likely to be relatively inelastic

➤ the price elasticity of demand for the final product: if the price elasticity of demand for the final product is relatively high, then the elasticity of demand for labour is likely to be high and if the price elasticity of demand for the final product is relatively low, then the elasticity of demand for labour is likely to be inelastic

➤ time: the elasticity of demand for labour is likely to increase over time, as firms have longer to find appropriate substitutes for labour.

★ Exam tip

Remember to also label the demand curve for labour as the MRP curve.

Factors affecting the supply of labour

If it is assumed that a firm is in a perfectly competitive market for labour and so cannot influence the price of labour, then the firm is a price taker and so the supply of labour is perfectly elastic, shown by a horizontal MC curve.

However, although this is the case for an individual firm, for the industry as a whole the supply curve of labour will be upward sloping from left to right because more people will make themselves available for work when there is an increase in the wage rate paid to labour. This can be seen in Figure 8.6. When the wage rate in an industry increases from 0W to 0W$_1$, the quantity of labour supplied increases from 0Q to 0Q$_1$. If there is a further increase in the wage rate to 0W$_2$, the quantity of labour supplied increases to 0Q$_2$.

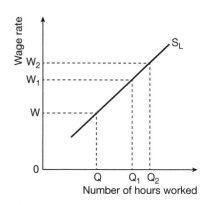

▲ **Figure 8.6** An industry supply curve for labour

It is possible that for an individual worker, an increase in the wage rate may persuade that worker to work fewer hours so as to be able to enjoy more leisure time. This shows the opportunity cost of working more hours in terms of the reduced leisure time. This situation gives rise to a backward-bending supply curve for a particular worker. This can be seen in Figure 8.7. When the wage rate is $0W_1$, the amount of hours worked is $0Q_1$. When the wage rate is increased to $0W_2$ or $0W_3$, the number of hours worked by the individual worker increases to $0Q_2$ or $0Q_3$. However, if there is an increase in the wage rate above $0W_3$, there is a decrease in the number of hours worked by the individual worker.

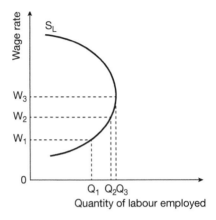

▲ **Figure 8.7** Backward sloping supply curve for labour

The slope of the labour supply curve will depend on the elasticity of supply of labour, i.e. the degree of responsiveness of the supply of labour in response to a change in the wage rate. Figure 8.8 shows differences in the elasticity of supply of labour. If the supply of labour is elastic, then a change in the wage rate will bring about a greater percentage change in the quantity of labour supplied. If the supply of labour is inelastic, then a change in the wage rate will bring about a smaller percentage change in the quantity of labour supplied.

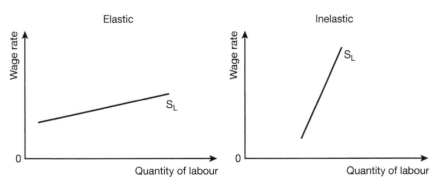

▲ **Figure 8.8** Differences in the elasticity of supply of labour

The supply curve of labour will be influenced by the occupational mobility of labour and the geographical mobility of labour.

Net advantages and the long-run supply of labour

Net advantages

There are various advantages of being in work. One of these is the reward to workers in the form of wages, salaries and any other kind of financial benefit. These financial advantages are known as pecuniary advantages.

However, there may be other advantages of being in work that are non-financial, such as the job satisfaction that a person gains from employment. These non-financial advantages are known as non-pecuniary advantages.

The balance between the financial, or pecuniary, advantages and the non-financial advantages, or non-pecuniary advantages, of any employment gives rise to what are termed the net advantages.

The long-run supply of labour

There are a number of possible factors that could influence the long-run supply of labour and these include the following:

➤ the size of the population of a country

➤ the extent of immigration into, and emigration out of, a country

➤ the labour participation rate

➤ the tax rates that are applied to income earned

➤ the level of benefits paid by the state

➤ improvements in the occupational mobility of labour

➤ improvements in the geographical mobility of labour.

Wage determination in perfect markets

Competitive product and factor market forces determining wage differentials

Equilibrium in a labour market is just like equilibrium in any other market and is achieved where demand is equal to supply. This can be seen in

Figure 8.9 where the equilibrium wage is 0W and the equilibrium quantity is 0Q. Figure 8.9 shows the situation for both the market and an individual firm; the wage rate is determined in the market where D_L is equal to S_L and all firms in the industry have to accept this wage, i.e. the firms are price, or wage, takers.

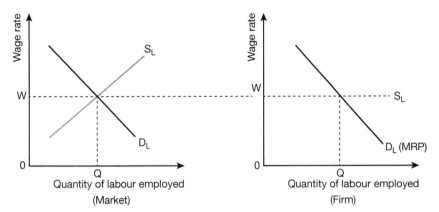

▲ **Figure 8.9** Wage determination in perfect markets

The characteristics of a perfect factor, e.g. labour, market are very similar to those of a perfect product market:

➤ a large number of firms employing labour

➤ a large number of homogeneous workers who are perfectly mobile within the industry

➤ perfect knowledge in the market for both employers and employees.

Transfer earnings and economic rent

Transfer earnings refer to those earnings that are the minimum that would be necessary to keep a factor production in a particular use.

Economic rent refers to the additional payment that a worker receives above transfer earnings.

Figure 8.10 shows the distinction between transfer earnings and economic rent. The area under the supply curve, 0BAQ, represents the transfer earnings, and the area between the supply curve and the horizontal line across from W, BWA, represents the economic rent.

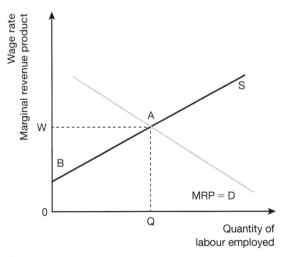

▲ **Figure 8.10** Transfer earnings and economic rent

Wage determination in imperfect markets

The influence of trades unions on wage determination

Wage determination in perfect markets has already been covered, but it is not necessarily the case that a labour market operates as a perfect market. For example, the workers may be members of a trades union and these organisations may be able to influence the process of wage determination in what would therefore be seen as an imperfect market.

Trades unions represent the interests of their members in wage negotiations with the employers through what is called collective bargaining. Sometimes a trades union will operate a closed shop to increase its bargaining power where the entire workforce employed in an industry belong to the trades union.

One way of doing this is by a reduction in the supply of labour, e.g. by forcing the employers to make it more difficult for workers to enter into an industry. The effect of this will be to bring about an increase in the level of wages. This can be seen in Figure 8.11. The trades union brings about a restriction on the entry of labour into a particular industry, such as through raising the minimum level of qualifications or period of training required to work in the industry. This will have the effect of shifting the supply curve of labour to the left, from S_L to S_{L1}. As a result of this, the wage rate will increase from $0W$ to $0W_1$, although the number of workers employed will fall from $0Q$ to $0Q_1$.

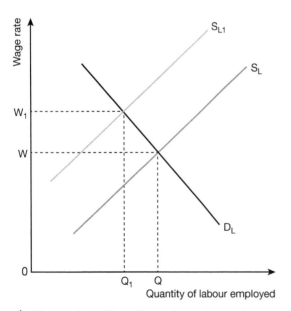

▲ **Figure 8.11** The effect of restricting the supply of labour in an industry

An alternative approach would be for the trades unions to negotiate wage increases for their members as a result of the increased productivity of the workers. For example, the trades unions could agree to the workers adopting more flexible working practices or to using new technology. This can be seen in Figure 8.12 where there is a shift of the demand curve to the right from D_1 to D_2. This has the effect of increasing the wage rate from $0W_1$ to $0W_2$ and increasing the quantity of labour from $0Q_1$ to $0Q_2$.

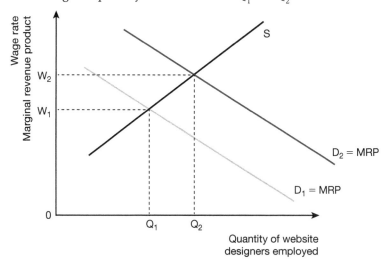

▲ **Figure 8.12** The effect of increasing the demand for labour in an industry

The influence of government on wage determination

The existence of an imperfect market has already been seen in the context of trades unions intervening in labour markets to try to increase the wage rates of their members. Another example of intervention is where a government intervenes to influence wage rates in a market, such as through the establishment of a national minimum wage.

Figure 8.13 shows the effect of a government intervening to establish a national minimum wage. The equilibrium wage rate in the market, without any government intervention, would be 0W, where demand and supply intersect, and the equilibrium quantity would be 0Q. However, a government may decide that the wage rate of 0W is too low and so decides to intervene in the market by passing a law to establish the wage rate at 0W1. This has the advantage that all those in employment now receive a wage rate of $0W_1$, rather than 0W, but the drawback of this government intervention is that although $0Q_2$ workers are willing to work at this rate of pay, only $0Q_1$ will be demanded at the higher rate of pay.

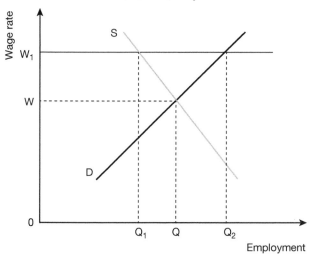

▲ **Figure 8.13** A national minimum wage

Monopsony

Another example of how wage determination can occur in an imperfect market is through the existence of a monopsony. It has been assumed, up to now, that there are likely to be a number of firms operating in an industry and so the demand for labour curve will be made up of a number of firms in an industry.

However, in the case of a monopsony, or single buyer, there is only one firm in the market that wishes to employ labour. Unlike the situation in a market where there are many firms in an industry, where each firm is a price, or wage, taker, accepting the prevailing wage rate in the market, if a firm is a monopsonist it would be able to pay a lower wage.

Labour is employed by a monopsonist, but supplied competitively

Figure 8.14 shows the situation of a single buyer of labour, the monopsonist, and labour supplied competitively. The average cost of labour is shown by AC_L and this is also the supply curve of labour (S_L). The marginal cost of labour curve (MC_L) is above the AC_L curve. The monopsonist will employ workers by equating the marginal cost paid to employ a worker with the marginal revenue product gained from this employment, i.e. where $MRP = MC_L$, with 0Q quantity of labour employed. This is the profit maximising position. The wage that the monopsonist pays to employ labour is 0W. However, because the marginal cost of labour is above and diverging from the average cost of labour, to employ more workers the monopsonist must increase the wage rate for the last worker and all the workers before.

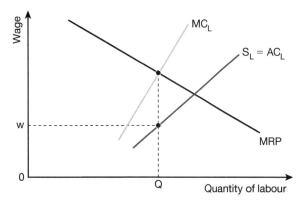

▲ **Figure 8.14** A monopsony labour market

As well as a single buyer of labour, the monopsonist, it is also possible that instead of being supplied competitively, labour is supplied by a monopoly, i.e. a trades union. This situation is known as a bilateral monopoly. The trades union will want to have a higher wage rate and a higher employment level. However, as already pointed out, the monopsonist will want to have a wage rate of 0W and an employment level of 0Q. The monopsony buyer and the monopoly seller will negotiate these wage and employment positions and the eventual wage and quantity established in the market will depend on the relative bargaining strengths of the monopsony buyer and the monopoly seller.

> **X | Common error**
>
> Be careful not to confuse the terms 'monopsonist' and 'monopolist'. A monopsony is a single buyer of labour in a market and a monopoly is a single seller of labour in a market.

Key term

Monopsony: a single buyer of a product or a factor of production, e.g. labour.

Key term

Bilateral monopoly: a situation where labour is being bought by a single buyer, the monopsonist, and being sold by a single seller, the trades union or monopolist.

⬆ Raise your grade

Discuss to what extent a country can increase the supply of labour in the long-run. [13]

It is possible that the supply of labour could be increased in the long-run. The size of the population of a country could increase over a period of time. This would be the case if there was net migration into a country.[1,2] The supply of labour would also increase if there was an increase in the labour participation rate, e.g. if more people could be allowed and encouraged to work.[3] The level of taxation on earned income could also influence supply, especially if tax levels increased substantially, as this could have a disincentive effect in an economy.[4] Improvements in the occupational mobility of labour could increase the supply of labour in particular industries, such as through improvements in the education and training provision in a country.[5]

It can therefore be seen that an increase in the supply of labour is more likely in the long-run.[6]

How to improve this answer

1   The candidate has referred to the potential impact of net migration into a country, but it would have been helpful if they had also stated that an increase in the size of a population could come about from a natural increase, i.e. when the birth rate exceeded the death rate.

2   The candidate has referred to net migration, but has not actually explained that this is the difference between immigration into, and emigration out of, a country.

3   The candidate refers to a possible increase in the labour participation rate, but has not included any examples of how this might be brought about, such as an increase in the retirement age in a country.

4   The candidate has referred to the level of taxation as a possible factor, but there could also have been a reference to the level of state benefits. This could have included a comment on the potential significance of the poverty trap.

5   The candidate has referred to the potential impact of improvements in the occupational mobility of labour, but they could also have referred to the potential impact of improvements in the geographical mobility of labour, such as through an improvement in the provision of information about job vacancies in other geographical areas.

6   The candidate has not considered any possible reasons to challenge the question and to assert that it may not necessarily be that easy to increase the supply of labour in the long-run. For example, there may be net migration out of a country, reducing the size of its population, and the level of benefits may be so high that people are discouraged from working.

Level 2 – 6/13

8.4 Government failure in microeconomic intervention AL 3(d)

This topic is concerned with:

➤ the effectiveness of government policies.

Unit 3 and this unit have indicated a number of different ways in which a government can intervene to reduce the extent of market failure in an economy. The effectiveness of government policies to achieve this aim will depend on a number of factors, including the following:

➤ information: government policies of microeconomic intervention will only be effective if a government has all the necessary information on which to base policy decisions, but this may not always be the case and so any inaccurate information is likely to undermine the effectiveness of any intervention

➤ incentives: a government may take one policy decision, such as a decision to make income tax more progressive so as to achieve a more equitable distribution of income, but as a result there may be a disincentive effect, causing some people to work less hours or even to leave the country and seek employment elsewhere.

Government failure can therefore occur where a government intervenes in order to correct market failure, but in doing so, creates other distortions or imperfections in the market.

> **Exam tip**
>
> Make sure that you are able to support any comments in the exam on government failure with appropriate examples.

> **Key term**
>
> **Government failure:** the failure of a government to achieve desired objectives as a result of intervention in a market.

Revision checklist

I can:

➤ understand how indirect taxes can be used to correct market failure ☐

➤ understand how subsidies can be used to correct market failure ☐

➤ be clear about what is meant by the term nationalisation ☐

➤ be clear about what is meant by the term privatisation ☐

➤ understand how price and output decisions will be taken under nationalisation and privatisation ☐

➤ appreciate how prohibitions can be used to correct market failure ☐

➤ understand how licences can be used to correct market failure ☐

➤ be clear about what is meant by property rights and why a government might decide to extend property rights ☐

➤ understand why a government might wish to intervene in a market to improve the information that is available ☐

➤ be clear about the regulations, rules and laws that may be introduced by a government and how these are supervised and enforced by regulatory bodies ☐

➤ be clear about the distinction between regulation and deregulation and understand why deregulation might take place in a market ☐

➤ be clear about why a government might decide to bring about the direct provision of goods and services in a market ☐

➤ understand what is meant by pollution permits and why they might be used in a market ☐

➤ be clear about how behavioural economics can provide insights into certain aspects of market failure ☐

➤ understand what is meant by 'nudge' theory and how governments can try to 'nudge' people to behave in certain ways ☐

➤ be clear about what is meant by the term efficiency ☐

➤ be clear about what is meant by the term equity ☐

➤ be clear about how a buffer stock scheme can be used to bring about a greater degree of price stabilisation in a market ☐

➤ be clear about what is meant by means-tested benefits and how they differ from universal benefits ☐

➤ understand what is meant by transfer payments and why a government may decide to make transfer payments to certain people in a society ☐

➤ be clear about what is meant by a progressive tax ☐

➤ understand what is meant by a progressive income tax, a progressive inheritance tax and a progressive capital tax ☐

➤ be clear about what is meant by a negative income tax and how this is different from an income tax ☐

➤ understand what is meant by a poverty trap and how it can come about in an economy ☐

➤ be clear about what is meant by a Gini coefficient ☐

- ➤ be clear about what is meant by a Lorenz curve ☐
- ➤ understand what is meant by inter-generational equity ☐
- ➤ be clear about the factors that can affect the demand for labour ☐
- ➤ understand how an individual firm's demand for labour can be derived using marginal revenue product theory ☐
- ➤ understand the significance of the elasticity of demand for labour ☐
- ➤ distinguish between marginal revenue product (MRP) and marginal physical product (MPP) ☐
- ➤ be clear about the factors that can affect the supply of labour ☐
- ➤ understand the significance of the elasticity of supply for labour ☐
- ➤ be clear about the significance of the geographical mobility of labour ☐
- ➤ be clear about the significance of the occupational mobility of labour ☐
- ➤ understand the distinction between pecuniary and non-pecuniary advantages of employment ☐
- ➤ be clear about what is meant by the net advantages of employment ☐
- ➤ be clear about the factors that can affect the long-run supply of labour ☐
- ➤ understand how wages are determined in perfect markets ☐
- ➤ be clear about what is meant by the term transfer earnings ☐
- ➤ be clear about what is meant by the term economic rent ☐
- ➤ understand the relationship between transfer earnings, economic rent and the elasticity of supply of labour ☐
- ➤ understand how wages are determined in imperfect markets ☐
- ➤ be clear about the distinction between perfect and imperfect labour markets ☐
- ➤ understand the potential influence of trades unions on wage determination in imperfect markets ☐
- ➤ understand the potential influence of a government on wage determination in imperfect markets ☐
- ➤ be clear about the meaning of monopsony ☐
- ➤ understand the potential influence of a monopsony on wage determination in imperfect markets ☐
- ➤ be able to comment on the effectiveness of government policies of microeconomic intervention ☐
- ➤ understand what is meant by government failure in microeconomic intervention and how such failure can come about. ☐

❓ Exam-style questions

1 An indirect tax will shift:

   A the demand curve to the left

   B the demand curve to the right

   C the supply curve to the left

   D the supply curve to the right. [1]

2 X-inefficiency in monopoly comes about as a result of:

   A external economies of scale in an industry

   B organisational slack in a firm

   C strong competition in an industry

   D technical efficiency in a firm. [1]

3 A pollution permit is also known as a:

   A capital tax

   B property right

   C tradable permit

   D transfer payment. [1]

4 A means-tested benefit is one which:

   A does not give rise to a poverty trap

   B does not target those people most in need of additional funds

   C is paid to a person depending on their income and wealth

   D is paid to a person irrespective of their income and wealth. [1]

5 A relatively high Gini coefficient indicates that:

   A prices are relatively stable in an economy

   B taxes in an economy are extremely progressive

   C the distribution of income in a country is relatively less even

   D the distribution of income in a country is relatively more even. [1]

6 If the demand for labour is elastic, then a change in the wage rate will bring about:

   A a greater percentage change in the quantity of labour demanded.

   B a larger proportion of workers in trades unions

   C a smaller percentage change in the quantity of labour demanded

   D no change in the quantity of labour demanded. [1]

7 A financial advantage of employment is known as a:

   A fringe advantage

   B net advantage

   C non-pecuniary advantage

   D pecuniary advantage. [1]

8 Transfer earnings refer to those earnings that are:

   A in excess of the opportunity cost of employment

   B paid by a government to those people not in employment

   C shown in a wage diagram by the area above the supply curve

   D the minimum that would be necessary to keep labour in a particular use. [1]

9 A closed shop is where:

   A a firm is unable to employ any additional workers

   B all workers in a particular industry are members of a trades union

   C all workers in a trades union are ordered to go on strike

   D it is impossible to calculate the marginal revenue product of the workers. [1]

10 A monopsony refers to:

   A a government establishing a national minimum wage

   B a monopoly buyer of labour

   C a monopoly seller of labour

   D an industry where 100% of workers are in a trades union. [1]

11 **(a)** Explain what is meant by a national minimum wage. [12]

   (b) Discuss whether the introduction of a national minimum wage will always be beneficial. [13]

12 Discuss to what extent a trades union will always be able to determine the wage rates that are paid to its members. [25]

9 The macro economy

AL 9(a)–(i)

Key topics

➤ economic growth, economic development and sustainability

➤ national income statistics

➤ classification of countries

➤ employment/unemployment

➤ the circular flow of income

➤ money supply (theory)

➤ Keynesian and Monetarist schools

➤ the demand for money and interest rate determination

➤ policies towards developing economies: policies of trade and aid.

9.1 Economic growth, economic development and sustainability

AL 4(a)

This topic is concerned with:

➤ the definition of economic growth, economic development and sustainability

➤ actual versus potential growth in national output; output gap; business (trade) cycle

➤ factors contributing to economic growth

➤ the costs and benefits of growth, including using and conserving resources.

Definition of economic growth, economic development and sustainability

Economic growth

Economic growth is defined as the increase in the national output of a country over a period of time. It is usually measured in terms of a change in gross domestic product.

> **Exam tip**
>
> It is important to be able to clearly distinguish between two types of growth: actual growth and potential growth in national output.

> **Key term**
>
> Economic growth: an increase in the national output of an economy over a period of time, usually measured through changes in real gross domestic product.

> **Remember**
>
> It is important to understand that the increase in output needs to be an increase in real output, i.e. the increase in output needs to needs to have taken inflation into account.

> **Exam tip**
>
> Whereas economic growth is concerned with increases in the national output of a country, as measured by changes in gross national product, economic development is a wider concept that includes the improvement of education, literacy, health care and life expectancy and the reduction of poverty and inequality.

A Level

Economic development

Economic development is a broader concept than economic growth. It puts the emphasis on the quality of life of people rather than just the material aspects of their standard of living.

Sustainability

Sustainability refers to the ability to use existing resources to satisfy the needs of the present generation without compromising the ability of future generations to satisfy their needs.

Actual versus potential growth in national output; output gap; business (trade) cycle

Actual versus potential growth in national output

It has already been pointed out that it is important to be able to distinguish between actual and potential economic growth.

Actual economic growth occurs when the existing factors of production in an economy are used more efficiently so as to achieve a higher level of output. For example, a higher level of output could be obtained through a reduction in the number of people unemployed in an economy. This can be seen in Figure 9.1. A movement from X, within the production possibility curve AB, to a position of Y, on the production possibility curve, shows actual economic growth.

Potential economic growth occurs when there is a shift outwards of a production possibility curve. In Figure 9.1, this is where the production possibility curve shifts out from AB to CD. This could come about as the result of an increase in the quantity of the factors of production available in an economy and/or an increase in the quality of those factors of production. The position Z was not possible to be reached on the AB production possibility curve, but it can now be reached on the CD production possibility curve. Potential growth therefore comes about as the result of an increase in the potential capacity of an economy, shown by an outward shift of the production possibility curve.

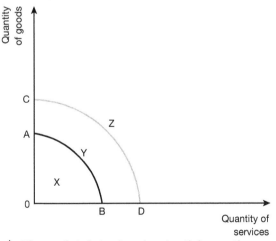

▲ **Figure 9.1** Actual and potential growth

✓ What you need to know

Actual economic growth involves a movement from a position inside a production possibility curve to a position on a production possibility curve, but this will involve an opportunity cost, i.e. if there is an increase in the quantity of goods produced, there will be a decrease in the quantity of goods produced. However, **potential economic growth** involves a shift outwards of a production possibility curve and this will not involve an opportunity cost, i.e. it will be possible to increase both the quantity of goods and the quantity of services produced.

Key terms

Economic development: an increase in the economic wealth of a country so as to benefit all of its people.

Sustainability: a situation where the needs of the present generation can be met without imposing costs on future generations.

Key terms

Actual economic growth: the rate of growth in the national output when all the resources in an economy are fully employed, indicated by a movement from inside to a position on a production possibility curve.

Potential economic growth: the rate at which an economy can grow, resulting from a greater quantity and/or quality of factors of production used in the production process, indicated by a shift outwards of a production possibility curve.

Output gap

The equilibrium level of income in an economy may not necessarily be at the full employment level of income. If there is a situation where the equilibrium income is greater than the full employment equilibrium, i.e. aggregate demand is greater than aggregate supply, this output gap will be called an inflationary gap.

If there is a situation where the equilibrium is less than the full employment equilibrium, i.e. aggregate demand is less than aggregate supply, this output gap will be called a deflationary gap.

The business (trade) cycle

A business cycle or trade cycle refers to fluctuations in output and employment that can occur in an economy over a period of time. The cycle involves four stages:

➤ slump

➤ recovery

➤ boom

➤ recession.

Figure 9.2 shows the business cycle. The wavy line shows the four stages of the cycle and the straight line shows the growth of real GDP over time.

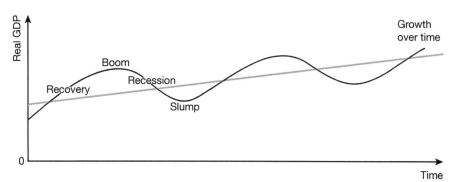

▲ **Figure 9.2** The business (trade) cycle

Make sure you understand how the two axes of a business cycle diagram are labelled. The vertical axis should be labelled 'Real GDP' and the horizontal axis should be labelled 'Time'.

Factors contributing to economic growth

Economic growth can be brought about in an economy by a number of factors, including the following:

➤ an increase in the number of workers

➤ an improvement in the quality of labour, e.g. the acquisition of new or improved skills, as a result of improved education and training, leading to a higher level of productivity

➤ a greater commitment to research and development, in terms of both invention and innovation

➤ an improvement in the state of technology

➤ an increase in investment in capital stock, e.g. machinery and equipment; this can also be called an increase in gross fixed capital formation

➤ a reduction in taxes on the profits of businesses to allow firms to keep more funds that can be used to finance investment

➤ encouragement given to saving, i.e. to bring about an increase in the savings ratio, because a high level of savings will provide the necessary funds to finance investment

➤ a move towards more capital-intensive, and away from labour-intensive, production

➤ increased mobility and flexibility of factors of production

➤ a more efficient allocation of resources

➤ the development of new markets, e.g. for exports

➤ an upturn or recovery in the business, or trade, cycle.

Key terms

Invention: the discovery of new products and new methods of production.

Innovation: the bringing of inventions to the market place.

Be careful not to confuse inventions and innovations. An invention simply refers to the discovery of a new product or a new method of production, but without any application to an economy. An innovation refers to the bringing of these new products and methods of production into economic use.

★ **Exam tip**

Economic growth comes about in an economy not only from an increase in the quantity of factors of production used in the production process, but also from an increase in the quality of those economic resources.

The costs and benefits of growth, including using and conserving resources

Economic growth clearly has benefits for a country, but it is also important to recognise that there can also be costs of growth.

This contrast between the potential benefits and costs of economic growth can be seen in relation to the use or conservation of resources. The use of resources can contribute significantly to economic growth, but it should not be forgotten that many natural resources are finite in supply, i.e. they will eventually run out some time in the future. This is why there is a strong argument in favour of the conservation of resources, stressing that this is a more sustainable approach that takes into account not only the needs of the present generation, but also the needs of future generations.

✓ **What you need to know**

The benefits of economic growth include the following:

➤ an increase in the number of goods and services produced in a country, leading to an increase in the standard of living and a reduction in poverty

➤ economic growth is an indication that an economy is doing well and this could lead to greater confidence and optimism in the long-term prospects of an economy, encouraging investment decisions

➤ it could lead to a decrease in the level of unemployment in an economy

➤ the increase in output, if exported, could lead to a reduction of a deficit in the current account of a country's balance of payments

➤ increased tax revenue could lead to an improvement in an economy's infrastructure, e.g. in relation to education and health care.

The costs of economic growth include the following:

➤ it can sometimes involve a shift away from consumer goods to capital goods which will be good in the long run, but not necessarily in the short run

➤ it may lead to a depletion of natural resources and possible damage to the environment, e.g. in relation to pollution, and so a certain rate of economic growth could be regarded as unsustainable

➤ the benefits of economic growth may not always be shared evenly in an economy

➤ there could be a reduction in the quality of life of people, e.g. if working hours are longer, this will reduce leisure time.

9.2 National income statistics `AL 4(b)`

This topic is concerned with:

➤ Gross Domestic Product(GDP)/Gross National Product (GNP)/Gross National Income (GNI)

➤ National debt (government or public sector debt)

➤ the use of National Income statistics as measures of economic growth and living standards.

Gross Domestic Product (GDP)/Gross National Product (GNP)/Gross National Income (GNI)

National Income is a generic term that can involve a number of different statistics.

Gross Domestic Product (GDP)

Gross Domestic Product (GDP) refers to all that is produced within the geographical boundaries of a country over a particular period of time, usually a year. It does not matter whether the productive assets are owned within the country or are foreign owned.

There are three different ways of measuring the value of a country's GDP:

➤ the output method

➤ the income method

➤ the expenditure method.

However, all three methods will produce the same value because they all measure the flow of income in an economy over a particular period of time.

Net Domestic Product (NDP) is obtained by deducting depreciation, or capital consumption, from GDP.

Key terms

National Income: a general term for the total income of an economy over a particular period of time.

Gross Domestic Product (GDP): the total value of all that has been produced within the geographical boundaries of a country over a given period of time, irrespective of the ownership of the productive assets.

Output method: a way of measuring GDP through the total value of what has been produced in a country over a given period of time.

Income method: a way of measuring GDP through the total income that has been received as a result of producing an output over a given period of time.

Expenditure method: a way of measuring GDP through the total expenditure that has been spent over a given period of time on the output produced.

Net Domestic Product (NDP): the GDP of a country minus depreciation or capital consumption.

Gross National Product (GNP)

This is calculated by adding net property income from abroad to the Gross National Product (GNP) value. Net Property Income from Abroad takes into account the total interest payments, profits and dividends, both entering and leaving a country.

★ Exam tip

If a question requires a discussion of the effects of economic growth, remember to refer to both the costs and benefits of growth.

💡 Remember

There are good arguments for both the use of resources and the conservation of resources. Sustainable economic growth requires that resources are both used and conserved for future use.

✗ Common error

It is fine to argue that a country should aim for as high a rate of economic growth as possible, but you need to recognise that it is possible for a country to have too high a rate of economic growth, e.g. if this leads to significant pollution and to the rapid depletion of scarce resources. It is important that reference is made to the concept of sustainable economic growth.

Key terms

Gross National Product (GNP): the GDP of a country plus the net property income from abroad over a given period of time.

Net Property Income from Abroad: the net inflow and outflow of interest, profits and dividends.

Net National Product (NNP) is obtained by deducting depreciation, or capital consumption, from GNP.

Gross National Income (GNI)

Gross National Income (GNI) refers to the sum of value added by all resident producers, plus any product taxes (minus subsidies) not included in the valuation of output plus net receipts of primary income (compensation of employees and property income) from abroad.

💡 Remember

The figure for net property income from abroad tens to be positive for developed countries and negative for developing countries. This means that in developed countries, the GNP is likely to be greater than the GDP, whereas in developing countries, the GDP is likely to be greater than the GNP.

✓ What you need to know

It is important to distinguish between nominal and real National Income statistics. If the statistics are nominal, i.e. they are at current prices, no adjustment would have been made to take into account the effects of inflation. If the statistics are real, i.e. they are at constant prices, an adjustment would have been made to take into account the effects of inflation. A GDP deflator is used to convert nominal National Income statistics into real GDP.

Key terms

Current prices: data at current prices have not been corrected to take account of inflation.

Constant prices: data at constant prices have been corrected to take account of inflation.

GDP deflator: a price index that is used to remove the effect of price changes, so that statistics can show changes in real output in an economy.

★ Exam tip

Gross National Income (GNI) is now being used more extensively than in the past. For example, the World Bank now uses GNI rather than GNP. The Human Development Index (HDI) now uses GNI rather than GDP.

National debt (government or public sector debt)

The national debt refers to the total of all debt that has been accumulated over a period of time by the government or the public sector of a country.

> ★ **Exam tip**
>
> Make sure you understand that a budget deficit only applies to a particular period of time and is brought about by the excess expenditure over revenue within a financial year, whereas the national debt refers to debt that has accumulated over centuries.

The use of National Income statistics as measures of economic growth and living standards

National Income statistics can be used as measures of economic growth and living standards. In terms of economic growth, GDP has tended to be used and, in particular, changes in real GDP over a period of time. In terms of living standards, GDP per capita has tended to be used and, in particular, changes in real GDP per capita or per head over time.

However, although real GDP per capita has generally been used to compare living standards in different countries, there are limitations in using such data. These include the following:

➤ the hidden, informal or underground economy in a country will not be included in GDP data because the income from such economic activity is not declared

➤ GDP data will only include goods and services that involve transactions through a market, but in many economies there will be examples of non-marketed products where there is no price attached, e.g. DIY (do it yourself) activities

➤ it may be that in some countries, a great deal of the increase in output involves weapons and military equipment, but this will not directly lead to an increase in living standards

➤ there may be an increase in short-run living standards resulting from economic growth, but this will not necessarily lead to a long-term increase in living standards if the economic growth is not sustainable

➤ real GDP can be divided by a country's population to give an average per head or per capita figure, but this average may be very misleading in countries with a very unequal distribution of income and wealth

➤ GDP statistics take into account the quantity of a country's output, but not the quality of the goods and services produced

➤ changes in the exchange rates between different currencies will make it difficult to compare the living standards of people in different countries, so to overcome this problem the comparisons of real GDP per capita are usually expressed in terms of purchasing power parities

➤ GDP data measures the output produced in a country, but it does not measure how that output is produced, e.g. there could be a substantial increase in working hours and a deterioration in working conditions, such as in relation to health and safety

➤ GDP will not include information about political freedom and civil and human rights in different countries and yet these can be regarded as important elements of the quality of life

➤ the level of literacy may vary between countries, making data collection and interpretation inaccurate.

Key term

National debt: the amount of money that a government, or public sector, owes both domestically and abroad which has accumulated over a number of years.

✗ Common error

Don't think that if there is a reduction in the size of a country's budget deficit in one year, then the size of the national debt will decrease. This is not the case. If a country's budget deficit falls, money will still need to be borrowed to pay for this debt, so the size of the country's national debt will continue to rise, even if it increases at a slower rate than before.

★ **Exam tip**

Remember that when living standards are being measured in different countries, it will involve comparisons of real GDP per capita at purchasing power parity.

Be careful not to confuse how GDP can be used to measure economic growth and living standards. If economic growth is being measured, changes in real GDP over a period of time should be used. If living standards are being measured, changes in real GDP per capita at purchasing power parity over a period of time should be used.

9.3 The classification of countries   AL 4(c)

This topic is concerned with:

➤ indicators of living standards and economic development, monetary, non-monetary, Human Development Index (HDI), Measure of Economic Welfare (MEW), Human Poverty Index (HPI), later supplanted by the Multidimensional Poverty Index (MPI), and the Kuznets curve

➤ characteristics of developed, developing and emerging (BRICS) economies: by population growth and structure, income distribution, economic structure, employment composition, external trade and urbanisation in developing economies – comparison of economic growth rates and living standards over time and between countries.

Indicators of living standards and economic development

Traditionally, real GDP per capita at purchasing power parity has been used to compare standards of living in different countries, but the possible limitations of using such statistics have already been referred to. Other indicators are now used, many of which combine both monetary and non-monetary elements.

The Human Development Index (HDI)

The Human Development Index (HDI) is a composite measure that takes into account three elements of living standards:

➤ average income in terms of real gross national income (GNI) per capita or per head at purchasing power parities in US dollars

➤ life expectancy

➤ years of schooling.

There is also an Inequality-adjusted Human Development Index (IHDI). This was introduced in 2010 to take into account the extent of inequality in different countries.

Measure of Economic Welfare (MEW)

The Measure of Economic Welfare (MEW) is a broader measure of living standards and economic development than real GDP per capita and takes into account such elements of living standards as:

➤ leisure hours

➤ crime rates

➤ the value of childcare and looking after the sick and the elderly

➤ depletion of natural resources and changes in the natural environment

➤ levels of pollution.

Human Development Index (HDI): a measure of economic development that uses average income in the form of real GNI per capita at PPP, years of schooling and life expectancy.

Inequality-adjusted Human Development Index (IHDI): the HDI after taking into account the extent of inequality in a country.

Measure of Economic Welfare (MEW): a measure of economic development that adds the value of leisure time and the amount of unpaid work in an economy and subtracts the value of the environmental damage caused by industrial production and consumption.

The Multidimensional Poverty Index (MPI)

The Human Poverty Index (HPI) was used as an indicator of living standards and economic development for many years, but in 2010 it was replaced by the Multidimensional Poverty Index. This uses ten indicators in three categories or dimensions (health, education and living standards):

➤ child mortality

➤ nutrition

➤ years of schooling

➤ child school attendance

➤ provision of electricity

➤ sanitation

➤ quality of drinking water

➤ type of floor

➤ type of cooking fuel

➤ ownership of assets.

Other indicators

A number of other indicators of living standards and economic development have been produced.

One of these is Gross National Happiness (GNH), which includes the following seven forms of wellness:

➤ economic

➤ environmental

➤ physical

➤ mental

➤ workplace

➤ social

➤ political.

There is also a Happy Planet Index that focuses on measuring how well countries are doing in terms of the achievement of sustainable wellbeing for all.

The Kuznets curve

The Kuznets curve shows that as an economy develops over time, economic inequality first increases and then decreases. This is shown in Figure 9.3 on the next page. The vertical axis shows the level of income and wealth inequality, or Gini coefficient, in a country and the horizontal axis shows the economic development, or income per capita, in the country. The curve is an inverted U-shape and shows that as an economy develops initially, the level of inequality increases, but after a certain level of economic development, and per capita income, has been reached, the level of inequality decreases as the benefits of economic growth and economic development extend to a greater number of people in the country.

Key terms

Human Poverty Index (HPI): a measure of the extent of poverty and deprivation in different countries, replaced by the Multidimensional Poverty Index in 2010.

Multidimensional Poverty Index: a measure of the poverty and deprivation in different countries, based on three dimensions and ten indicators.

Key terms

Gross National Happiness (GNH): a measure of the level of happiness in different countries, based on seven forms of wellness.

Happy Planet Index: a measure of the achievement of sustainable wellbeing in different countries.

Kuznets curve: a curve which shows that as an economy develops, economic inequality first increases and then decreases.

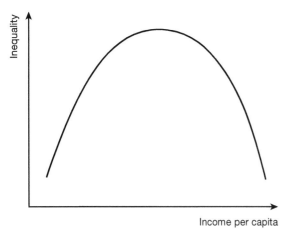

▲ **Figure 9.3** The Kuznets curve

The characteristics of developed, developing and emerging (BRICS) economies

Developed economies, developing economies and emerging economies can be distinguished by a number of key characteristics:

Characteristic	Developed economies	Developing and emerging economies
Population growth	Relatively low birth rates, death rates and infant mortality rates, leading to slow rate of population growth	Relatively high birth rates, death rates and infant mortality rates, leading to high rate of population growth
Population structure	Relatively large ageing population	Relatively large young population
Income distribution	Income relatively more evenly distributed	Income relatively less evenly distributed
Economic structure	Relatively high proportion of output from tertiary sector; proportion of output from primary and secondary sectors declining	Developing countries have a relatively high proportion of output from primary sector (although this will vary enormously); in emerging economies, the tertiary sector will be more significant than in developing economies
Employment composition	Relatively high proportion of employment in tertiary sector; proportion of employment in primary and secondary sectors declining	Developing economies have a relatively high proportion of employment in primary sector (although this will vary enormously); in emerging economies, the tertiary sector will be more significant than in developing economies
External trade	In the past, developed economies relied heavily on the exports of manufactured products, but now there is more reliance on the exports of services	Developing economies have relied heavily on the exports of primary products; in emerging economies, there has been an increase in the exports of manufactured products
Urbanisation	A relatively high proportion of the population live and work in urban areas	In developing economies, a relatively high proportion of the population have lived and worked in rural areas, but the extent of urbanisation is now increasing; in emerging economies, the extent of urbanisation is also increasing

Developed economies: economies characterised by a relatively low birth rate, a relatively high life expectancy, a relatively high level of literacy and a relatively high gross domestic product.

Developing economies: economies characterised by a relatively high birth rate, a relatively low life expectancy, a relatively low level of literacy and a relatively low gross domestic product.

Emerging economies: economies that are rapidly growing and going through a relatively fast rate of economic development, mainly located in parts of Asia, Africa and South America.

Birth rate: the number of live births per thousand of population in a year.

Death rate: the number of deaths per thousand of population in a year.

Infant mortality rate: the number of deaths of infants under one year old per thousand live births in a year.

BRICS: an acronym referring to the emerging economies of Brazil, Russia, India and China; sometimes South Africa is added as a fifth country.

MINT: an acronym referring to the emerging economies of Mexico, Indonesia, Nigeria and Turkey.

CIVETS: an acronym referring to the emerging economies of Colombia, Indonesia, Vietnam, Egypt, Turkey and South Africa.

VISTA: an acronym referring to Vietnam, Indonesia, South Africa, Turkey and Argentina.

★ **Exam tip**

Emerging economies are sometimes collectively referred to by an acronym, such as BRICS, MINT, CIVETS or VISTA. It will be useful in the exam if you could refer to at least a few of these and the countries that are included within them.

X **Common error**

Although the rate of population growth in a developing economy is likely to be higher than in a developed economy, don't assume that this means that all developing economies have relatively large populations and that all developed economies have relatively small populations. This is clearly not the case.

Also, don't assume that all people in a developed economy are rich and that all people in a developing economy are poor. This is not the case. Some people in developed economies will be very poor and some people in developing or emerging economies will be very rich.

⬆ **Raise your grade**

Explain the main characteristics of a developing economy.   [12]

A developing economy will have a number of key characteristics.

It is likely to have a relatively high rate of population growth, resulting from the difference between the birth rate and the death rate.[1] There is also likely to be a relatively high proportion of young people.

Income levels will tend to be lower than in a developed economy[2] and it is likely that a majority of the population will be employed in the primary and secondary sectors, with a lower proportion employed in the tertiary sector compared with a developed economy. A relatively smaller proportion of women are likely to be employed in a developing economy compared with a developed economy.[3]

In terms of external trade, many developing economies will rely on the export of primary products, such as agricultural produce.[4] There is likely to be a high degree of urbanisation taking place in developing economies.[5] Many developing economies have accumulated a great deal of external debt.[6]

A developing economy is likely to have a lower Human Development Index value than a developed economy.[7]

How to improve this answer

1   Although the candidate has referred to the difference between the birth rate and the death rate, they could have pointed out that this refers to the natural increase in the country's population. They could also have pointed out that the actual increase in a country's population will also be affected by the rate of net migration.

2   The candidate could also have pointed out that there is likely to be a relatively high level of inequality in the distribution of that income.

3   The candidate could have indicated some possible reasons for this, such as a variety of social, cultural and religious reasons.

4   The candidate could have pointed out that there is often a high level of price instability associated with such products.

5   The candidate could have pointed out that this rural-urban migration can put a great deal of pressure on resources in the urban areas.

6   This point could have been developed more fully, e.g. by pointing out that in some developing economies, the level of debt can be over 100% of gross national product.

7   It is good that the candidate has referred to the Human Development Index, but they could have developed this point more fully, e.g. by stating the three elements that are included in the HDI and by giving an indication of the difference between the HDI values for developing economies and developed economies, such as stating that whereas a developed economy is likely to have an HDI value of 0.8 or 0.9, a developing economy is likely to have an HDI value of 0.3, 0.4 or 0.5.

Level 2 – 6/13

9.4 Employment/unemployment AL 4(d)

This topic is concerned with:

➤ the size and components of a labour force

➤ labour productivity

➤ full employment and the natural rate of unemployment

➤ the causes of unemployment

➤ the types of unemployment

➤ the consequences of unemployment

➤ the unemployment rate; patterns and trends in (un)employment

➤ the difficulties involved in measuring unemployment

➤ policies to correct unemployment.

The size and components of a labour force

The labour force of a country refers to all the people who are employed or who are actively looking for work. It therefore consists of both the employed and the unemployed in an economy, i.e. it is the number of people in an economy who are available for work.

Another way of expressing the number of people in a country who are available to work is to refer to the working population. The participation rate refers to the proportion of the population that is employed or officially registered as unemployed.

The size of a country's labour force depends on a number of factors, including the following:

➤ the total size of a country's population

➤ the birth rate

➤ the death rate

➤ the school leaving age

➤ the number of people who stay in full-time education after leaving school

➤ the retirement age

➤ the availability and value of transfer payments to those who do not have a job

➤ the availability and cost of childcare

➤ the attitudes in a country to women working

➤ the economic state of a country.

The components of the labour force refer to the sector of employment, e.g. the primary, secondary or tertiary sectors, and the classification of workers by age and gender.

> **Key terms**
>
> **Labour force**: the number of people in a country who are available for work.
>
> **Working population**: the number of people in a country who are currently working or who are actively seeking work.
>
> **Participation rate**: the proportion of a country's population that is either employed or officially registered as unemployed.

> ✗ **Common error**
>
> Make sure you understand that 'labour force' or 'working population' don't only refer to those people in employment. In fact, the two terms include **both** the employed and the unemployed, i.e. all the people in a country who are in work or who are available for work.

Labour productivity

Labour productivity refers to the efficiency of labour in terms of the output per worker per period of time. Levels of productivity can vary for a number of reasons, including the following:

➤ education

➤ training

➤ skills

➤ experience

➤ technical knowledge

➤ level of capital available

➤ working methods and practices

➤ motivation and engagement.

X Common error

Be sure not to confuse 'production' and 'productivity'. Production refers to the total output from a given number of resources, whereas productivity refers to the efficiency of an input, such as labour, into the production process.

Full employment and the natural rate of unemployment

Unemployment refers to a situation where people are able and willing to work, but are unable to find employment.

Full employment generally refers to a situation where everyone in an economy who wants a job has a job, with the exception of those who are frictionally unemployed. This is usually about 4%–5% of the working population.

The natural rate of unemployment stresses the link between the level of unemployment and the level of inflation in an economy. It is that level of unemployment associated with a non-accelerating level of inflation, often referred as NAIRU: the non-accelerating inflation rate of unemployment.

✓ What you need to know

The natural rate of unemployment, or NAIRU, is an equilibrium position where the aggregate demand for labour is equal to the aggregate supply of labour at the current real wage rate. As a result of this situation of equilibrium, there is no upward pressure on the level of prices in an economy, i.e. it is non-accelerating.

It is often associated with monetarist economists, such as Milton Friedman, who argued that the natural rate of unemployment could not be reduced as any increase in aggregate demand would lead to higher inflation and higher unemployment.

★ Exam tip

Full employment does not mean that the unemployment rate in an economy is 0.0% because there will always be an element of frictional unemployment where people are in the process of leaving one job and searching for another.

The causes of unemployment

It is possible to distinguish between two distinct explanations of the cause of unemployment in an economy.

The Monetarist school states that the cause of unemployment is external interference in the labour market which leads to a situation where the supply of labour does not equal the demand for labour in the labour market. For example, minimum wage laws, restrictive trades union practices, taxes on companies, transfer payments in the form of unemployment benefits, occupational immobility, geographical immobility and various rules and regulations all prevent the labour market from clearing.

The Keynesian school states the unemployment in an economy is largely caused by the trade, or business, cycle. The lack of aggregate demand for goods and services reduces the demand for workers to produce those goods and services.

✓ **What you need to know**

It is important to be able to distinguish between these two explanations of the causes of unemployment, with the Monetarists explaining unemployment as the result of excessive interference in the labour market and Keynesians emphasising the cyclical nature of unemployment.

The types of unemployment

Just as it is possible to distinguish between different causes of unemployment, it is also possible to distinguish between different types of unemployment. These include the following:

➤ structural unemployment: changes in the conditions of demand in an economy can lead to some industries declining and so unemployment occurs as a result of such changes in the structure of an economy

➤ regional unemployment: this occurs as the result of structural changes in an economy taking place in particular areas or regions of a country

➤ cyclical unemployment: this is where unemployment is more widespread in an economy, resulting from a downturn or recession in an economy; it is therefore called cyclical as it is related to changes in the trade, or business, cycle, although it is also known as demand-deficient unemployment.

Key terms

Structural unemployment: a situation where unemployment occurs as a result of changes in the structure of an economy.

Regional unemployment: a situation where unemployment is much higher in particular regions of a country.

Cyclical unemployment: a situation where unemployment occurs as a result of adverse changes in the trade, or business, cycle.

Demand-deficient unemployment: another name for cyclical unemployment, stressing the lack of aggregate demand in an economy.

➤ **frictional unemployment**: a situation where at any one moment in time, some people will be between jobs, i.e. they are only unemployed for a relatively short period of time. It is possible to distinguish between three different types of frictional unemployment: search employment, casual employment and seasonal employment

➤ **technological unemployment**: a situation where some people lose their jobs as a result of a move away from labour-intensive methods of production towards capital-intensive methods of production

➤ **real wage unemployment**: a situation where some people are unemployed in an economy because real wages are too high, e.g. as a result of the negotiating strength of trades unions; this is also known as classical unemployment

➤ **voluntary unemployment**: a situation where some people are not willing to work at the current wage level.

Key terms

Frictional unemployment: a situation where unemployment occurs for a relatively short period of time, when people are between jobs.

Search unemployment: a situation where people are prepared to spend time searching for the best possible job available rather than taking the first one offered.

Casual unemployment: a situation where employment in certain occupations is irregular, causing unemployment at certain times.

Seasonal unemployment: a situation where people are unemployed because of a lack of demand for them in certain seasons of the year, such as in the agriculture or tourism industries.

Technological unemployment: a situation where some people lose their jobs as a result of a greater use of technology compared with labour.

Real wage unemployment: a situation where some people are unemployed in an economy because real wages are too high.

Classical unemployment: this is another term for real wage unemployment.

Voluntary unemployment: a situation where some people are not willing to work at the current real wage level.

 Exam tip

Although it is possible to consider unemployment in a generic sense, it is also important to be able to distinguish between different types of unemployment that could occur in an economy and to give appropriate examples to indicate that these differences have been understood.

✓ **What you need to know**

It is important to understand that frictional unemployment can actually be regard as a positive sign in an economy, indicating dynamic change, with some sectors expanding while others are declining.

The consequences of unemployment

Unemployment can have a number of consequences in an economy, including the following:

➤ economic resources are scarce and so any unemployment will involve a waste of scarce resources

➤ an economy with a relatively high level of unemployment will be underperforming because the level of national output produced will be lower than would otherwise have been the case

➤ this will mean that the standard of living and quality of life will be lower than would have been the case if there had been a lower level of unemployment

➤ tax revenue will be less that it would otherwise have been, both in terms of direct taxes, such as income tax, and indirect taxes, such as a goods and services tax

➤ government expenditure is likely to be more, e.g. as a result of spending on transfer payments in the form of unemployment benefits and on the provision of training schemes to give the unemployed the necessary skills to enable them to gain employment

➤ the budget deficit is likely to increase as a result of the fall in revenue and the rise in expenditure

➤ if the unemployment is persistent, the unemployed could find that their skills become outdated, leading to a low level of confidence and motivation as employment becomes increasingly difficult to find (known as the hysteresis effect)

➤ a relatively high level of unemployment can be associated with an increase in social problems in a country, such as an increase in the divorce and crime rates.

> **Key term**
>
> **Hysteresis effect**: the tendency for unemployment to lead to longer-term unemployment as workers find that their skills and knowledge become increasingly outdated.

> **✗ Common error**
>
> Make sure that you read any question in the exam on the topic of unemployment very carefully, especially in terms of distinguishing between the 'causes' and the 'consequences' of unemployment. It is easy to confuse the two words.

The unemployment rate; patterns and trends in (un)employment

It is important to be able to distinguish between the number of people who are unemployed in a country and the unemployment rate. The unemployment rate refers to the total number of people who are unemployed in a country divided by the labour force.

Although economists will be interested in the unemployment rate in an economy at any one moment in time, they will also be interested to discover patterns and trends in employment and unemployment over a longer period of time. They will be particularly interested in finding out whether the trend in the unemployment rate is upward or downward.

> **Key term**
>
> **Unemployment rate**: the number of unemployed people in an economy divided by the labour force.

> **★ Exam tip**
>
> If you are asked to comment in the exam on a pattern or a trend, make sure that you do focus on the overall pattern or trend over time and not simply describe every figure that is included in the data.

> **💡 Remember**
>
> It is important to be able to distinguish between the number of people who are unemployed in an economy and the unemployment rate, which will be expressed as a percentage of the unemployed as a proportion of the labour force.

Difficulties involved in measuring unemployment

There are various difficulties involved in measuring unemployment and this is why there are two different ways of measuring it. One method is the claimant account. This is where the number of people who officially register as unemployed is counted. One difficulty of this method is that not everybody who is able and willing to work actually register as officially unemployed. Another difficulty is that some people who register do so in order to receive certain transfer payments, e.g. unemployment benefits, and yet have no intention to work.

Another method is the labour force survey. This is where a survey is conducted to find out the people who are able and willing to work, but who

> **Key terms**
>
> **Claimant count**: the number of people in an economy who officially register as unemployed.
>
> **Labour force survey**: this includes not only those who are officially registered as unemployed in the claimant count, but those who have not registered, including those who do not qualify for any transfer payment given by the state.

have not officially registered themselves as unemployed, and this number is then added to the claimant count. The difficulty of this method is that not all of those who are able and willing to work, and who have not officially registered as unemployed, will necessarily be identified in the labour force survey. Another difficulty, like any survey, is that it uses a sample of households and there is no guarantee that this ample will be entirely representative.

> ★ **Exam tip**
>
> Make sure you indicate that there are a number of potential difficulties involved in measuring unemployment and that there are two different methods involved in the process of measurement: the claimant count and the labour force survey.

Policies to correct unemployment

There are a number of different policies that can be used to correct unemployment and they are of three types: fiscal policy, monetary policy and supply side policy.

Fiscal policy, when used to correct unemployment in an economy, will involve the reduction of taxation, both direct and indirect, to increase the level of consumption. Taxes on the profits of companies can also be reduced to encourage greater investment. Government expenditure can also be increased. A reduction in taxation and/or an increase in government expenditure will increase the level of aggregate demand in an economy and this is likely to correct unemployment.

Another possible approach to the correction of unemployment is through the use of monetary policy. Interest rates could be lowered and/or the money supply increased to encourage the level of spending in an economy. If the cost of borrowing is reduced, this will encourage people to spend more and save less. Also, if interest rates in an economy are lowered, this is likely to lead to a fall in the exchange rate. If this did happen, it would make a country's exports more price competitive in international markets and this could lead to an increase in the demand for them and therefore an increase in the demand for labour to produce them, correcting unemployment. This assumes that the demand for the exports is price elastic.

Whereas fiscal policy and monetary policy operate to influence the level of aggregate demand in an economy, another way to correct unemployment is through the use of supply side policy measures. Policies could be adopted with the aim of allowing markets to work more efficiently and this would be likely to reduce the level of unemployment. For example, policies to make the labour market more flexible, such as fewer regulations and more restrictions on trades unions, would be likely to bring about a greater level of employment. Government initiatives, such as training and retraining schemes, would also help to make workers more employable.

9.5 The circular flow of income   AL 4(e)

This topic is concerned with:

➤ closed and open economies

➤ the circular flow of income between households, firms, government and the international economy; the multiplier, average and marginal propensities to save and consume

➤ the Aggregate Expenditure (AE) function: meaning, components of AE and their determinants; income determination using AE and income approach; and withdrawal (leakage) and injection approach; inflationary and deflationary gaps; full employment level of income and equilibrium level of income; autonomous and induced investment; the accelerator.

Closed and open economies

A closed economy is one where it is assumed that a country does not engage in trade with any other countries in the world. If there is a movement of incomes between households and firms, then this form of closed economy is known as a two sector economy. If a government is then added, in addition to households and firms, then this form of closed economy is known as a three sector economy.

However, a more realistic approach would be to assume that a country does engage in trade with other countries in the world. In this case, it would be described as an open economy. If the trade in goods and services that are exported from, and imported to, a country is added to the households and firms and to the government, then it is described as a four sector economy.

> **✓ What you need to know**
>
> A two sector economy involves the flow of incomes between households and firms. A three sector economy involves the flow of incomes between households, firms and the government. Both the two sector economy and the three sector economy are examples of a closed economy. A four sector economy involves the flow of incomes between households and firms, the government and the international economy. A four sector economy is an example of an open economy.

The circular flow of income between households, firms, government and the international economy

The circular flow of income refers to movements of income around an economy. At any one time, there will be a number of injections into the economy and a number of withdrawals or leakages out of the economy.

There are three types of injection into the circular flow of income:

➤ investment spending by private sector firms (I)

➤ government spending (G)

➤ income received from exports sold abroad (X).

There are three types of withdrawal or leakage out of the circular flow of income:

➤ savings (S)

➤ taxation (T)

➤ income spent on imports bought from abroad (M).

Key terms

Closed economy: an economy that does not trade with any other countries in the world.

Open economy: an economy that trades with other countries in the world.

Key term

Circular flow of income: the flow or movement of incomes around an economy, involving a mixture of injections into the economy and leakages or withdrawals out of the economy.

Key terms

Injection: spending which adds to the circular flow of income in an economy; this can come from investment (I), government expenditure (G) and expenditure on exports (X).

Withdrawal (or leakage): income which leaks out of the circular flow of income in an economy; this can be as a result of savings (S), taxation (T) and expenditure on imports (M).

The multiplier

The multiplier measures the extent to which an increase in an injection into the circular flow of income of an economy brings about a multiplied effect on the level of income. However, it is also important to understand that an increase in an injection into the circular flow of income is also likely to have an effect on the withdrawals or leakages out of the circular flow of income. Each successive increase in aggregate demand, as a result of the injection into the circular flow of income, will therefore become progressively less.

In order to calculate the size of the multiplier, it is necessary to understand what is meant by the marginal propensity to withdraw. It is also necessary to understand the difference between an average propensity and a marginal propensity.

An average propensity measures the total of, say, consumption or saving, as a proportion of total income. The average propensity to consume (APC) will therefore show the proportion of total income that is spent. The average propensity to save (APS) will show the proportion of total income that is saved.

However, economists are also interested in marginal propensities. A marginal propensity measures the proportion of any change in income that is, say, spent on consumption or saved. The marginal propensity to consume (MPC) will therefore show the proportion of any change in income that is spent on consumption. The marginal propensity to save (MPS) will show the proportion of any change in income that is saved.

The size of the multiplier is calculated through marginal propensities. In a two sector economy, involving only households and firms, it is calculated by 1 divided by the marginal propensity to save, i.e. $\dfrac{1}{MPS}$

In a three sector economy, involving households, firms and the government, it is calculated by 1 divided by the marginal propensity to save + the marginal rate of taxation, i.e. $\dfrac{1}{MPS + MRT}$

In a four sector economy, involving households, firms, government and the international economy, it is calculated by 1 divided by the marginal propensity to save + the marginal rate of taxation + the marginal propensity to import, i.e. $\dfrac{1}{MPS + MRT}$

The size of the multiplier is usually simplified by expressing it as 1 divided by the marginal propensity to withdraw, i.e. $\dfrac{1}{MPW}$

> ★ **Exam tip**
>
> Even if an exam question does not explicitly refer to the multiplier, this does not mean that it should not be included in an answer. In any question on the determination of the level of income in an economy, you should assume that you will need to include an explanation of the multiplier and the multiplier process in your answer.

> ★ **Exam tip**
>
> Make sure, when you are writing about injections into, and leakages or withdrawals from, the circular flow of income, that you are able to give examples of the injections and leakages.

> **Key terms**
>
> **Multiplier:** the amount by which an increase in an injection into the circular flow of income will bring about an increase in the total income in an economy.
>
> **Average propensity to consume (APC):** the proportion of total income that is spent.
>
> **Average propensity to save (APS):** the proportion of total income that is saved.
>
> **Marginal propensity to consume (MPC):** the proportion of any change in income that is spent.
>
> **Marginal propensity to save (MPS):** the proportion of any change in income that is saved.
>
> **Marginal rate of taxation:** the proportion of any change in income that is paid in direct tax.
>
> **Marginal propensity to import:** the proportion of any change in income that is pent on imports.
>
> **Marginal propensity to withdraw:** the total of MPS, MRT and MPM.

The Aggregate Expenditure (AE) function

The meaning of AE; the components of AE and their determinants

Aggregate expenditure (AE), or aggregate demand (AD), means the total expenditure on, and the total demand for, all that is produced in an economy. It can be represented as follows: AE or AD = C + I + G + (X − M).

The first component of AE is consumption. Consumption refers to the expenditure by households in an economy over a period of time. The main influences on consumption include the following:

➤ the level of disposable income in an economy; the consumption function indicates the relationship between income and consumption

➤ the distribution of income and wealth

➤ the rate of interest on borrowing money to finance consumption

➤ the availability of credit

➤ expectations about the future prospects of the economy.

> **✓ What you need to know**
>
> It is possible that consumption actually exceeds income. In this situation, the difference between consumption and income would need to be financed by the use of past savings. This is known as dissaving.
>
> Saving is generally regarded as good for an individual, enabling a person to be able to buy something in the future. However, it can be viewed as potentially bad for an economy as a whole because it is a leakage or withdrawal from the circular flow of income and so could lead to a fall in national income. This contradiction is known as the paradox of thrift.

The second component of AE is investment. Investment refers to the expenditure by firms in an economy over a period of time, such as expenditure on factories, machinery and equipment. The main influences on investment include the following:

➤ the rate of interest on funds to finance investment expenditure

➤ changes in technology

➤ the cost of capital goods

➤ changes in consumer demand

➤ government policies, such as in relation to taxes and subsidies

➤ expectations about the future prospects of the economy.

The third component of AE is government expenditure. Government expenditure refers to the money spent by a government, such as the wages and salaries of those who are employed in the public sector and the money spent on public sector investment projects, such as the building of a new road. The main influences on government spending include the following:

➤ government policies on expenditure decisions

➤ tax revenue

➤ demographic changes.

The fourth component of AE is net exports. Net exports refer to the difference between the value of the exports that leave a country and the value of the

> **✓ What you need to know**
>
> It is important that you understand what is involved in the multiplier process. If there is an injection into the circular flow of income, the increase in national income will be greater than the size of the injection. The extra income creates extra expenditure and this creates extra income, as the multiplier process is based on the idea that one person's spending is another person's income. There will be successive rounds of spending, but in each successive round the multiplier effect will be reduced because of the impact of leakages or withdrawals from the circular flow of income.

> **Key terms**
>
> Dissaving: a situation when consumption exceeds income and so this shortfall has to be financed by using savings that have accumulated in the past.
>
> Paradox of thrift: the contradiction between the potential advantages and the potential disadvantages for an economy of people deciding to save.

imports that enter a country. The main influences on net exports include the following:

➤ a country's GDP

➤ the GDP of other countries

➤ the relative prices of a country's exports

➤ the quality, reliability and reputation of a country's exports

➤ exchange rate movements.

Key term

Aggregate expenditure (AE): the total expenditure on, or demand for, goods and services in an economy; it comprises consumption, investment by private sector firms, government expenditure and net exports. It is also known as aggregate demand.

Income determination using AE and income approach; and withdrawal (leakage) and injection approach

There are two ways to determine the level of income in an economy: one way is by using the AE and income approach and the other way is by using the withdrawal (leakage) and injection approach.

The AE and income approach

The level of equilibrium income in an economy is determined where aggregate expenditure is equal to output. This is shown in Figure 9.4. Real GDP is shown on the horizontal axis and aggregate expenditure is shown on the vertical axis. The 45 degree line shows where planned expenditure equals real national income. The economy is in equilibrium at E where AE crosses the 45 degree line at Y.

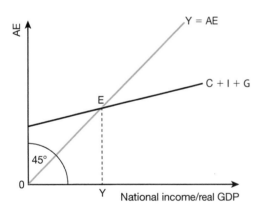

▲ **Figure 9.4** The AE and income approach to income determination

The withdrawal (leakage) and injection approach

The level of income in an economy is also determined where the injections into the circular flow of income of an economy are equal to the withdrawals or leakages. This is shown in Figure 9.5 on the next page. Real GDP is shown on the horizontal axis and the injections and withdrawals are shown on the vertical axis. The economy is in equilibrium at E where injections (J) are equal to withdrawals (W).

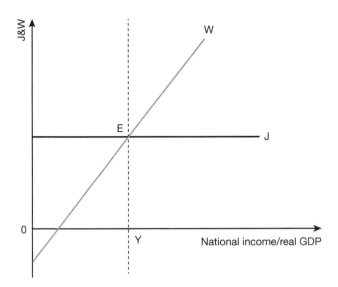

▲ **Figure 9.5** The withdrawal and injection approach to income determination

✓ What you need to know

The two different methods will produce the same level of equilibrium income.

Inflationary and deflationary gaps; the full employment level of income and the equilibrium level of income

It is important to understand that an equilibrium level of income in an economy may not necessarily be at the full employment level of income.

Inflationary gap and the level of income

An inflationary gap shows a situation where the equilibrium level of income in an economy is greater than the full employment level of income, i.e. aggregate demand is greater than aggregate supply.

This can be seen in Figure 9.6. At the equilibrium level of income of $0Y$, where the 45 degree line $(AD = Y)$ intersects with AD_0, the level of aggregate demand in the economy is actually AD_1, i.e. the level of aggregate demand exceeds the level of output at full employment, causing upward pressure on prices. The inflationary gap is shown by the vertical distance between AD_0 and AD_1.

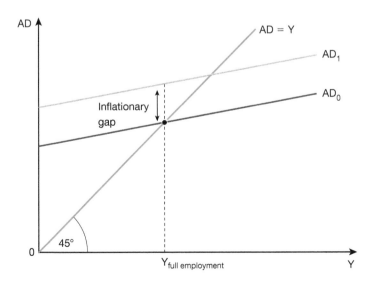

▲ **Figure 9.6** Inflationary gap

Deflationary gap and the level of income

A deflationary gap shows a situation where the equilibrium level of income in an economy is less than the full employment level of income, i.e. aggregate supply is greater than aggregate demand.

This can be seen in Figure 9.7. The full employment level of income is at $0Y$, determined by where the 45-degree line intersects with AD_1. However, the level of aggregate demand in the economy is shown by AD_0 and this is less than AD_1. The equilibrium level of income is at $0Y_1$, less than the full employment level of income. A deflationary gap therefore occurs when the level of aggregate demand in an economy is below the level of output at full employment. The deflationary gap is shown by the vertical distance between AD_0 and AD_1.

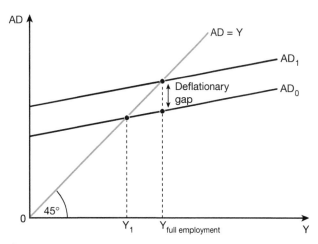

▲ **Figure 9.7** Deflationary gap

Common error

Don't assume that the equilibrium level of income and the full employment level of income in an economy will be the same. This will not necessarily be the case. It is possible that an output gap in the form of either an inflationary gap or a deflationary gap could occur.

Autonomous and induced investment; the accelerator

It is important to be able to distinguish between two different types of investment: autonomous investment and induced investment.

Autonomous investment

This refers to investment that is not the result of any changes in the level of national income in an economy, i.e. it is independent of any such changes.

Induced investment

This refers to investment that is the result of any changes in the level of national income in an economy, i.e. it is dependent on any such changes.

Key terms

Inflationary gap: a situation where the level of aggregate demand in an economy is greater than the level of aggregate supply at full employment, causing a rise in the general level of prices in the economy.

Deflationary gap: a situation where the level of aggregate demand in an economy is less than the level of aggregate supply at full employment, causing unemployment in the economy.

Key terms

Equilibrium level of income: a situation where the aggregate demand for goods and services is equal to the aggregate supply of goods and services in an economy.

Full employment level of income: a situation where the aggregate demand for goods and services is equal to the aggregate supply of goods and services in an economy where there is full employment of resources, i.e. real GDP = potential GDP.

Autonomous investment: capital investment that is not related to changes in the level of national income in an economy.

Induced investment: capital investment that is related to changes in the level of national income in an economy.

The accelerator

The concept of the accelerator is based on the relationship between changes in the level of national income in an economy and changes in induced investment. It assumes that there is a fixed capital : output ratio and states that investment is a function of a change in national income.

It is important to understand that the accelerator is concerned with the relationship between investment and the rate of change of output. It is not the level of output that is important, but the rate of change of that output.

✗ **Common error**

Be careful not to confuse the multiplier and the accelerator. The multiplier shows the effect of an injection on the level of national income in an economy, whereas the accelerator shows the effect of the rate of growth of demand on the level of investment.

9.6 Money supply (theory)   AL 4(f)

This topic is concerned with:

➤ the quantity theory of money (MV = PT)

➤ broad and narrow money supply

➤ sources of money supply in an open economy (commercial banks and credit creation, the role of a central bank, deficit financing, quantitative easing, total currency flow)

➤ the transmission mechanism of monetary policy.

The quantity theory of money

The quantity theory of money shows the relationship between the money supply, the general level of prices and the level of output in an economy. It is usually expressed in terms of MV = PT, where:

➤ M is the quantity of money or the money supply

➤ V is the velocity of circulation, i.e. the number of times money changes hands

➤ P is the general price level

➤ T is the number of transactions or output.

✓ **What you need to know**

It is assumed that V (the velocity of circulation of money) and T (the number of transactions) are constant over a period of time. In this situation, M (the quantity of money or money supply) and P (the general level of prices) are directly linked, although there is likely to be a time lag before this is seen of perhaps 12, 18 or 24 months.

However, the theory has been challenged, especially as to whether it is correct to assume that V and T will be constant over a period of time. It has also been challenged for being less of a theory and more of an identity that is necessarily true, i.e. MV represents total spending in an economy and PT represents the total money received for the goods and services. In essence, it is the same situation looked at from different perspectives.

Key terms

Accelerator: a way of calculating the effect of a change in national income on investment in an economy, i.e. the extent to which the level of investment depends on the rate of growth of aggregate demand.

Capital : output ratio: the amount of capital required to produce a particular level of output.

Key term

Quantity theory of money: the MV = PT equation shows that changes in the general price level (P) are directly proportional to changes in the money supply (M).

Broad and narrow money supply

The money supply refers to the total amount of money in an economy at any one time. It includes both broad money supply and narrow money supply.

A broad money supply reflects the total purchasing power in an economy at a particular time. It is sometimes called M3 or M4 and includes not only notes and coins but also a wide range of deposits held with different financial services providers.

A narrow money supply is mainly the cash in an economy at a particular time. It is sometimes called M0 or M1 and mainly includes the notes and coins held by people and in balances with financial institutions. It is also sometimes known as the monetary base.

Key terms

Money supply: the amount of money available to the general public and the banking system in an economy at any one time.

Broad money supply: a measure of the stock of money which reflects the total purchasing power in an economy.

Narrow money supply: a measure of the stock of money in an economy which is mainly cash, i.e. notes and coins.

Monetary base: the cash held by the general public and by the banking system, including the balances of the financial institutions with the central bank of a country.

⭐ **Exam tip**

There are no agreed definitions of broad and narrow money supply and the situation will vary from one country to another in terms of how these are expressed in particular financial systems.

The sources of money supply in an open economy

Commercial banks and credit creation

Financial institutions, such as commercial banks, are able to create 'new' money as a result of additional cash deposits. This is termed credit creation. It is understood that only a small proportion of such deposits need to be available to give out to people, allowing the institutions to, perhaps, have a cash ratio of 10%, enabling them to lend out the remaining 90%. This process is known as fractional reserve banking and the ratio of new money created to the initial money deposited is known as the credit multiplier.

Key terms

Fractional reserve banking: the idea that financial institutions only need to keep a fraction of their reserves in cash, enabling them to lend the remainder.

Credit multiplier: the ratio of the new money created to the size of the initial deposit.

Key terms

Commercial bank: a financial institution in which individuals and firms can save money and obtain loans.

Credit creation: the process by which financial institutions are able to use some of the money deposited to expand their lending.

Cash ratio: the ratio of the total liabilities of a financial institution that is held in the form of cash reserves.

The role of a central bank

A central bank might want to control the ability of **commercial banks** to lend money, such as through open market operations. This is the process of buying and selling government securities, i.e. bonds or shares that are issued by a government.

✓ **What you need to know**

If a central bank wants to encourage bank lending, it will buy government securities. If a central bank wants to discourage bank lending, it will sell government securities.

✗ **Common error**

Be careful not to confuse a commercial bank and a central bank. A commercial bank has direct dealings with individuals and firms, whereas a central bank has a broad oversight of the entire banking system of a country and can come to the rescue of commercial banks by providing funds in its capacity as a lender of last resort. A central bank is also likely to have responsibility for the issuing of notes and coins and for the setting of key interest rates in an economy.

Deficit financing

A government can plan for a budget surplus, a balanced budget or a budget deficit. If there is a budget deficit, this can be financed by the government borrowing money from the central bank and/or the commercial banks. This will lead to an increase in the money supply in the economy. The method is termed deficit financing.

Quantitative easing

Quantitative easing refers to a process whereby a government, through the central bank, buys securities, such as bills and bonds, creating more liquidity in the financial system, leading to an increase in bank deposits.

★ **Exam tip**

It would be useful if you understood how quantitative easing has been used by a number of countries since the financial crisis of 2007-2008 to stimulate economic activity, increasing the level of aggregate demand in such countries and so helping the countries to get out of a situation of recession.

Total currency flow

Total currency flow refers to the total inflow and outflow of money as a result of a range of international monetary transactions which are shown in the balance of payments.

The transmission mechanism of monetary policy

This refers to the process connecting changes in the stock or supply of money in an economy to changes in the level of income and output. This monetary transmission mechanism shows how increased lending by financial

Key term

Central bank: the main bank in a country that is responsible for the monitoring and oversight of the banking system.

Key terms

Budget deficit: a situation where projected revenue is less than planned expenditure.

Deficit financing: the different ways in which a government could finance a budget deficit where there is a gap between public revenue and public expenditure.

Quantitative easing: the process whereby the government of a country deliberately buys bonds and bills in order to increase the money supply in an economy.

Key terms

Total currency flow: the total inflow and outflow of money as a result of international transactions with other countries, which are shown in the balance of payments.

Transmission mechanism: the theoretical process which connects changes in the stock of money in an economy to changes in the level of income and output.

institutions leads to an increase in both investment and consumption. This then leads to an increase in the level of aggregate demand and then finally to an increase in the general level of prices in an economy.

Figure 9.8 shows the transmission mechanism of monetary policy.

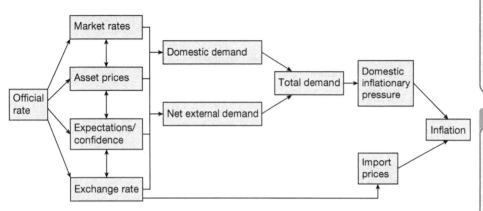

▲ **Figure 9.8** Transmission mechanism of monetary policy

 Raise your grade

Discuss how useful is the quantity theory of money in explaining the existence of inflation in an economy. [13]

The quantity theory of money, MV = PT, is very useful in explaining the existence of inflation in an economy.[1] It shows that there is a direct link between the money supply in an economy and the general level of prices in that economy.[2]

However, although the theory is useful in explaining how inflation can come about in an economy, it has been criticised. It assumes that T is constant over a period of time, but this may not always be the case.[3]

The theory has also been challenged for being more of an identity than a theory, in that it could be argued that MV and PT are essentially the same. MV represents total spending in an economy and PT represents the total money received for the goods and services.[4]

Therefore, it can be seen that while the quantity theory of money is quite useful in explaining the existence of inflation in an economy, and is an important element in the Monetarist approach, stressing the link between changes in an economy's money supply and changes in the general level of prices in that economy, it is not without its critics. This is especially the case with regard to the assumptions on which the theory is based and the fact that some economists have argued that it is not really a theory at all, but simply a situation of looking at the same thing from two different angles.[5]

How to improve this answer

1 The candidate has given the quantity theory of money, MV = PT, but has not attempted to explain what M, V, P and T represent.

2 The candidate has pointed out that there is a direct link between the money supply in an economy and the general level of prices in that economy, but has not emphasised that there is likely to be a time lag involved of 12, 18 or 24 months before the effect can be noticed.

3 The candidate has pointed out that one of the assumptions on which the theory is based is that VT is constant over a period of time, which may not necessarily be the case, but they could also have made the point that another assumption of the theory is that it is assumed that V is constant over a period of time.

4 This is a good point that the candidate has made.

5 This is quite a good conclusion that does address the 'how useful' aspect of the question.

Level 3 – 7/12

9.7 Keynesian and monetarist schools AL 4(g)

This topic is concerned with:

➤ different theoretical approaches to how the macro economy functions.

The Keynesian school

The Keynesian approach to Economics is associated with the economist John Maynard Keynes (1883–1946). He believed that an economy, if left to market forces, would not necessarily achieve a full employment level of GDP and so it would sometimes be necessary for a government to intervene in an economy to influence the level of economic activity, especially in relation to a reduction in the level of unemployment. The concept of the multiplier was very important in this support for government intervention. If aggregate demand in an economy was too low, it was the role of the government to intervene in order to stimulate the level of demand. Keynesians tend to favour the use of fiscal policy as an instrument to influence the level of demand in an economy.

The Monetarist school

The Monetarist approach to Economics is associated with the economist Milton Friedman (1912–2006). He believed that it was generally better if an economy was left to market forces rather than relying on extensive government intervention. Whereas Keynes was primarily concerned with reducing the level of unemployment in an economy, Friedman was mainly concerned with reducing the level of inflation. Friedman stated that "inflation is always and everywhere a monetary phenomenon". Friedman believed that

Key terms

Keynesian approach: an approach to the macro economy based on the views of the economist John Maynard Keynes (1883–1946) who believed that unemployment was the main economic problem that needed to be overcome.

Monetarist approach: an approach to the macro economy based on the views of a number of economists, of which the best known are Milton Friedman (1912–2006) and Friedrich Hayek (1899–1992), who believed that inflation was the main economic problem that needed to be overcome.

if a government attempted to reduce unemployment through an increase in spending, it would be most likely to bring about a higher rate of inflation. Monetarists tend to favour the use of monetary policy as a macroeconomic policy instrument, especially through reductions in the growth of the money supply in an economy.

> **Remember**
>
> The Keynesian approach stresses the importance of bringing down the level of unemployment in an economy, whereas the Monetarist approach stresses the importance of bringing down the level of inflation.
>
> Also, remember that whereas Keynesians generally favour government intervention to solve economic problems, monetarists are generally more inclined to believe that economic problems are better solved through the operation of market forces.

> **Exam tip**
>
> Make sure that you are able to compare and contrast these two different theoretical approaches to how the macro economy functions.

9.8 The demand for money and interest rate determination `AL 4(h)`

This topic is concerned with:

➤ Liquidity preference theory.

The demand for money in an economy, and the determination of interest rates, can be analysed through the liquidity preference theory.

This Keynesian approach to the demand for money and the determination of interest rates is based on the fact that there are three possible motives for holding money.

Firstly, there is the transactions demand for money. This is where money is used to pay for everyday purchases. This is an active balance and is interest inelastic.

Secondly, there is the precautionary demand for money. This is where money is used to pay for unexpected expenses. It is also an active balance that is interest inelastic.

Thirdly, there is the speculative demand for money. This is where money is used to buy government bonds. Unlike the transactions and the precautionary demand for money, it is regarded as an idle balance and it is interest elastic. An important influence on the demand for a bond is the yield; this is the annual income obtained from the bond as a proportion of its current market price. The price of government bonds and the rate of interest will move in opposite directions. Whereas the transactions demand for money and the precautionary demand for money is price inelastic, shown by a straight vertical line, the speculative demand for money is interest elastic, shown by a downward sloping demand curve, i.e. as the rate of interest falls there will be a rise in the demand for money. It is even possible, at a relatively low rate of interest, the liquidity preference (or demand) curve could become horizontal. At this point, the demand for money is perfectly elastic and this is known as the liquidity trap.

> **Key terms**
>
> Liquidity preference: the relationship between the quantity of money that people wish to hold and the rate of interest.
>
> Active balance: the demand for money that is not responsive to changes in the rate of interest; it applies to both the transactions and the precautionary demand for money.
>
> Idle balance: the demand for money that is responsive to changes in the rate of interest; it applies to the speculative demand for money.
>
> Yield: the annual income that is obtained from a bond as a proportion of its market price.
>
> Transactions demand for money: money that is demanded to pay for everyday purchases; it is an active balance that is interest inelastic.

> **Key terms**
>
> Precautionary demand for money: money that is demanded to pay for unexpected expenses; it is an active balance that is interest inelastic.
>
> Speculative demand for money: money that is demanded to pay for bonds; it is an idle balance that is interest elastic.

This can be seen in Figure 9.9 below. The transactions and precautionary demand for money can be shown by the vertical straight line at M. The speculative demand for money curve is downward sloping. The demand, or liquidity preference, curve D is the combination of the three motives for holding money. Eventually, at a low rate of interest, the demand curve will become perfectly elastic and horizontal and at this point it is known as the liquidity trap.

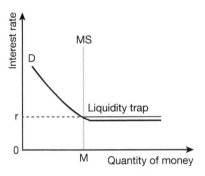

▲ **Figure 9.9** The liquidity preference curve

Key term

Liquidity trap: a situation at relatively low rates of interest when changes in the money supply will have no effect on the rate of interest and where the demand for money is perfectly elastic, i.e. totally unresponsive to any changes in the rate of interest.

✓ What you need to know

The demand for money is based on three motives for holding money. The transactions demand and the precautionary demand for money are both active balances and in both cases will not respond to changes in interest rates. The speculative demand for money, on the other hand, is an idle, rather than an active, balance and is interest elastic, i.e. it will respond to changes in interest rates.

It is important you understand that the price of bonds and the rate of interest will move in opposite directions, i.e. there is an inverse relationship between them. If the interest rate rises, this will reduce the desire to hold money and the price of the bonds will fall. If the interest rate falls, there will be less of an incentive to switch out of money into other assets and the price of bonds will rise.

Whereas the transactions and the precautionary demand for money are interest inelastic, the speculative demand for money is elastic and so the demand curve for money is downward sloping, until at low rates of interest it becomes perfectly elastic, shown by a horizontal demand curve. This is known as the liquidity trap.

✗ Common error

Make sure you fully understand the speculative demand for money. There are three aspects that need to be stressed:

➤ whereas the transactions and the precautionary demand for money are active balances, the speculative demand for money is an idle balance

➤ whereas the transactions and the precautionary demand for money are interest inelastic, the speculative demand for money is interest elastic

➤ the price of bonds and the rate of interest are inversely related, i.e. when one rises, the other falls.

9.9 Policies towards developing economies: policies of trade and aid

AL 4(i)

This topic is concerned with:

➤ types of aid, the nature of dependency

➤ trade and investment, the role of multinationals and Foreign Direct Investment (FDI)

➤ external debt, the role of the IMF and the World Bank

➤ the impact of corruption and the importance of the legal framework in an economy.

Types of aid and the nature of dependency

One policy approach towards developing economies is the provision of aid. There are various types of aid from developed to developing economies, including different types of financial grants and loans. Sometimes the aid is bilateral aid, involving just two countries, and sometimes the aid is multilateral aid, involving a number of different countries and/or agencies.

It is possible to distinguish between the following types of aid:

➤ humanitarian emergency assistance

➤ food

➤ investment projects

➤ military assistance.

There have, however, been a number of problems in relation to aid and it has been criticised as contributing towards a situation of dependency where developing countries have become, to some extent, dependent on the help of the governments of other countries and/or international agencies.

Key terms

Aid: the process of developed economies and/or international agencies providing different types of financial support to developing economies.

Bilateral aid: aid that involves just two countries.

Multilateral aid: aid that involves a number of countries and/or international agencies.

Dependency: a situation in which one country depends on the help of another country and/or an international agency, or a number of countries and/or international agencies.

✓ What you need to know

There are a number of potential problems of the aid given to developing economies, including the following:

➤ some aid has been in the form of financial support for investment projects that have been relatively unsuccessful once they have started operation

➤ some of the aid has been 'tied', i.e. there have been conditions attached to the grants and loans given to the developing economies

➤ there is some evidence of an element of corruption in a few countries where the aid has been concentrated in the hands of a few

➤ some aid has been counterproductive and has made a situation worse, e.g. the provision of food has reduced prices, making it more difficult for the farmers to survive

➤ some of the financial aid has involved the payment of interest, putting many countries in a state of debt.

★ Exam tip

Make sure that you are aware of the different types and forms of aid that can exist and that you are able to consider both the potential advantages and the potential disadvantages of aid.

Remember

Although there are a number of potential advantages of aid to developing economies, there is a chance that it will create a situation of dependency.

Trade and investment, the role of multinationals and Foreign Direct Investment (FDI)

Trade and investment

The theory of comparative advantage shows that all countries can benefit from free trade as long as there are differences in the opportunity cost ratios of production in the different countries. International trade will therefore lead to an increase in world output and this will lead to an improvement in the standard of living and quality of life, including developing economies. The World Trade Organisation, consisting of 164 member countries, exists to promote trade between countries. It deals with the global rules of trade between countries and its main function is to ensure that trade flows as smoothly, predictably and feely as possible.

It will also be useful if investment is encouraged in developing economies. Investment is often relatively low in developing economies because of the lack of savings (the savings ratio tends to be lower in developing economies compared with developed economies) and/or the lack of financial institutions with the funds to substantially support investment. However, if investment can be encouraged, with the help of developed economies and/or international agencies, it may be possible to create a virtuous circle.

Key terms

World Trade Organisation: an international organisation, established in 1995, replacing the General Agreement on Tariffs and Trade (GATT) which had been set up in 1948, to promote free trade in the world through the reduction of trade barriers; it establishes, monitors, reinforces and regulates the rules of trade between countries.

Virtuous circle: the links between an increase in investment, an increase in productivity, an increase in income and an increase in savings.

Although the encouragement of trade between developing economies and developed economies should be encouraged, there are potential problems with such trade, including the following:

➤ many developing economies rely on the production of primary products and the prices of these tend to be generally lower than those of manufactured products

➤ the prices of primary products also tend to be less stable than those of manufactured products

➤ the demand for primary products tends to be more income inelastic than the demand for manufactured products.

The role of multinationals and foreign direct investment (FDI)

Investment in developing economies can come about through the decisions of multinationals to locate in such countries, such as by building a factory, and this is known as foreign direct investment (FDI).

The potential advantages of a multinational locating in a developing economy include the following:

➤ there can be an increase in employment, creating more income and through the multiplier effect, this can lead to an increase in the standard of living and quality of life

➤ they can provide more choice for consumers

➤ they can lead to an increase in the revenue received from taxation, such as from taxes on the profits of the multinationals

➤ the multinationals can bring technical knowledge which could lead to an increase in levels of productivity in the developing economy

➤ they can contribute to an increase in economic growth

➤ if some of the output produced is exported to other countries, this could lead to an improvement in the current account of the balance of payments.

However, there are also potential disadvantages of a multinational locating in a developing economy, including the following:

➤ they may use capital-intensive, rather than labour-intensive, methods of production, with the result that any increase in employment will be relatively small

➤ the jobs that are created may be relatively unskilled (such jobs are sometimes called 'screwdriver' jobs)

➤ although some of the profit made may be taxed by the developing economy, much of it will be repatriated to the home country and not re-invested in the local economy

➤ the operation of the multinationals may lead to damage to the environment, in the form of additional pollution, and they may contribute to the further depletion of natural resources

➤ the multinationals may attempt to influence the government of the country, giving rise to the possibility of corruption.

External debt and the role of the IMF and the World Bank

External debt

The existence of external debt can be a major obstacle to the economic growth and economic development of a country. The repayment of the debt, including any interest payments, can become a major burden for a country, despite the efforts of such organisations as Jubilee 2000 and Make Poverty History to cancel or reschedule the debt.

There is also an opportunity cost involved with external debt, as there is with any form of expenditure. The funds that are being used to pay the debt could have been used in other ways that would have been more productive in terms of the economic development of a country, such as spending on health care and education.

The role of the International Monetary Fund (IMF)

The International Monetary Fund (IMF) was established in 1944 to promote international trade through such measures as providing financial support in the form of a loan to help a country overcome, or at least reduce, a deficit in the current account of the balance of payments. It has 189 member countries.

The role of the World Bank

The World Bank was established in 1944 to provide finance to countries, particularly developing economies, to help with various kinds of capital investment projects. It actually consists of five agencies, the most well known of which is the International Bank for Reconstruction and Development (IBRD). It has 180 member countries.

The impact of corruption and the importance of the legal framework in an economy

It has already been pointed out, in relation to the potential disadvantages of multinationals, that they may try to influence the decisions of a government, giving rise to the possibility of corruption. Corruption would appear to have occurred in a number of countries, although its impact will vary a great deal from one country to another. It can undermine the process of economic development in a country, leading to a lower rate of economic growth than would otherwise be the case.

One way to reduce the impact of corruption is to ensure that there is a respected and well established legal framework in an economy which will help to minimise the opportunities for corruption to take place. An economy will be better able to function effectively if legal rights, especially property and contractual rights, are legally enforced and protected. The International Monetary Fund has stated that those countries with strong and established legal frameworks have performed better, in terms of economic growth and development, than those countries without such legal frameworks.

> **Key terms**
>
> **International Monetary Fund (IMF)**: an international organisation that offers advice to governments and central banks and provides loans to countries in severe economic difficulties.
>
> **World Bank**: an international organisation that provides loans to developing economies to facilitate capital investment.

Revision checklist

I can:

- ➤ understand what is meant by economic growth ☐
- ➤ be clear about the meaning of economic development and of how it differs from economic growth ☐
- ➤ understand what is meant by sustainability ☐
- ➤ distinguish between the actual and the potential growth in national output ☐
- ➤ understand what is meant by an output gap
- ➤ understand what is meant by a business (trade) cycle and the different stages that the cycle passes through ☐
- ➤ understand the different possible factors contributing to economic growth ☐
- ➤ distinguish clearly between the costs and benefits of economic growth ☐
- ➤ contrast the use and the conservation of resources ☐
- ➤ understand the differences between GDP, GNP and GNI ☐
- ➤ be clear about the meaning of national (government or public sector) debt ☐
- ➤ appreciate the use of National Income statistics as measures of economic growth and living standards ☐
- ➤ be clear about the distinction between monetary and non-monetary indicators of living standards ☐
- ➤ be clear about the different indicators of living standards and economic development: the HDI, the MEW, the HPI and the MPI ☐
- ➤ understand what is shown by the Kuznets curve ☐
- ➤ distinguish between the characteristics of developed, developing and emerging (BRICS) economies by: population growth and structure, income distribution, economic structure, employment composition, external trade and urbanisation in developing economies ☐
- ➤ make comparisons of economic growth rates and living standards over time and between countries ☐
- ➤ understand the size and the components of a labour force ☐
- ➤ explain what is meant by productivity ☐
- ➤ understand the meaning of full employment ☐
- ➤ understand the meaning of the natural rate of unemployment ☐
- ➤ be clear about the different possible causes of unemployment in an economy ☐
- ➤ differentiate between the different types of unemployment in an economy ☐
- ➤ be clear about the possible consequences of unemployment in an economy ☐
- ➤ be clear about what is meant by the unemployment rate in an economy ☐
- ➤ discern patterns and trends in unemployment data ☐
- ➤ appreciate the possible difficulties involved in measuring unemployment in a country ☐
- ➤ understand the different policies that can be used to correct unemployment ☐
- ➤ distinguish between closed and open economies ☐

- ➤ be clear about the circular flow of income between households, firms, government and the international economy ☐
- ➤ understand the meaning and significance of the multiplier ☐
- ➤ distinguish between average and marginal propensities to save and consume ☐
- ➤ understand what is meant by the aggregate expenditure (AE) function ☐
- ➤ be clear about the meaning of the components of AE and their determinants ☐
- ➤ understand the theory of income determination using the AE and income approach ☐
- ➤ understand the theory of income determination using the withdrawal (leakage) and injection approach ☐
- ➤ be clear about what is meant by an inflationary gap ☐
- ➤ be clear about what is meant by a deflationary gap ☐
- ➤ distinguish between the full employment level of income and the equilibrium level of income ☐
- ➤ be clear about the difference between autonomous and induced investment ☐
- ➤ understand the meaning and significance of the accelerator ☐
- ➤ understand what is meant by the quantity theory of money $(MV = PT)$ ☐
- ➤ distinguish between broad money and narrow money ☐
- ➤ understand the different sources of money in an open economy: commercial banks and credit creation, the role of a central bank, deficit financing, quantitative easing, total currency flow ☐
- ➤ be clear about the meaning of the transmission mechanism of monetary policy ☐
- ➤ understand the different theoretical approaches of the Keynesian and Monetarist schools to how the macro economy functions ☐
- ➤ be clear about the demand for money and interest rate determination though the liquidity preference theory ☐
- ➤ appreciate the different types of aid ☐
- ➤ understand the nature of dependency ☐
- ➤ be clear about the potential importance of trade and investment ☐
- ➤ understand the role of multinationals in economies and of the potential importance of foreign direct investment (FDI) ☐
- ➤ be clear about the significance of a country's external debt ☐
- ➤ be clear about the role of the IMF ☐
- ➤ be clear about the role of the World Bank ☐
- ➤ understand the potential impact of corruption in an economy ☐
- ➤ appreciate the importance of the legal framework in an economy. ☐

? Exam-style questions

1   Sustainability can be defined as a situation where:

    A   actual growth is always greater than potential growth

    B   the economic growth of a country is never more than 2% per annum

    C   the needs of the present generation are met without affecting the needs of future generations.

    D   the standard of living is guaranteed to be higher in the future than it is today.   [1]

2   The four stages of the business (trade) cycle are:

    A   boom, output, recession, slump

    B   recovery, boom, recession, depression

    C   slump, inflation, boom, recession

    D   slump, recovery, boom, recession.   [1]

3   Net Domestic Product is obtained by:

    A   adding depreciation, or capital consumption, to GDP

    B   adding net property income to GDP

    C   deducting depreciation, or capital consumption, from GDP.

    D   deducting the rate of inflation from GDP.   [1]

4   The MPI is the:

    A   measure of poverty index

    B   monetary poverty index

    C   multidimensional poverty index

    D   multinational production index.   [1]

5   When people are between jobs, it is known as:

    A   cyclical unemployment

    B   demand-deficient unemployment

    C   frictional unemployment

    D   structural unemployment.   [1]

6   The aggregate expenditure function is:

    A $C + I + G + (X + M)$

    B $C + I + G + (X - M)$

    C $C + I + T + S$

    D $C + I + X + M$ [1]

7   The multiplier is calculated by 1 divided by:

    A   APS + ART + APM

    B   MPS + MPC + MPM

    C   MPS + MRT + MPM

    D   MPS + MRT + MPX   [1]

8   The quantity theory of money is:

    A $MP = VT$

    B $MT = VP$

    C $MV = PT$

    D $TV = PM$ [1]

9   The speculative demand for money is:

    A   an active balance with interest elastic demand

    B   an active balance with interest inelastic demand

    C   an idle balance with interest elastic demand

    D   an idle balance with interest inelastic demand.   [1]

10   A liquidity trap shows the situation when the demand for money is:

    A   perfectly elastic

    B   perfectly inelastic

    C   relatively elastic

    D   relatively inelastic.   [1]

11   **(a)** Explain what is meant by structural unemployment.   [12]

    (b) Discuss whether frictional unemployment is likely to have a more damaging effect on an economy than cyclical unemployment.   [13]

12   Discuss whether a decision by a multinational to produce in a country will always be of benefit to that country.   [25]

Government macro intervention

Key topics

➤ government macro policy aims

➤ inter-connectedness of problems

➤ effectiveness of policy options to meet all macroeconomic objectives.

10.1 Government macro policy aims

AL 5(a)

This topic is concerned with:

➤ inflation

➤ balance of payments

➤ exchange rates

➤ unemployment

➤ economic growth and development.

Governments usually have a wide range of aims in relation to macroeconomic policy, but in most cases they tend to concentrate on a combination of these five aims.

Inflation

One aim is in relation to changes in the general level of prices in an economy over a period of time. Governments generally aim for a relatively low and stable rate of inflation, although what might be considered a relatively low and stable rate of inflation is likely to vary from one country to another.

Balance of payments

A government would aim for the balance of payments to be in equilibrium over a period of time. This means that the inflows of money equal the outflows of money taking into account all aspects of the balance of payments.

Exchange rates

Governments generally aim to avoid large fluctuations in the external value of the currency. This will be easier to achieve with a fixed exchange rate where the government intervenes in the foreign exchange markets on a regular basis in order to maintain a particular rate of exchange with other currencies. If there is a floating exchange rate, this will be more difficult to achieve because the rate of exchange with other currencies will be determined by changes in the demand for, and the supply of, the currency on foreign exchange markets. However, some governments aim to reduce any large fluctuations in a floating exchange rate system through a degree of intervention and this is known as a managed float.

Unemployment

Governments aim to achieve full employment, although this may vary from one country to another. Full employment is defined as the situation which exists when all those willing and able to work at the given real wage rate are either in employment or about to take up employment, i.e. they are frictionally unemployed.

Economic growth and development

Governments aim for a high economic growth rate, although there is increasing recognition that the growth rate needs to be sustainable. This means that there should be conservation as well as use of non-renewable resources so that the interests of future generations, and not just those of the present generation, are taken into account.

Economic development is a broader aim, focusing not just on growth in terms of real national output, but also on other factors that influence the standard of living and the quality of life of people, such as in relation to the provision of education and health care.

10.2 Inter-connectedness of problems AL 5(b)

This topic is concerned with:

➤ the relationship between the internal and external value of money

➤ the relationship between the balance of payments and inflation

➤ the trade-off between inflation and unemployment; the Phillips curve.

The relationship between the internal and external value of money

It is important to distinguish between the internal and external value of money, but it also needs to be stressed that the two values of money are interrelated. For example, if a country is experiencing a relatively high rate of inflation, this will reduce the internal value of a currency. Exports will become more expensive and if demand for those exports is price elastic, the demand for them will fall, as will the demand for the currency to pay for them. This will lead to a fall, or depreciation, in the external value of the currency.

The relationship between the balance of payments and inflation

If there is a relatively high rate of inflation in a country, this will make exports more expensive. This is likely to reduce the demand for them, assuming that the price elasticity of demand for the exports is elastic. The demand for imports, however, may remain unchanged. In such a situation, the money received from exports will fall but the money paid for imports will remain the same. This will lead to a deterioration in the current account of the balance of payments.

The trade-off between inflation and unemployment; the Phillips curve

If a country is experiencing a relatively high rate of inflation, its government may decide to deliberately bring down the rate of aggregate demand to reduce the inflation rate, especially if the country is experiencing demand-pull inflation. For example, monetary policy could be used to reduce aggregate demand through an increase in the interest rate or fiscal policy could be used through an increase in taxation. If there is a reduction of aggregate demand in an economy, it is likely to lead to an increase in the level of unemployment.

This trade-off between inflation and unemployment can be seen through the Phillips curve, as shown in Figure 10.1.

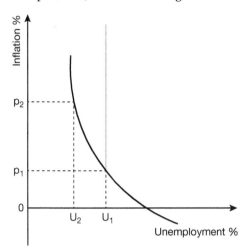

▲ **Figure 10.1** The Phillips curve

The diagram shows that if there is a fall in the level of unemployment from $0U_1$ to $0U_2$, this will have the effect of increasing the general level of prices in the economy from $0P_1$ to $0P_2$. However, some countries experienced stagflation, i.e. a situation of both relatively high inflation and relatively high unemployment, suggesting that the trade-off did not always apply.

This absence of a trade-off between inflation and unemployment was particularly noticeable in the long run. This was because of the expectations of consumers in terms of future prices and the expectations of producers in terms of future costs. This has given rise to the expectations-augmented Phillips curve in the long run. This is a vertical line that shows what is called NAIRU: the non-accelerating inflation rate of unemployment. This is shown in Figure 10.2.

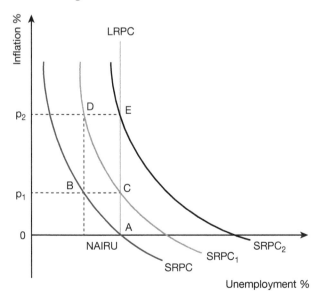

▲ **Figure 10.2** The expectations-augmented Phillips curve

This diagram shows three Phillips curves in the short run: SRPC, $SRPC_1$ and $SRPC_2$. However, although the trade-off relationship can be seen in the short run, in the long run LRPC is a vertical straight line to indicate NAIRU.

Key terms

Stagflation: a situation characterised by both a high rate of inflation and a high level of unemployment.

Phillips curve: a way of showing the trade-off between the rate of inflation and the level of unemployment in an economy. It is shown as a curve in the short run, but in the long run it becomes a vertical line.

NAIRU: the non-accelerating inflation rate of unemployment

It is important to be able to show the distinction between the short-run Phillips curve and the long-run Phillips curve. In the short run, it is a curve because as the price level in an economy rises, the level of unemployment falls and as the level of unemployment rises, the level of inflation falls. However, in the long run, the Phillips curve is not a curve but a vertical straight line. Any attempt to reduce unemployment by increasing demand will just lead to inflation. This long-run curve is known as the expectations-augmented Phillips curve, i.e. it takes into account the expectations that consumers and producers have in relation to prices, wages and costs. This vertical line will show NAIRU, which is the level of unemployment in an economy that does not cause the rate of inflation to increase.

10.3 Effectiveness of policy options to meet all macroeconomic objectives

AL 5(c)

This topic is concerned with:

➤ problems arising from conflicts between policy objectives on inflation, unemployment, economic growth, balance of payments, exchange rates and the redistribution of income and wealth

➤ the existence of government failure in macroeconomic policies

➤ Laffer curve analysis.

Problems arising from conflicts between policy objectives on inflation, unemployment, economic growth, balance of payments, exchange rates and the redistribution of income and wealth

It is not always easy for governments to achieve success in all policy objectives and it is often the case that there are conflicts between different policy objectives. For example, a depreciation or a devaluation in the value of an exchange rate could increase the demand for exports and decrease the demand for imports, assuming that the price elasticity of demand for both is elastic (for a devaluation to be successful, the Marshall-Lerner condition states the sum of the two elasticities must be greater than one). However, if the price elasticity of demand for imports is relatively inelastic, the demand for them will not change significantly and the effect of this is that it will contribute to a relatively high rate of inflation in an economy, both in terms of the price of imported raw materials/component parts and imported finished goods.

The Phillips curve shows the possible conflict when a government tries to reduce both the rate of inflation and the level of unemployment in an economy. Policies to reduce the level of unemployment will not usually conflict with a policy of achieving economic growth, but there may be a conflict between the policy objective of high economic growth and the need to protect the environment, especially if the rate of growth is unsustainable, i.e. it does not sufficiently take into account the needs of future generations.

A policy objective of redistributing income and wealth, such as through progressive taxation, may have a disincentive to work effect on those workers paying high rates of taxation on their earnings and this could have a dampening effect on the rate of economic growth in an economy.

The existence of government failure in macroeconomic policies

It is possible that a government may fail in its macroeconomic policies. For example, policies to bring about a more equitable distribution of income and wealth in an economy through the use of progressive tax could not only create a disincentive to work effect, as already indicated, but could also lead to people deciding to leave a country in protest at the high rate of tax being paid. Such people are likely to be the most educated and the most skilled in an economy, and this is why such a situation has been referred to as a 'brain drain'.

Information failure could have an impact on the success or otherwise of a government's macroeconomic policies. For example, there may be a time lag between when a policy is introduced and when it begins to have an effect, but during this time lag the economic situation has changed. It has been estimated by economists that a change in interest rates can take up to 18 or 24 months to be fully effective.

A country may be experiencing a relatively high rate of inflation and so the government decides to take appropriate measures to reduce the level of demand in the economy. However, the level of inflation then falls for reasons that have nothing to do with the measures taken, leading to a rise in the level of unemployment as a result of the measures taken, an unintended consequence of the measures taken.

Laffer curve analysis

A Laffer curve shows the relationship between the percentage tax rates in an economy and the revenue received by government from the taxation. Figure 10.3 shows the Laffer curve.

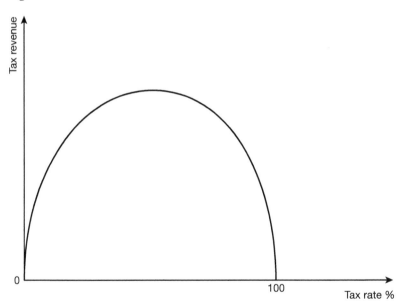

▲ **Figure 10.3** The Laffer curve

The Laffer curve shows that as the tax rate is increased along the horizontal axis, the revenue received from this taxation at first increases and then falls. At relatively high rates of tax, the tax is not worthwhile as it actually brings in less revenue than at lower rates of tax.

> ★ **Exam tip**
>
> Make sure that you are able to refer to different examples of problems arising from conflicts between policy objectives on a wide range of macro policy aims.

> ★ **Exam tip**
>
> Make sure that you are able to refer to different examples of government failure in relation to macroeconomic policies.

> ✓ **What you need to know**
>
> A Laffer curve shows the relationship between changes in the rate of tax and changes in the revenue that is received from that taxation. As the tax rate is increased, the tax revenue first begins to rise until a certain percentage of tax is reached and then falls. This shows the disincentive effect of high rates of taxation on both workers and firms. The name of the curve that shows this relationship comes from the name of an economist, Arthur Laffer.

> **Key term**
>
> Laffer curve: a curve that shows the relationship between tax rates and the revenue received from those taxes.

I can:

- ➤ understand the macro policy aims of governments ☐
- ➤ understand the relationship between the internal and the external value of money ☐
- ➤ understand the relationship between the balance of payments and the rate of inflation in an economy ☐
- ➤ understand the relationship between the rate of inflation and the level of unemployment in an economy ☐
- ➤ distinguish between the short-run and the long-run Phillips curve ☐
- ➤ be clear about what is meant by NAIRU ☐
- ➤ appreciate that problems can arise from possible conflicts between the different policy objectives of a government ☐
- ➤ understand the implications of government failure in macroeconomic policies ☐
- ➤ understand what is involved in a Laffer curve analysis in relation to the tax rates in an economy and the revenue generated by those taxes. ☐

? Exam-style questions

1 Governments generally aim for a:

- **A** relatively high and stable rate of inflation
- **B** relatively high and unstable rate of inflation
- **C** relatively low and stable rate of inflation
- **D** relatively low and unstable rate of inflation. [1]

2 When a government intervenes in a floating exchange rate system, it is known as:

- **A** a managed float
- **B** a special float
- **C** a stable float
- **D** an interventionist float. [1]

3 Stagflation refers to a situation where there is a combination of:

- **A** high inflation and high unemployment
- **B** high inflation and low unemployment
- **C** low inflation and high unemployment
- **D** low inflation and low unemployment. [1]

4 The long-run Phillips curve is a:

- **A** downward sloping straight line
- **B** horizontal straight line
- **C** upward sloping straight line
- **D** vertical straight line. [1]

5 For a devaluation to be successful, the Marshall-Lerner condition states that the price elasticities of demand for exports and imports should be:

- **A** equal to one
- **B** equal to zero
- **C** greater than one
- **D** less than one but more than zero. [1]

6 The Laffer curve shows that as the tax rate increases:

- **A** the tax revenue at first falls and then rises
- **B** the tax revenue at first rises and then falls
- **C** the tax revenue continually falls
- **D** the tax revenue continually rises. [1]

7 (a) Explain the main macroeconomic policy aims of a government. [12]

(b) Discuss to what extent these macroeconomic policy aims are likely to give rise to a conflict between them. [13]

8 Discuss whether the Phillips curve adequately shows the trade-off between the levels of inflation and unemployment in an economy. [25]

11 Raising your achievement

Sharing some ideas about how to achieve the best you can in your Economics examinations.

During your course of study

Let's start with some ideas about how to make good use of your study time.

Recent research shows that there are some important things you can do from the very start to make sure you achieve your best.

The first thing is to set yourself some definite goals. Here are some important questions for you to answer:

Question 1

What grade do you want to achieve in Economics to ensure that you are pleased with your result and to ensure that you can gain acceptance for the next stage in your education or employment? Setting a specific goal will motivate you and give you something to focus on.

> **Exam tip**
> Setting a specific goal will motivate you and give you something to focus on.

Question 2

How much time do you spend out of class working on developing your skills in Economics? You may already spend many hours in private study, but if you feel this is not the case, it is a good idea to set yourself some definite plans to increase your study time. This can be done gradually; for example you could plan to add an extra hour to your normal study time for the next few weeks. Then you could add an extra hour to this increased time, and so on.

> **Exam tip**
> Make definite plans to increase your study time.

Question 3

What is your reaction when you have received some work back in Economics and you have not done quite as well as you had hoped, despite having made a real effort to get a good mark? Many students will, understandably, answer by saying they are a bit deflated and hope they can get over the disappointment quickly. However, maybe if this is your typical response, you could think a little differently. Research shows that students who say to themselves something along the lines of: "Okay, this did not go so well; let me have a look at what I did wrong and learn from my mistakes" turn a negative experience into something far more positive which then leads to real progress.

> **Exam tip**
> Try to learn from your mistakes.

Question 4

What do you do with all the work you do during your course of study? Maybe your answer is: "Well, I have it all here somewhere, it just needs sorting out". Many students would find it extremely helpful to keep a carefully organised collection of the work they do. Have a separate section for each topic with your notes, all the answers you have produced together with the questions or at least a reference to where these questions can be found. When it comes to preparing for the examination, having a well-organised file will mean you can get on with revision without wasting time trying to find the relevant materials.

> **Exam tip**
> Organising your work will make it easier to revise.

So, at this stage you could be working towards the following position:

➤ you have a definite goal (the examination grade that you would like to achieve)

➤ you have a plan to increase the time spent on private study

➤ you view each result you achieve for the work you do as an opportunity to learn from your mistakes

➤ you are building up a well-organised file of work which will be invaluable for revision.

Some practical ideas to help you learn more effectively during your course of study

Self-assessment: this means that you mark your own work making use of a model answer or mark scheme provided with past examination papers. Research has shown that there are many benefits to doing this if you carry out the process on a regular and frequent basis, for example:

➤ you find out for yourself how well you have done as quickly as you wish after completing a task

➤ you can get immediate information about any errors or omissions in your answer, so you can start to learn from your mistakes right away

➤ if you use mark schemes (for example examination paper mark schemes) you can learn a great deal about how marks are allocated to answers so that you are better prepared to produce the answers expected in an examination situation.

Peer-assessment: an alternative to marking your own work is to get a friend to mark your work, while you mark your friend's work – the same benefits will arise in this situation.

'Repairing' your answers: the more substantial benefits of checking your own work arise when you then go on to look more closely at any aspect of your answer which was not correct or where something was missing. It is a good idea to spend a little time trying to understand why the model answer is showing a particular outcome which is different to the answer you have provided. Try and work out for yourself how the right answer was achieved, or maybe ask your teacher or a friend to explain the right answer to you if you really cannot see how it was done. It is as this point you will find you are making real progress by focusing on any shortcomings in your own work. Do make a point of adding some notes about the correct answer to your work; these notes will be useful when you look back at the question and the answer.

Here are some straightforward situations to illustrate what is meant by 'repairing' answers.

Example 1: repairing an answer where a calculation is incorrect

Calculate the price elasticity of demand for a product from the information provided.

Original price per unit: $6

New price per unit: $8

Original demand: 200 units

New demand: 300 units

Student's answer	Model answer
The price elasticity of demand for a product is percentage change in price divided by percentage change in quantity demanded.	The price elasticity of demand for a product is percentage change in quantity demanded divided by percentage change in price.
This is 33.3%/50.0% = 0.66	This is 50.0%/33.3% = 1.5

Action taken to repair the answer:

Student's answer	Repair
The price elasticity of demand for a product is percentage change in price divided by percentage change in quantity demanded. This is 33.3%/50.0% = 0.66	I should have learned the formula for the calculation of price elasticity of demand better. I must remember in the examination that it is the percentage change in the quantity demanded of a product divided by the percentage change in the price of the product, not the other way round as I had mistakenly thought.

Example 2: repairing an answer where a written response is incorrect

Describe the factors that could bring about a shift of the demand curve for a product to the right.

Extract from the student's answer	Extract from the model answer
A shift of the demand curve for a product to the right is caused by a fall in the price of a product. The fall in price of the product will make more consumers want to buy the product and this can be seen in the shift of the demand curve to the right.	The factors that could bring about the shift of the demand curve for a product to the right: ➤ an increase in the incomes of consumers ➤ an increase in the price of a substitute product ➤ a decrease in the price of a complementary product ➤ an advertising campaign stressing the positive features of the product ➤ an increase in population ➤ a change in the tastes and preferences of consumers in favour of the product ➤ a decrease in the rate of interest, making borrowing more affordable.

Action taken to repair the answer:

Extract from the student's answer	Repair
A shift of the demand curve for a product to the right is caused by a fall in the price of a product. The fall in price of the product will make more consumers want to buy the product and this can be seen in the shift of the demand curve to the right.	I should have remembered that a change in the price of a product only causes a movement along a demand curve, **not** a shift of a demand curve. I must remember the difference between a change in demand and a change in the conditions of demand in the examination. I need to make sure I am able to distinguish between a movement along a demand curve and a shift of a demand curve, so that I do not make this mistake in the examination.

So why is assessing my own work and then 'repairing' answers such a good idea?

Well, the answer is that much international research has shown that this approach carried out systematically will make a big difference to what an individual can gain from all the practical work which is carried out *and* over a course of study can boost an individual's performance by as much as two examination grades!

In the first illustration the student has focused attention on how the price elasticity of demand for a product should be calculated. If this process is repeated whenever this type of error is made, then very soon it is likely that the student will have learned the correct formula for the calculation of this important concept.

In the second illustration, the student has focused attention on how they have completely misunderstood the question, confusing a movement along a demand curve and a shift of a demand curve. As a result, they now have their own personal record of what is needed to avoid repeating the error, and if they repeat this process for similar questions it is much more likely they will remember this distinction between a movement along a curve and a shift of a curve. Remember each correction you make represents a step - maybe just a small step - towards improving your examination performance.

Making progress with written answers

In order to make progress on demonstrating knowledge and understanding of key Economics ideas and concepts, you could try the following process in a situation where you are reading through a passage in a textbook or handout about a particular topic.

The process helps you organise information and consists of several steps:

Step 1: highlight key points in the text.

Step 2: prepare a table in which you make some notes which summarise key points about a particular aspect of the topic.

Step 3: prepare a second table this time making some notes which summarise key points about a different aspect of the topic, and so on. More tables can be added if necessary.

Example 3: using tables to analyse knowledge and ideas in an AS level topic: factors of production

Having highlighted key points in a textbook about the factors of production, you could produce tables along the following lines:

Table 1: The definitions of the factors of production	
Land	The factor of production that is concerned with the natural resources of an economy, such as farmland or mineral deposits.
Labour	The factor of production that is concerned with the workforce of an economy in terms of both the physical and mental effort involved in production.
Capital	The factor of production that relates to the human-made aids to production, such as tools and equipment.
Enterprise	The factor of production that takes a risk in organising the other three factors of production. The individual who takes this risk is known as an entrepreneur.

Table 2: The rewards to the factors of production	
Land	Rent
Labour	Wages or salaries
Capital	Interest
Enterprise	Profit

You can keep creating tables, looking at other aspects of factors of production or looking at certain factors of production in particular, such as the role of the factor enterprise in a modern economy.

The benefit of using this type of approach is that it makes information more accessible because the focus is on one particular aspect of the topic at a time. As a result, the ideas become more understandable and more memorable because they are separated out and carefully organised.

Example 4: using tables to analyse knowledge and ideas in an A level topic: cost benefit analysis

You have just been reading some passages in a textbook about cost benefit analysis.

Step 1: highlight each key point

Step 2: set up a table to organise some key information about the topic focusing on just one aspect

Step 3: set up a second table to organise some key information about the topic focusing on a different aspect, and so on. More tables can be added if necessary.

Table 1: The advantages and disadvantages of cost benefit analysis	
Advantages	**Disadvantages**
All the costs and benefits of an investment project can be analysed, not only the private costs and benefits.	Not all of the costs and benefits will have a market price, such as the price of pollution.
It can take a wide view of an investment project, considering its full impact on an economy and society.	It will be difficult to compare the interest of present and future generations.
It can consider the impact of an investment project not just at one moment in time, but over a period of time.	An investment project is likely to have third party, or spillover, effects, but it may be difficult to establish what these are and how far they extend.

Table 2: Possible solutions to the limitations of cost benefit analysis		
Problem	**Solution**	**Drawbacks**
Not all of the costs and benefits will have a market price, such as the price of pollution.	In the absence of market prices, values will need to be estimated through the use of shadow prices.	Shadow prices will not always be accurate, such as the valuation of time or an accident.
It will be difficult to compare the interest of present and future generations.	Future costs and benefits can be converted into present values through the process of discounting.	It is difficult to establish the future values of costs and benefits and discounting is quite a complex process.
An investment project is likely to have third party, or spillover, effects, but it may be difficult to establish what these are and how far they extend.	The cost benefit analysis can attempt to include all of the possible third party, or spillover, effects.	It can be very difficult to establish how far such effects extend, such as the advantages of constructing a new road and the disadvantages of the pollution that may be caused.

Again, the process of analysing text and organising the key points into tables which have a clear focus can act as a powerful aid to learning.

Avoiding the most common weaknesses in exam answers

When you look at the 'Raise your grade' feature in the units in this book, you will soon become aware of a number of common errors to be avoided. It is important that you know how to avoid some of the most common weaknesses in examination answers.

Weakness 1: not reading the question carefully

You may think that you have read an examination question, but have you read it carefully? Have you looked at every word in a question and established exactly what the examiner requires you to do? There are many examples where candidates will have thought that they were answering an examination correctly, when in fact the reality was very different. For example, the case where an examination required candidates to write about the consequences of inflation, and one candidate misread the question and wrote about the causes of inflation instead, an entirely different question requiring an entirely different answer.

Weakness 2: not reading the 'hint' words

This follows on very closely from the first weakness and arises from a failure to read an examination question carefully enough. Examination questions in Economics often contain strong hints to guide you in terms of what you need to write. This can be the case in 'discuss' questions where the questions may contain words such as 'to what extent', 'whether' or 'always'. These can be extremely helpful in terms of giving candidates a steer as to how they need to answer the question.

Weakness 3: not looking closely at the 'command' or 'directive' word used in an examination question

Many candidates, when they read and answer an examination question, tend to focus on the content covered by the question in terms of a particular topic on the syllabus, such as inflation or unemployment. However, it is also important to look carefully at the command or directive word being used in a question as this indicates what the examiners are actually asking you to do. For example, there is a great deal of difference between an examination question that asks you to state or identify something and one that asks you to discuss or evaluate something.

Weakness 4: not including both points of view and a conclusion in a 'discuss' question

This follows on very closely from the previous weakness and arises from a failure to look closely at the command or directive word used in a question. In Economics, a 'discuss' question will usually ask you to contrast two alternative viewpoints or perspectives and then come to a conclusion in the form of a judgement or recommendation. However, many candidates in a 'discuss' question only look at one point of view and/or do not include a conclusion. This will limit the number of marks that can be awarded for such an answer. It is also important to stress that the conclusion must be logical, i.e. it must follow on sensibly from what the candidate has written. For example, there was one answer to a question on whether monetary policy or fiscal policy was the best solution to the problem of inflation where the candidate, having written throughout the answer that monetary policy was likely to be more effective, concluded that fiscal policy was the best solution, completely contradicting what had gone before.

Weakness 5: not structuring and presenting the answer clearly

One other problem which can frequently arise is that answers are not well presented. To some extent this is understandable under examination conditions and, of course, it is accepted that corrections and alterations may need to be made to answers. However, there is no real reason why answers should not be set out properly. For example, it is very helpful if candidates can structure their longer answers into coherent and logical paragraphs. This makes it easier for the examiner to follow the argument or line of thought that is being presented.

So the important ideas arising from this review of the most common weaknesses in examination answers are to:

➤ read questions very carefully

➤ look for possible 'hint' or 'steer' words in a question

➤ look closely at the 'command' or 'directive' word used in a question

➤ include both points of view and a conclusion in a 'discuss' question

➤ present and structure answers as clearly as possible from the very start of your course.

Understanding what is expected by different types of question

Each question in an examination will start with a particular command or directive word which asks you to do something, as has already been explained. It is important to understand why particular words are used and what they mean, otherwise it is possible you will waste time by misunderstanding what is required and lose marks for not doing what is expected of you.

Examination papers will be designed:

To test	By asking you to
Knowledge	Identify State Define Outline
Understanding	Describe Illustrate
Application of knowledge and understanding in particular situations	Explain/how Compare Calculate Consider
Investigate a situation or a problem	Analyse Comment upon
Ability to look at a situation or a problem from different points of view, consider a range of factors, make a judgement and provide a conclusion	Discuss Justify Assess Evaluate

Words used	What is expected	Examples of questions	
Identify State Define Outline	A brief response, enough to show you can remember some facts or ideas. Identify: name the key knowledge point State: give a concise answer with little or no supporting argument required Define: give the exact meaning of Outline: describe the key points without detail	AS Level	**Identify** two functions of money. **State** two canons of taxation. **Define** cross elasticity of demand. **Outline** the differences between a tariff and a quota.
		A Level	**Identify** two pricing policies. **State** the quantity theory of money. **Define** labour productivity.
Describe Illustrate	A fuller written statement giving facts and (especially where explain is used) requiring some development; that is a further statement designed to show understanding. Sometimes the development can take the form of examples. **Describe:** give a description of, explain the main features of **Illustrate:** give examples, use a diagram	AS Level	**Describe** the causes of inflation. **Illustrate** with a diagram the meaning of the J curve.
		A Level	**Describe** the equi-marginal principle. **Illustrate** with examples the meaning of economies of scale.
Explain/how Compare Calculate Consider	Answers are required about a particular situation. **Explain/how:** give clear reasons or make clear the meaning of, use examples and explain the theory behind the question **Compare:** explain the similarities and differences between **Calculate:** work out using the information provided **Consider:** give your thoughts about, with some justification	AS Level	**Explain** what is meant by consumer surplus. **Compare** a depreciation and an appreciation of a currency. **Calculate** the price elasticity of demand for this product. **Consider** who might benefit from a trade war despite the advantages of free trade.
		A Level	**Explain** what is meant by Pareto optimality. **Compare** internal and external diseconomies of scale. **Calculate** the value of the multiplier. **Consider** why small firms continue to exist despite the advantages of large firms.
Analyse Comment upon	Where you study some information in some depth, separating out different aspects of the information. **Analyse:** explain the main points in detail, examine closely, separate into parts and show how all the parts connect and link **Comment upon:** give your reasoned opinion on, with explanations	AS Level	**Analyse** the effect of providing a subsidy in a market. **Comment** upon the view that all important decisions in Economics are taken at the margin.
		A Level	**Analyse** the effect of increasing interest rates in an economy. **Comment** upon the view that a relatively high rate of economic growth is always of benefit to an economy.

| Discuss Justify Evaluate Assess | Where you look at both sides of a particular proposal or idea, pointing out the benefits but also the drawbacks. You may be asked to make a judgement and give reasons to support it. **Discuss:** give the important arguments for and against, often requires a conclusion; this command word requires 'analysis' and 'evaluation'. **Justify:** explain why the arguments for an opinion are stronger than the arguments against **Evaluate:** discuss the importance of, judge the overall worth of, make an attempt to weigh up your opinions **Assess:** show how important something is, give your judgement on | AS Level | **Discuss** whether monetary policy or fiscal policy is likely to be more effective in reducing the rate of inflation in an economy. **Justify** your answer. **Evaluate** the decision of a government to devalue its currency to reduce the deficit in the current account of the balance of payments. **Assess** the arguments in favour of protectionism. |
| | | A Level | **Discuss** whether the consequences of unemployment are always negative. **Justify** your answer. **Evaluate** the decision of a country to concentrate on using, rather than conserving, its natural resources. **Assess** the arguments in favour of a multinational deciding to build a factory in a developing economy. |

Preparing for the exam

Before the exam

You need to approach the examination in a professional way. The key to success is preparation!

Here are eight top tips to help you prepare for the examination:

1 Read and appreciate the aims and objectives of the syllabus.

2 Look through the details of the five topic areas of the syllabus; check that you have covered everything.

3 Make sure that you have your file of notes organised: complete and in the right order. The importance of this has already been stressed.

4 Make sure that you are familiar with at least one good, up-to-date, textbook and one dictionary of Economics (very useful for definitions of key terms and concepts and for mastering the underlying ideas of the subject).

5 Keep up-to-date with recent developments by reading appropriate newspaper and magazines, such as changes in interest, exchange and growth rates, levels of inflation and unemployment and significant economic events around the world.

6 Go through each part of the syllabus and make sure that you have revision cards, spider diagrams or bullet points on each of the main areas and topics.

7 Look at specimen and past papers and at any examples of model or worked answers, but remember that they are answers to previous questions – the questions on your examination paper will be different.

8   Make sure that you allocate sufficient time to revision, in sensible blocks of time, and in an appropriate working environment. Draw up a realistic revision timetable and aim to use your revision time effectively. Some further advice on revision is given below.

Revision

As the examinations draw nearer, you will be thinking about the best way to revise. Just how much revision is done and how frequently it is done will, of course, vary from one student to another. In Economics it is important that a substantial portion of your revision time is spent actually answering questions. This will ensure that you remember the key points to be made in your answers.

You will find it useful to make a checklist of all the main topics in the AS/A Level specification and work your way through the list finding questions to try on each topic. This is where that well-organised course file will prove invaluable because you should easily be able to find suitable questions with your answers, including your own notes on points you learned when you did the question originally, plus a model answer. If you feel confident about a topic just try the trickier parts of the question again. Avoid looking at the model answer unless you really get stuck. If you are less sure about a topic, be prepared to spend more time on it. Try working through the entire question rather than just a few selected elements. Again, have a model answer available to help you if you get stuck. In the end you will find that actually answering questions will restore your confidence far more effectively than just reading through notes and looking at answers to past questions.

The key concepts

In addition to the five topic areas of the Economics syllabus, there are also five key concepts. These refer to essential ideas, theories, principles or mental tools that will help you to understand the subject better. They will also help you in your revision for the examination, making you better able to make links between the different topics in the syllabus. These key concepts are listed and explained in the table below.

Key concept	Description
Scarcity and choice	The fundamental problem in economics is that resources are scarce and wants are unlimited, so there is always a choice required between competing uses for the resources.
The margin and change	Decision-making by individuals, firms and governments is based on choices at the margin; that is, once behaviour has been optimised, any change will be detrimental as long as conditions remain the same.
Equilibrium and efficiency	Prices are set by markets, are always moving in to, and out of, equilibrium, and can be both efficient and inefficient in different ways and over different time periods.
Regulation and equity	There is a trade-off between, on the one hand, freedom for firms and individuals in unregulated markets and, on the other hand, greater social equality and equity through the government regulation of individuals and markets.
Progress and development	Economics studies how societies can progress in measurable money terms and develop in a wider, and more normative, sense.

The exam

Here are seven top tips to help you do as well as you possibly can in the examination:

1   Don't panic. Stay calm. The examiners want to give you the chance to show what you know, not what you don't know.

2   Read the examination questions carefully; it is so easy to overlook some detail or some particular wording which can drastically affect the quality of your answer. This is a point that has already been stressed.

3   Answer all parts of the question and use the marks allocated to each part as a guide to how long you should spend on each section. Some parts will only gain you two marks while other parts may be worth as many as 12 or 13 marks.

4   Look carefully at the command or directive words in the questions, such as explain, consider, analyse, compare, discuss, distinguish, identify, how far or to what extent. These words indicate what the examiners want you to do; the more you discuss, analyse or evaluate, rather than just describe, the higher the mark you will get. This point has already been stressed.

5   Wherever possible, use diagrams to aid your explanations, but make sure that they are accurately drawn, fully labelled and that you refer to them in your answer.

6   You should also try and bring in appropriate examples of current economic issues and problems to support the points you are making.

7   Time management is crucial. Ensure that you manage your time in the examination as effectively as possible. There is a lot that will need to be done in the time but you should try and leave time to read through your answers and correct any mistakes and/or add anything you feel is missing. An indication of how much time should be allocated to answering questions in the different examination papers is given below.

Time management

AS Level exam

In Paper 1, you will have 1 hour to answer 30 multiple choice questions. The time allocation for each question is therefore two minutes.

In Paper 2, you will have 1 hour 30 minutes to answer 2 questions (one will be Question 1 and the other will be Question 2, Question 3 or Question 4). The time allocation for each question is therefore 45 minutes.

A Level exam

In Paper 3, you will have 1 hour 15 minutes to answer 30 multiple choice questions. The time allocation for each question is therefore two and a half minutes.

In Paper 4, you will have 2 hours 15 minutes to answer 3 questions (one will be Question 1 and the other two will be chosen from Questions 2, 3, 4, 5, 6 or 7). Question 1 carries 20 marks, whereas the other questions carry 25 marks each. The time allocation is therefore approximately 39 minutes for Question 1 and 48 minutes for each of the other two questions.

These timings per question are a guide only. You may need to spend a little more time on a particular question and a little less on another. However, don't forget that every minute over the target time will be a minute less available on another question.

12 Exam-style questions

Assessment for A Level Economics

The assessment structure for A Level Economics is shown in the table below.

Component	Type of Paper	Marks	Time	AS Level Weighting	A Level Weighting
Paper 1	Multiple Choice 30 multiple choice questions based on the AS Level syllabus content	30	1 hour	40%	20%
Paper 2	Data Response and Essay Section A: one data response question (20 marks) Section B: one structured essay from a choice of three (20 marks) Based on the AS Level syllabus content	40	1 hour 30 minutes	30% 30%	15% 15%
Paper 3	Multiple Choice 30 multiple choice questions based on the Additional A Level syllabus content	30	1 hour 15 minutes		15%
Paper 4	Data Response and Essays Section A: one data response question (20 marks) Section B: two essays from a choice of six (50 marks) Based on the additional A Level syllabus content	70	2 hours 15 minutes		10% 25%

Note: Papers 3 and 4 test the additional syllabus content for A Level, but also require a knowledge and understanding of the AS Level syllabus content.

The following questions, covering each of the four papers, are an indication of what you will be required to answer in the examination.

Paper 1

In Paper 1, all of the multiple choice questions have only one correct answer.

1   When it is said that economic goods are scarce, it means that:

   A production has not kept pace with other goods

   B the goods have opportunity costs

   C the supply of the goods has decreased

   D very few items of the goods exist   [1]

2   Which of the following is closest to being a 'pure' public good?

   A defence

   B education

   C electricity supply

   D health care   [1]

3   Which of the following would cause a market demand curve to shift to the right?

   A a fall in the real disposable incomes of consumers

   B a rise in the price of a complementary product

   C a rise in the price of a substitute product

   D an increase in interest rates   [1]

4   Which of the following would cause the market supply curve for a good to shift to the left?

   A a fall in the price of the good

   B a subsidy on the production of the good

   C an increase in the number of producers

   D an increase in the price of factors producing the good   [1]

5   A benefit given by a government to those in financial need is called:

   A a specific tax

   B a transfer earning

   C a transfer payment

   D an ad valorem tax   [1]

6   A maximum price, to have any effect, needs to be introduced in a market:

   A above the equilibrium price

   B below the equilibrium price

   C equal to the equilibrium price

   D where there is a guaranteed price floor   [1]

7   Which of the following will definitely occur if the inflation rate in an economy is 10%?

   A Real personal disposable income will fall

   B The level of investment will fall

   C The value of money will fall

   D The volume of exports will fall   [1]

8 Which of the following is not a valid argument in favour of a tariff?

    A It may give protection against the arrival of cheap foreign labour

    B It may give protection to an infant industry

    C It may prevent a rise of unemployment in declining industries

    D It may protect industries that are essential to national defence   [1]

9 Which of the following is an example of a supply side policy to reduce inflation?

    A A reduction in money supply

    B An increase in interest rates

    C An increase in money supply

    D An increase in spending on training   [1]

10 Deflation occurs in an economy when:

    A the general level of prices is falling

    B the general level of prices is increasing at a more rapid rate

    C the general level of prices is increasing at a less rapid rate

    D the general level of prices is neither increasing nor decreasing   [1]

Paper 2

In Paper 2, you are required to answer the question in Section A and **one** question from Section B. Each of the two questions carries 20 marks.

Section A

1 The Economics Minister of a country is concerned about the relatively high rate of inflation her country has been experiencing in recent years. For example, last year the inflation rate reached 10.6%. She realises that this could have a significant effect on the standard of living of workers, especially in terms of their real wages, because the average increase in wages last year was only 3.8%. The minister is aware that inflation can be caused by a range of different factors in an economy.

She is determined to try to reduce the level of inflation in the country as she understands that a relatively high rate of inflation can have a number of negative consequences, especially in terms of international trade. The minister appreciates that monetary, fiscal and supply side policies are all methods that can be used to bring down the rate of inflation and that they each have various advantages and disadvantages.

(a) What is meant by a 'real wage'? [2]

(b) Calculate the change in the real wage rate of workers in the country over the last year. Show your workings. [2]

(c) Explain what is meant by 'supply side policies'. [2]

(d) Compare demand-pull and cost-push causes of inflation. [4]

(e) Describe the main negative consequences of a relatively high rate of inflation in an economy on its international trading position. [4]

(f) Discuss whether monetary or fiscal policy is likely to be more effective in reducing a relatively high rate of inflation in an economy. [6]

TOTAL: [20]

Section B

1 (a) Explain why a government might decide to provide a public good, such as national defence, rather than leaving it to be provided by the private sector. [8]

(b) Discuss whether a government should substantially increase the indirect tax on a demerit good, such as cigarettes, in an attempt to reduce the level of consumption of such a good. [12]

TOTAL: [20]

Paper 3

As in Paper 1, all of the multiple choice questions in Paper 3 have only one correct answer.

1   A reduction in unemployment in an economy can be shown on a production possibility curve (PPC) by a:

    A movement along the PPC

    B movement from within the PPC to a point on the PPC

    C movement from within the PPC towards the origin

    D shift of the PPC to the right   [1]

2   A social cost is defined as:

    A external cost minus private cost

    B private cost plus external cost

    C social benefit minus private cost

    D social benefit plus external cost   [1]

3   Which of the following is not a feature of perfect competition?

    A Advertising by firms

    B Free entry and exit of firms

    C Normal profits in the long-run

    D Perfectly elastic supply of factors of production   [1]

4   Which of the following is a condition for price discrimination to exist?

    A It is possible to buy in one market and resell in another

    B It is possible to separate the markets

    C The firms are in a perfectly competitive market

    D The price elasticity of demand must be the same in the markets   [1]

5   A tax is defined as progressive if:

    A a high-income earner pays more tax than a low-income earner

    B the average rate of tax increases as income increases

    C the marginal rate of tax is constant as income increases

    D the same amount of tax is paid at all income levels   [1]

6   A trades union will be less likely to raise the wages of its members if:

    A the larger the proportion of workers who belong to the union

    B the lower the price elasticity of demand for the product produced

    C the more easily labour may be substituted for other factors of production

    D the more effectively it can control the supply of labour   [1]

7   Which type of unemployment is directly caused by a deficiency in the level of aggregate demand in an economy?

    A Cyclical

    B Frictional

    C Seasonal

    D Structural   [1]

8 Liquidity is defined as the:

   A degree of solvency of an individual or firm

   B ease with which an asset can be changed into money

   C number of transactions that take place in an economy

   D velocity of circulation of circulation of money in an economy   [1]

9 The Phillips curve shows the trade-off between inflation and:

   A deflation

   B economic growth

   C the equality of income distribution

   D unemployment.   [1]

10 A Laffer curve shows that:

   A an increase in tax rates always leads to an increase in tax revenue

   B higher tax rates act as an incentive to people to work

   C higher tax rates will lead to a fall in tax revenue

   D higher tax rates will lead to an increase in tax revenue.   [1]

Paper 4

In Paper 4, you are required to answer the question in Section A and **two** questions from Section B. The question in Section A carries 20 marks and each of the questions in Section B carries 25 marks.

Section A

1   The Employment Minister of a country is concerned that the rate of unemployment in his country is substantially higher than that of nearby countries. He understands that some of this unemployment is due to structural factors and some of it to cyclical factors.

He believes that one approach to the problem of unemployment would be to take measures to increase the rate of economic growth and he is aware that a number of different measures could be taken to increase the rate of economic growth in the country.

However, the Environment Minister has reminded him that it is important to understand that a relatively high rate of economic growth may not be sustainable.

(a) Explain what is meant by the term 'rate of unemployment'.   [2]

(b) Explain what the Employment Minister means when he states 'that some of this unemployment is due to structural factors and some of it to cyclical factors'.   [4]

(c) Consider what is meant by a sustainable rate of economic growth.   [6]

(d) Discuss what are likely to be the most significant measures that could be taken to increase the rate of economic growth in this country.   [8]

TOTAL: [20]

Section B

1   (a) Explain how an economist would compare different market structures.   [12]

(b) Discuss whether a natural monopoly is always in the interests of consumers.   [13]

2   Discuss whether cost-benefit analysis will always lead to the correct decision being made in relation to an expensive investment project.   [25]

TOTAL: [50]

Appendix: Maths skills for AS and A Level Economics

Price elasticity of demand

It is important to remember that when calculating price elasticity of demand, it is necessary to compare percentage or proportionate changes in price and quantity demanded and not absolute changes.

Worked example

To convert $\dfrac{30}{80}$ into a percentage, the numerator (30) is divided by the denominator (80), and the answer multiplied by 100.

30 divided by 80 = 0.375

$\qquad$ 0.375 × 100 = 37.5%

Worked example

To calculate the price elasticity of demand for a product, it is necessary to divide the percentage change in quantity demanded of a product by the percentage change in the price of a product.

If the price of a product increases by 25% and the quantity demanded decreases by 10%, price elasticity of demand $= \dfrac{10\%}{25\%} = 0.4$

> **Remember**
>
> If the PED figure is less than 1, PED is inelastic.
>
> If the PED figure is equal to 1, PED is unitary elastic.
>
> If the PED figure is greater than 1, PED is elastic.

Income elasticity of demand

It is important to remember that when calculating income elasticity of demand, it is necessary to compare percentage or proportionate changes in income and quantity demanded and not absolute changes.

Worked example

To calculate the income elasticity of demand for a product, it is necessary to divide the percentage change in quantity demanded of a product by the percentage change in income.

If income increases by 10% and the quantity demanded increases by 20%, income elasticity of demand $= \dfrac{20\%}{10\%} = 2$.

It is also important to remember it is possible that a change in income will make no difference at all to the quantity demanded of a product. In this case, YED is zero.

It is also possible that a situation of negative income elasticity of demand occurs in the case of an inferior good, as the following example shows:

If income decreases by 5% and the quantity demanded increases by 10%, income elasticity of demand $= \dfrac{+10\%}{-5\%} = -2$

> **Remember**
>
> If the YED figure is less than 1, YED is inelastic.
>
> If the YED figure is equal to 1, YED is unitary elastic.
>
> If the YED figure is greater than 1, YED is elastic.

Cross elasticity of demand

It is important to remember that when calculating the cross elasticity of demand for a product, it is necessary to divide the percentage change in quantity demanded of a product by the percentage change in price of another product.

Worked example

To calculate the cross elasticity of demand for a product, it is necessary to divide the percentage change in quantity demanded of product A by the percentage change in price of product B.

If the price of tea increases by 20% and the quantity of coffee demanded increases by 30%, cross elasticity of demand $= \dfrac{30\%}{20\%} = 1.5$

In this case, when XED is a positive number, it is clear that tea and coffee are substitutes.

However, if the price of tea increases by 20% and the quantity of milk demanded decreases by 10%, cross elasticity of demand $= \dfrac{-10\%}{+20\%} = -0.5$

In this case, when XED is a negative number, it is clear that tea and milk are complements.

Price elasticity of supply

It is important to remember that when calculating the price elasticity of supply of a product, it is necessary to divide the percentage change in quantity supplied of a product by the percentage change in the price.

Worked example

To calculate the price elasticity of supply for a product, it is necessary to divide the percentage change in quantity supplied by the percentage change in price.

If the price of a product increases by 30% and the quantity supplied increases by 40%, price elasticity of supply $= \dfrac{40\%}{30\%} = 1.33$

In the case of many products, PES is likely to be relatively inelastic in the short run and relatively elastic in the long run, although the actual extent of elasticity of supply will depend on the particular product. For example, the supply of manufactured products generally tends to be more elastic than the supply of agricultural products.

> **Remember**
>
> If the PES figure is less than 1, PES is inelastic.
>
> If the PES figure is equal to 1, PES is unitary elastic.
>
> If the PES figure is greater than 1, PES is elastic.

Nominal and real GDP

It is important to remember than when calculating the Gross Domestic Product (GDP) of a country it is necessary to take into account the possible effect of inflation. For example, if the GDP of a country increased by 5% in a year and the rate of inflation in that country over the year was 5%, it would be clear that once the effect of inflation was taken into account, the GDP had not really increased at all. It is therefore necessary to adjust any increase in a country's GDP by the rate of inflation. In order to convert a country's nominal GDP to real GDP, a price index is used as a price deflator or GDP deflator.

Worked example

To convert nominal GDP to real GDP, the following formula is used:

$$\text{Real GDP} = \frac{\text{nominal GDP}}{\text{price index}} \times 100$$

If the nominal GDP of a country has increased from US$100 billion (bn) in one year to US$106 bn the next year and the price index of the country has increased from 103 to 105, then in Year 1 real GDP was $\frac{100}{103} \times 100 = \text{US\$97.08}$ bn and in Year 2 real GDP was $\frac{106}{105} \times 100 = \text{US\$100.95}$ bn.

Current account of balance of payments

It is important to remember that when calculating the current account of a country's balance of payments, it consists of the following four parts:

- the trade in goods, i.e. the balance of trade in relation to the exports and imports of goods

- the trade in services, i.e. the balance of trade in relation to the exports and imports of services

- net primary income, i.e. incomes from interest, profits, dividends resulting from investment and migrant remittances

- net secondary income, i.e. contributions to international organisations and overseas development aid.

Worked example

To calculate the current account of a country's balance of payments, it is necessary to add together the following four parts:

Part of current account	Value in US$ bn
Trade in goods	−188.6
Trade in services	241.2
Net primary income	17.9
Net secondary income	−21.4
Total	49.1

Balance of payments

It is important to remember that the components of the balance of payments include the following four parts:

- the current account
- the capital account
- the financial account
- the balancing item.

Worked example

To calculate a country's balance of payments, it is necessary to add together the following four parts:

Part of balance of payments	Value in US$ bn
Current account	49.1
Capital account	31.7
Financial account	−8.6
Balancing item	1.3
Total	73.5

Exchange rates

It is important to remember that it is possible to distinguish between three different forms of measurement of exchange rates:

- nominal exchange rates
- real exchange rates
- trade-weighted exchange rates.

Worked example

The nominal exchange rate is simply the rate at which currency can be exchanged in the foreign exchange market, i.e. it is the amount of foreign currency that can be purchased for one unit of domestic currency. Therefore, if the nominal exchange rate between the Great British Pound and the US Dollar is $1.30, it simply means that £1 can buy $1.30 dollars and no calculation is required.

However, the real exchange rate takes into account the prices in different countries. It refers to exchange rates that have been adjusted to take into account the inflation differential between two countries. While two currencies may have a certain nominal exchange rate on the foreign exchange market, this does not mean that goods and services purchased with one currency cost the equivalent amount in another currency; this is due to different inflation rates in the two countries. Real exchange rates are thus calculated as a nominal exchange rate adjusted for the different rates of inflation. It is calculated by using the following formula:

$$\frac{\text{nominal exchange rate} \times \text{domestic price index}}{\text{foreign price index}}$$

If the nominal exchange rate between the GBP and the US Dollar is $1.30, the price index in the UK is 110 and the price index in the US is 107, the real

$$\text{exchange rate} = \frac{\$1.30 \times 110}{107} = \$1.34$$

The trade-weighted exchange rate is an average of a country's bilateral exchange rates with other countries, weighted by the amount of trade with each of these countries. The UK has:

- 50% of its trade with the Eurozone

- 30% of its trade with the USA

- 20% of its trade with Japan.

Using these figures, it is possible to calculate the trade weighted exchange rate.

Currency	Value of £, Year 1	Base year price index, Year 1	Weighted index	Value of £, Year 2	Price index, Year 2	Price index, Year 2 × weight
Euro	1.3	100	500	1.20	92.4	46 200
Dollar	2.0	100	300	1.75	87.5	26 250
Yen	170.0	100	200	180.00	106.0	21 200
						93 650

The trade-weighted exchange rate: $\dfrac{95360}{1000} = 93.65$

Depreciation, appreciation, devaluation and revaluation

It is important to remember that changes in exchange rates are easier to compare when they are expressed in percentage or proportionate, rather than absolute, terms.

These four terms need to be clearly distinguished:

- depreciation refers to the fall in the external value of a currency in a floating exchange rate system

- appreciation refers to a rise in the external value of a currency in a floating exchange rate system

- devaluation refers to a fall in the external value of a currency in a fixed exchange rate system

- revaluation refers to a rise in the external value of a currency in a fixed exchange rate system.

Worked example

If the exchange rate between the Great British Pound and the US Dollar has depreciated from £1 = US$1.50 to £1 = US$1.20, it has fallen in value by 30 cents. In percentage terms, this is calculated by $\dfrac{0.30}{1.50} = 20\%$.

If the exchange rate between the Great British Pound and the US Dollar has appreciated from £1 = US$1.50 to £1 = US$2.01, it has increased in value by 51 cents. In percentage terms, this is calculated by $\dfrac{0.51}{1.50} = 34\%$.

The terms of trade

The terms of trade measures the change in export prices and the change in import prices and the ratio between these changes.

Comparative advantage

This is the idea that countries can benefit from specialisation and trade even if one country had an absolute advantage in all products. The theory was put forward by David Ricardo in the early 19th century and stressed that international trade is beneficial if there is a difference in the opportunity cost ratios between two countries. Through such trade, world output is increased and consumers can have a wider range of products at a cheaper price than would otherwise be the case if trade did not take place.

Worked example

There is a situation where resources are allocated between two goods, X and Y, in two countries, A and B. The output is shown in the table below.

	Good X	Good Y
Country A	1	4
Country B	2	3

A key part of the theory of comparative advantage is the importance of differences in the opportunity costs of production. These are shown in the table below.

	Opportunity cost of 1X	Opportunity cost of 1Y
Country A	4Y	0.25X
Country B	1.5Y	0.66X

If each of the two countries specialises in the production of the good in which it has a comparative advantage, country A will make good Y because the opportunity cost is 0.25X rather than 0.66X. Country B will make good X because the opportunity cost is 1.5Y rather than 4Y. If all of the resources are diverted into the production of these goods, then assuming constant returns to scale and no transport costs, the output will double in each country because there are twice as many resources in the production of the goods. This is shown in the table below.

	Good X	Good Y
Country A	0	8
Country B	4	0

Without the existence of international trade, the two countries produced 3X and 7Y. With trade, they make 4X and 8Y. There is therefore a greater production of both goods.

Gross Domestic Product and Gross National Product

It is important to be able to clearly distinguish between Gross Domestic Product and Gross National Product. GDP refers to the value of everything that is produced within the geographical boundaries of a country over a particular period of time, e.g. one year. GNP also includes the value of everything produced by the nationals of a country abroad.

Worked example

GNP is calculated by adding net property income from abroad to GDP, as the following example shows.

GDP	$2456 bn
Net property income from abroad	$216 bn
GNP	$2672 bn

In this case, the GNP is greater than GDP. However, it is possible that a country's net property income from abroad is negative. In this case, GDP will be greater than GNP, as the following example shows.

GDP	$1856 bn
Net property in come from abroad	–$189 bn
GNP	$1667 bn

The multiplier

The multiplier (k) refers to the amount by which an increase in injections into the circular flow of income in an economy will increase total income in that economy. The injections into an economy can come from investment (I), government expenditure (G) or exports (X). However, the effect of any increase in injections will be affected by the level of leakages or withdrawals from the circular flow of income and these will comprise savings (S), taxation (T) or imports (M).

In order to calculate the multiplier, it is necessary to distinguish between a two-sector economy, a three-sector economy and a four-sector economy. A two-sector economy consists of one injection (investment) and one withdrawal (saving). A three-sector economy consists of two injections (investment and government expenditure) and two withdrawals (saving and taxation). A four-sector economy consists of three injections (investment, government expenditure and exports) and three withdrawals (saving, taxation and imports).

Worked example

In a two-sector economy, the level of national income is in equilibrium and a business invests \$10 m in new equipment. The level of national income will start to increase and will continue to increase until investment and saving are equal. If it is assumed that people save $\frac{1}{5}$ of their extra income, the marginal propensity to save (MPS) will be 0.2. This means that the marginal propensity to consume (MPC) will be $1 - 0.2 = 0.8$. When national income has risen by \$50 m, then 0.2 will be saved and 0.2 of \$50 m is equal to \$10 m which equals the original injection.

The formula for k is $\dfrac{\$50}{\$10} = 5$

Another way of looking at the multiplier in a two-sector economy is that

$$k = \frac{1}{\text{MPS}} = \frac{1}{1 - \text{MPC}}$$

Therefore, $k = \dfrac{1}{1 - 0.8} = \dfrac{1}{0.2} = 5$

In a three-sector economy, there is an additional injection (government) and an additional withdrawal or leakage (taxation). In this case, the multiplier is now: $\dfrac{1}{\text{MPS} + \text{MRT}}$

If it is assumed that $\frac{1}{5}$ of the extra income is taxed, the multiplier will now be $\dfrac{1}{0.2} + 0.2 = \dfrac{1}{0.4} = 2.5$. This is much less than the multiplier in the two-sector economy and so the initial investment of \$10 m, assuming that the government does not inject any money into the economy, will bring about a national income of \$10 m $\times$ 2.5 = \$25 m.

In a four-sector economy, there is an additional injection (exports) and an additional leakage or withdrawal (imports). In this case, the multiplier is now: $\dfrac{1}{\text{MPS} + \text{MRT} + \text{MPM}}$

If it is assumed that $\frac{1}{5}$ of the extra income is spent on imports, the multiplier will now be $\dfrac{1}{0.2} + 0.2 + 0.2 = \dfrac{1}{0.6} = 1.67$. This is again much less than the multiplier in the two-sector or the three-sector economy and so the initial investment of \$10 m, assuming no further injections into the economy, will bring about a national income of \$10 m $\times$ 1.67 = \$16.7 m.

The accelerator

The concept of the accelerator stresses the relationship between investment and the rate of change of output. It is important to understand that investment will be determined not by the level of output, but by the rate at which output changes. If output grows faster than before, the rate at which new productive capacity is created will need to increase. However, if output stabilises, no additional investment will be needed, other than that needed to replace worn-out machines, so investment will actually fall. It can therefore be seen that the concept of the accelerator causes investment to fluctuate much more than output.

Worked example

Year	Demand	Number of machines	Machines needed	Replacement investment	Induced investment	Total investment
1	1000	10	10	1	0	1
2	1100	10	11	1	1	2
3	1400	11	14	1	4	5
4	1400	14	14	1	0	1
5	1300	14	13	0	0	0

At the start, the firm has 10 machines. One of these needs to be replaced each year to be able to produce 100 units each year. The table shows how investment will respond to a change in demand. In Year 4, constant demand means that there is no induced investment (induced investment refers to investment that responds to changes in national income), while the fall in demand in Year 5 leads to no investment.

An important feature of the accelerator is that it assumes a constant capital-output ratio, i.e. the ratio of capital used to produce a unit of output in a given time period. However, this ratio is likely to change over a period of time as new technology can make capital more productive as newer machines are likely to be able to produce a greater output.

Useful formulae for the exam

Concept	Formula
Price elasticity of demand	$\dfrac{\text{percentage change in quantity demanded}}{\text{percentage change in price}}$
Income elasticity of demand	$\dfrac{\text{percentage change in quantity demanded}}{\text{percentage change in income}}$
Cross elasticity of demand	$\dfrac{\text{percentage change in quantity demanded of good A}}{\text{percentage change in price of good B}}$
Price elasticity of supply	$\dfrac{\text{percentage change in quantity supplied}}{\text{percentage change in price}}$
Real GDP	$\dfrac{\text{nominal GDP}}{\text{price index}} \times 100$
Current account of balance of payments	trade in goods + trade in services + net primary income + net secondary income
Balance of payments	current account + capital account + financial account + balancing item
Real exchange rate	$\dfrac{\text{nominal exchange rate} \times \text{domestic price index}}{\text{foreign price index}}$
Terms of trade	$\dfrac{\text{index of average export prices}}{\text{index of average import prices}} \times 100$

Gross National Product	Gross Domestic Product + Net Property Income from Abroad
Injections into the circular flow of income of an economy	government expenditure (G), investment (I) and exports (X)
Leakages or withdrawals from the circular flow of income	savings (S), taxation (T) and imports (M)
Aggregate demand	consumption (C) + investment (I) + government expenditure (G) + net exports (X – M)
Multiplier in a two-sector economy	$\dfrac{1}{MPS}$
Multiplier in a three-sector economy	$\dfrac{1}{MPS + MRT}$
Multiplier in a four-sector economy	$\dfrac{1}{MPS + MRT + MPM}$ or $\dfrac{1}{\text{marginal propensity to withdraw}}$
Value of multiplier	$\dfrac{\text{change in income}}{\text{change in injection}}$
Accelerator coefficient	$\dfrac{\text{net investment}}{\text{rate of change of national output}}$

Index